ABOUT THE AUTHOR

Charlie is from London, England. This is his first book. Visit www.hiredfiredfled.com for more on travel, career, and his upcoming projects. Join in the conversation, leave feedback, and be directed to this book's Amazon page. Please share the link with friends, family, and colleagues, and be sure to write a review.

HIRED, FIRED, FLED

Charlie Raymond

[signature]

24/1/17

Saxon Nomad Media
www.saxonnomad.com

The right of Charlie Raymond to be identified as author of this work has been assured by him in accordance with the Copyrights, Designs and Patents Act, 1988.

ISBN 978-0-9954527-2-5

Published by Saxon Nomad Media

This is a work of creative non-fiction, and while based on the author's experiences a number of names and locations have been changed in order to respect the privacy of others, recognising that his recollection of events is a subjective take on the past.

www.hiredfiredfled.com
www.charlieraymondauthor.com
www.saxonnomad.com

For Chloe, Hector, and everyone facing *the ultimate question*

PROLOGUE

Live. Work. Die.

Nothing levels us more. Whether you're in the streets of London, the towers of Dubai, or the paddy fields of Asia, there's no escape.

But while living and dying are natural, work's a bitch. It keeps us on edge, sweating over exams, fretting over interviews, losing sleep over retirement. It drives us; it defines us; it keeps the world spinning. We're all part of it, this great game, striving to earn, advance, and prosper.

The Great Game.

It's a term used to describe how the UK and Russia vied for Central Asian supremacy in the mid-1800s, but it's far better suited to the working world. That's because we're all tied to the workplace, vying for supremacy, desperate to leave victorious. Yet for something so integral to our everyday lives, so central to who we are, it's a game with no rules, no instructions, leaving most of us to wonder how the hell it should be played.

And that brings us to the question, the one that torments and inspires, that demands clarity and self-awareness; it's a question so challenging it often goes unanswered to the end, surrounded by memories of a life misunderstood.

It's no less than… *the ultimate question*:

What should I be doing with my days on Earth?

It's a riddle we try to solve from an early age, but one that many grapple with into their thirties, forties, and beyond. It's a question that led me to pen this tale, for mine is a story that's seen me flirt with insanity in search of an answer, going to extreme lengths to ensure I become one of society's success stories.

It's been tough, it's been an adventure, but above all it's given me an understanding of the working world, and why being able to answer that question right is so very important, because the way you spend your nine-to-five affects every aspect of your life, and ultimately, your happiness.

A WORLD OF OPTIONS

"I want to look into women's handbags."

It was the statement I innocently announced to my mother at the age of five after a trip to London's Science Museum.

Once we'd returned home, sitting round the kitchen table, I proudly told her what I wanted to be when I grew up: "A museum man." It was the first time I'd expressed any interest in a career, and she was delighted, assuming I wanted to curate one of world's great institutions, consumed by a life of academia.

Then she asked why.

"'Cause, Mummy, I want to look into women's handbags…"

"But that's not…"

"…like the museum welcome man, who takes the hats and coats."

That life of academia vaporised.

Yet to her credit she didn't seem disappointed or perplexed, she just smiled sweetly, not showing any concern as to her son's voyeuristic ambition. Maybe she was just happy I had a goal. Any goal.

It wasn't to last.

Like most kids I regularly changed my, "What do you want to be when you grow up?" answer. Fireman, policeman, astronaut, *The A-Team's* Hannibal Smith, they all made the list. An adult's working life seemed like a pic 'n' mix theme park; a magical place of fire hoses, flashing lights, rocket ships, and the ability to turn Tupperware into explosives. It was something to love and enjoy, so why settle on just one line of work?

Enjoy them all, seemed the obvious theory.

So I did.

After two decades in the working world my inauspicious list of jobs now includes: pizza delivery boy for one night (I quit, debt being easier and more in vogue), safari guide, second assistant director, junk removal man, locations assistant, barman, ski rep, marketing exec, charity phone salesman (sorry to everyone I called), caterer, tour operations manager… and that's just the half of it.

It's not surprising I still ponder the ultimate question, wondering if I'm on the right path. And if I am, could I have got to where I am faster? How did I take so many wrong turns? Are some people just 'late-starters'? Should there have been better guidance to help me find my path sooner? Why wasn't it easier?

Answering all that depends on how much you know about yourself from an early age, whether you know what you want out of life – at any age – and how much help you get, or ask for. I was born into a supportive family and went to a decent school, but it didn't lead me to run a major corporation, or start a trans-Atlantic airline; with a similar background, nor did it for Sir Richard Branson. His work ethic did. That's because, wherever you're from, it's down to your drive and your goals.

It's a dog-eat-dog world; navigating it isn't easy, but the hardest part for most people is step one, the ultimate question.

And I was clueless.

But everyone needs an answer, whatever it may be, so I set about finding mine. Not knowing where to start, I began with a simple goal, focusing on something I loved, something I thought should define my life from the day I left school:

Travel.

Of course everyone says they love travel, much like everyone loves watching movies, eating chips, and breathing air. A generic love of travel is an obvious offshoot of cheap fares, but I wanted travel to be integral to my working life, not just my time off. I knew

3

it was possible, as I'd been told so for years, having repeatedly heard a phrase that first appeared in Shakespeare's *The Merry Wives of Windsor*, 'The world's mine oyster.' Growing up I heard it over and over again, and started to believe it.

I mean truly believe it.

I mean take it as gospel.

I wanted to experience the planet in its entirety, working from the mountains to the deserts, from the cities to the wilds. My thinking was, *we live on a massive ball of rock floating in a big bundle of nothing, and it's there for me to explore,* so that became the plan. I assumed that following it would make for a happy life, but it left me facing yet another question: What career would match the plan?

Unsure, I fixated purely on my desire to travel, believing the answer would materialise… somewhere, in a foreign land.

How naïve.

My story is of a regular man undertaking a universal task, that of finding his path in life. Things didn't go *quite* according to plan, but I still believe in 'the oyster theory' – of being able to go anywhere and do anything – even though I now know it's a theory that requires finesse.

Yet as a teenager I thought it a theory beyond limits, and wanting to deploy my travel plan straight off, the first corner of the globe I chose to experience was a long, long way from home, deep inside a country ruled by a geriatric despot.

It was time to put the theory to the test.

It was time to start my search for the ultimate answer.

It was time to put on the shortest shorts a man should ever wear.

CHAPTER ONE

London, 1996.

Fuelled by a teenage obsession with Land Rovers, coupled with an ability to sing the entire score of Disney's *The Lion King*, on leaving school the scene was set. There was no fighting it. I had to follow my destiny. I had to become a safari guide in Africa… and so began my first ever job hunt.

Fully supportive of the decision to dispatch her son to the far side of the world, my mother put me in touch with a friend at the South African tourism board, and in turn she suggested I contact Tusker Game Reserve. It was a private ranch, not in South Africa, but in northern Zimbabwe; its owner, she'd heard, was on the prowl for staff. I took down the number, fingers crossed.

After a few days exchanging calls and faxes with the reserve's owner I was amazed to be offered a trainee guiding position, starting as soon as my paperwork could be processed. The owner – a dour man with Scottish heritage – told me that all I had to do was arrange a work permit at the Zimbabwe High Commission; once done I could pack, fly south, and so fulfil my safari guide goal.

The world really is my oyster, I thought. The only hurdle was the work permit, but I expected it to be a simple procedure, probably a half-hour of form-filling and fee payment, resulting in an exotic new passport stamp.

If only.

At eighteen years of age, one wide-eyed Englishman trooped off to the heart of central London, and so entered the world of bureaucratic hell that is the Zimbabwe High Commission. In later years I'd learn that most nations possess such places of torturous rubber-stamping idiocy, the pen pushers that populate them creating wastelands of red tape in order to infuriate all who dare enter.

5

Rain-streaked, leaden, and imposing from the outside, the High Commission's interior welcomed without awe, stale furniture reeking of better times, long past. I stepped up to the reception desk, interrupting a bespectacled lady and her coffee break crossword, asking as pleasantly as possible what form I'd need to request a work permit. It would be the first of many times.

Soon enough I'd be reminded of the film *The Twelve Tasks of Asterix* where our intrepid Gallic hero has to find Permit A38 in 'The Place That Sends You Mad', an official Roman building full of uncooperative staff, confusing corridors, and lethal stairs. After I'd been sent to half a dozen disparate offices, ordered to fill out nonsensical paperwork, told to wait at each stop, only to be dispatched to yet another distant department, I too found myself going steadily insane.

As the staff began to filter home for the day, I found myself back at the reception desk, exhausted. The bespectacled lady glared at me, pondering my work permit query, then she sat back, shaking her head. I prepared to be sent to yet another corner of that labyrinthine building.

"You can't get it here," she said. "It has to be done by your future employer in Zimbabwe."

Surely this was a cruel joke, obscure revenge for Britain's colonial past? Whatever it was, it didn't fit the oyster theory. The receptionist smiled, deliberately: *Yes, we've been fucking with you*. I meekly turned tail, soaking up my first lesson in international employment rules, yet I was determined I wouldn't let a building of vindictive civil servants alter my chosen path.

Calling the ranch owner only confused the situation. He assured me my work permit had to be dealt with in the UK, stating there was absolutely no way it could be processed at his end. I said I'd take care of it, mulled over a return to the High Commission, discarded the idea within seconds (fearing fast-tracked insanity), and decided instead to rely on a tourist visa.

I'm only going for six months; the tourist visa covers six months, so why bother with the paperwork? It was an instinctive decision, based on weighing up the odds, coupled with above-average laziness, and a schoolboy mentality of manipulating the system.

Case in point: the school cross-country marathon. Its figure of eight design meant the lazier children – read myself and esteemed associates – dodged the first loop of the race, only running the second loop. Other boys had tried telling the Head of Sports they were 'legally entitled' to withdraw from marathon running, but I could see it wouldn't wash. It wasn't worth the hassle. Far better to pretend you've run the full race. It was an attitude that led to a line of spectators aghast at my arrival, because having missed half the marathon I was able to jog to the finish line behind the fittest and fastest in the school.

Yet it's one thing manipulating an institution designed to keep children under control, a whole different story when you're breaking the rules of a foreign government. But that was my strategy, one that boasted as much foresight as an American war in the Middle East.

I wasn't oblivious to the pitfalls of working on a tourist visa, but assumed that as long as I made it through passport control I'd have the system beat.

It turned out that Zimbabwe had far bigger fish to fry.

One illegal safari guide was the least of their worries.

"What's the purpose of your visit?" was the acceptable question thrown my way, after a nineteen-hour journey connecting in Paris and Johannesburg.

"Tourism."

Stamp!

"Have a nice stay," beamed the uniformed officer.

"I'll try," I beamed back, as unseen my heart rate hit 180, cold beads of sweat bullying their way to my brow.

I raced to the baggage hall, grabbed my backpack, and fled the scene, entering Zimbabwe on a sizzling September's day. As the stress of the journey abated, my pulse calming, I scoured the dusty airport exterior. Safari jeeps and minibus taxis carpeted the scene. Arriving tourists stripped off layers, acclimatising. Hotel staff unloaded departing bags; unused dollars exchanged hands. African beats thumped from waiting cars. I scanned the lot, searching for my ride.

It didn't take long.

The boss had said to look for Martin, who'd be wearing a Tusker Game Reserve shirt. No further detail was needed. Martin was unmistakable. A South African in his thirties, there he was, standing proud in groin-hugging shorts, khaki shirt, and wide-brimmed Akubra sun hat. We made contact, him showing me to the company's clapped-out minibus, elephant logo on its side. I smiled. I couldn't believe it. *This is really happening.*

Once on board, he cranked the engine; it sputtered into life, and we departed Harare Airport, entering the city's purple-blooming, jacaranda-lined streets. It was a short urban swing, as within twenty minutes we were clear, pushing into the breadbasket of Africa, Zimbabwe's once profitable and productive farmlands.

After England's manicured gardens and surreal gnome collections, it was liberating to bump along mile after mile of open road, surrounded by beige land and sprinkler-fed crops, dodging tractors, and antelope road-kill. The insanity of the High Commission was instantly forgotten as Africa seduced me.

I revelled in the change. It was the opposite of everything I knew. Out here there was no safety net, no mother's voice, no government advice. I was on my own, thousands of miles from home. Nobody knew me, and I knew nobody. It was exhilarating, challenging; it was adult.

With that in mind, I began to consider the job at hand, my first proper job. I'd worked before, but nothing more than odd days for family friends, painting sheds and picking fruit. Those are jobs that if done poorly carry nothing more than the threat of a parental reprimand; most people are thrilled if their job's completed, let alone finished with finesse.

This was different. Cocking up the safari job would mean an early return home, tail tucked firmly between legs. Failure was not an option, which left me stressing as to what I'd be doing for a little known employer in a little known corner of the world. What I'd been told about the job was limited: the medium-sized property of forty thousand acres needed someone to guide tourists around the reserve – that much I knew – but quite why they'd let a teen-age Englishman join the team was a mystery. I mulled over the work required, coming to the same conclusion I'd reached before: it can't be that hard.

Do training. Meet tourists. Show animals.

I presumed part of the reason they'd employed me was that I'd accepted the eye-wateringly low salary of £50 a month, enough to buy the local Newbury brand of cigarettes, an ice cream or two, and a few trinkets in the village market. Yet beyond tobacco, sugary treats, and mass-produced gifts my expenses were limited. Everything was provided for: a room in the staff bungalow, food, drink, and a fast education in Africa's wildlife.

I can do this. I can do this. I can do this.

And then, worry vanished, adrenaline rose, as we'd arrived. On either side of the road soared thick stone pillars, iron letters arching between them, their wondrous message silhouetted against the sky:

Tusker Game Reserve Welcomes You.

We bounced into the reserve, leaving behind the towering green and yellow maize of the neighbouring farms. Martin told me that due to its populated, agricultural location, the ranch's carnivores – lion, leopard, hyena, and cheetah – had to be kept in enclosures for safety, leaving the grazing plains strewn with some of the most confident antelope in Africa. We swept past them, Martin clocking the species. The unmistakable black and white zebra was all I recognised. The rest sounded like items off a mythological menu: kudu, sable, impala, hartebeest, waterbuck, wildebeest, buffalo, roaming before me, no longer confined to a textbook.

After a ten-minute drive we pulled up to the staff bungalow, a beige concrete block, four rooms long, two wide, rusting chairs out front, whereupon Martin dispensed the most critical lesson of all: "Check your room every night for bugs and beasts." There weren't many places to hide, my bedroom containing a single bed, wooden chair, and prefab wardrobe, so I wasn't particularly concerned; but less than an hour later Martin was proved right, as I spotted a small, demonic-looking scorpion scampering into a shoe I'd just unpacked.

Big scorpions can hurt, the guidebook told me, but it's the small ones that pack the biggest punch. I eyed the shoe.

Should I crush it?

No, I'm here for the animals. No, no, no.

I gingerly picked up the trainer, as carefully as a parent waking a teething toddler. Hands shaking, I opened the window, flipped over the shoe, and dumped the lethal stinger into the bushes below, at which point it disappeared into the darkness, its hidden location haunting me for weeks to come.

In need of a drink, I raced to the guest lodge to meet Martin. The traditional wood and thatch building had a high roof over a simple dining area, its walls adorned with antlers and animal hide. Outside was a large wooden deck, wicker chairs lining its edge, giving way to a gentle, grassy slope that ended in a moat, beyond which the antelope gathered around a muddy watering hole.

Sipping a beer that first night, hearing the white noise of cicadas, the low rumble of lion and thunder, overlooking grazing animals feeding under floodlight, confirmed I'd made the right move. It was classic, clichéd Africa, as promised by a thousand brochures, and a Disney cartoon.

The following day, a different scene, roused not by a fairy-tale chorus of African birdsong, but by Martin revving the engine of his tan 1974 Series III Land Rover, shouting at me to join him. It was 6am. Cool, but not cold. Crisp, but not brittle. I jumped out of bed, peered inside my trainers – all clear – and was outside within five minutes.

School was in session.

From that moment on I'd follow Martin everywhere, learning the lie of the land (the hills, plains, lakes, and caves), mastering the route of the game drive, being shown how to take care of visitors, and being tested to identify the reserve's most common animals, birds, and plants. It was 'Safari Guiding for Dummies', rather than a Masters in Zoology, but I didn't need to know everything, just the basics, so I absorbed what I could, and after three weeks of shadowing, taking notes, and revising the route, was deemed ready to take a tour.

To mark the auspicious day I was given my uniform: a khaki shirt and a pair of shorts so tight an American cheerleader would think twice before donning them. But it was an honour; I was part of the team. And so, adjusting tackle every five minutes, I rolled out on my first ever solo tour, cruising deep into the reserve, entrusted with a group of chattering tourists. As I'd witnessed on Martin's safaris, they fired off predictable queries, and in turn I spewed out the same stats that guides have been repeating for decades.

The top tourist questions are always about cheetah speed, hippo aggression, giraffe height, lion appetite, and elephant poo. Once you master the 'Top Five' there's little to fear. The golden rule was to radio to Martin if I didn't know something. Never guess, not unless it's about varieties of poo. Big poo = big animal. Just prod it with a stick, or sniff at it knowingly. Tourists love that Bear Grylls touch.

After a few outings I knew when and where questions would pop up, the game drive following the same route every day, beginning in the plains for an hour, after which we'd canoe a reservoir for forty-five minutes, eat a sadza (maize-based) lunch, visit the big cat pens, ending back at the lodge for farewell drinks.

It was simple, physical, rewarding employment, beginning at sunrise, ending at sundown. Anyone who hasn't worked outdoors should experience it, at least once, if possible in southern Africa surrounded by the world's finest natural beauty. I challenge anyone not to fall for that rugged terrain.

Every day it impressed me more, and as it did, the job became easier, my confidence growing, reaping fatter tips. But as I became comfortable with the nine-to-five, the 'honeymoon period' slipped away, allowing the realities of the working world to surface, soon to tear the grin off another fresh-faced grunt.

Number one reality: The Boss.

With every job there's a chief, and that person makes or breaks your working life. As a safari guide I had a direct manager, a cheerful, blonde, thirty-something lady who made life easy, even fun; but her immediate boss was the tall, seventy-something, white-bearded farmer of Scottish descent, Mr Douglas.

Old man Douglas lived on extensive farmland near the reserve, but not on the reserve, so he was detached from our day-to-day operations. His main business was the highly profitable tobacco plant, grown on most of the farms in the area, as I was to see when Martin took me up a *kopje* (hill) to point out the local properties.

Tusker Game Reserve extended far into the distance, but beyond it you could make out green swathes of farmland where Martin told me they grew tobacco, along with peas for Marks & Spencer, lettuce for Tesco, sweetcorn for Sainsbury's, and so on. It seemed the region's farmers were growing most of Britain's food, and half the world's tobacco, but of course it wasn't *them* doing the labour – they owned the land – it was the native population whose hard graft was putting baby carrots on dinner plates across the Home Counties.

Seeing the scale of the industry, and knowing ours was merely one of many agricultural areas, my 'honeymoon period' blinkers slipped off, and I began to see Zimbabwe for what it really was: a post-colonial conundrum that relied on its rural black population to toil away, existing as second-class citizens.

The issue of land ownership sustained that status quo, the divide exacerbated by the comfort in which the white farmers lived

compared to their black employees. The imbalance was so significant that it seemed, to an outsider, as if the country were still under
white rule. That's because land means power, particularly in an
agrarian economy, and seeing as the whites owned the lion's share
of the most fertile farmland, yet accounted for less than one per
cent of the population, the power imbalance was clear-cut.

For a young Londoner it was puzzling; here was a country that
in 1996 still had significant white control, even though its native
president, Robert Mugabe, had held power since 1980 (initially as
prime minister), having taken over from Ian Smith's illegitimate
white-rule government, which itself had declared independence
from the British in 1965; and the Brits, of course, had started it all
when Cecil Rhodes colonised tribal lands in the late-1800s creating
Southern Rhodesia. Considering the country's turbulent, divisive
history it amazed me that Mugabe hadn't immediately imple-
mented land reform on becoming PM. What had he been doing
with his sixteen years in power? Perfecting his golf swing? Learning
Spanish?

Something was amiss, and it remained unclear until I learnt
of the small print in the Lancaster House Agreement (LHA), a
UK-negotiated treaty that oversaw the 1980 transition to Mugabe's
regime. Besides its peace-not-war objectives, there was a contentious clause ruling out land reform for ten years, unless white owners *wanted* to sell their property. If they did, they could do so under
a 'willing buyer, willing seller' policy that guaranteed market prices,
funded by a 'land resettlement grant' backed by the UK and international donors.

Peace, cheap labour, and the option to sell at a market rate?

Unsurprisingly, Zimbabwe barely changed.

Most farmers liked things the way they were. They opted to
stay put. Even after the LHA's ten-year clause expired there was
little push for land reform, Mugabe's government maintaining a
policy of 'fair compensation'. Despite the introduction of the Land
Acquisition Act in 1992, pressure to sell prime farms remained low,

leaving the state of affairs to kick on into the mid-90s.

And so, as neighbouring South Africa abolished apartheid, electing Nelson Mandela to office in 1994, Zimbabwe was stuck in the past; yet change lurked over the horizon, firstly due to the 'land resettlement grant' expiring in 1996, and secondly due to a polished politician sweeping to victory in London, celebrated to the sound of D:Ream's 'Things can only get better'.

Not so for Zimbabwe's white farmers.

Following the election of Tony Blair's government in 1997, New Labour changed tack on post-colonial relations, distancing itself from Britain's past. Clare Short, the new Secretary of State for International Development, said her administration was, "without links to former colonial interests…" and therefore had no "… special responsibility to meet the cost of land purchases."

Mugabe, one assumes, was livid. He believed white farmers to be a distinctly British problem. New Labour, it appeared, did not.

Of course in 1996 it was way too early to foresee the 'fast track' land grab that would see white farmers, often violently, forced off their properties from July 2000; but even so, hints were in the air.

And I was to get a personal taste of those hints, on bumping into two groundsmen as they tended to a broken fence at the edge of the safari reserve. On spotting me they stopped their work, apparently keen to chat; I stopped too, not realising I'd soon be trapped in a particularly awkward conversation.

Discussing salaries is not the done thing.

This is what I should have said to the blue-overall-clad pair, but it might have dented our nascent friendship, so when they told me they knew what I earned I didn't say what I was thinking, I merely asked them what they'd heard. The answer was spot on: £50 or 600 Zimbabwe dollars a month. (This was years before hyperinflation pushed the currency into the absurd, the government famously issuing a 100 trillion dollar bill in 2008.) Telling them they were right, I leant against a tree, trying to be nonchalant, but in reality I was livid, embarrassed at my pittance of a wage.

Before I could ask how they knew, they asked me why I needed to be on such a high salary. *Excuse me? High?*

They continued, on a roll:

"We're earning half that amount, and have families to support, so why should you earn so much? Is it because you're European? Is this fair? Why should a white man earn more when we've been with the Douglas family all our lives, and we know more about the ranch and its animals?"

I was speechless, unsure what to say.

"It, it, it, it, it, it's because I, I, I, I come from the same place that many of the, er, er, tourists come from… and they can, I, I, I guess, easily talk to me."

Nonplussed faces stared back, but it was all I had. Fortunately they could see I was as surprised as them, or they didn't want the moment to become any more awkward, as one of them swung the conversation from my tycoon earnings to inviting me to their 'compound' to see how they lived.

I smelled a rat, and made my paranoid suspicions clear by declining the offer in the most English of ways possible:

"What a lovely invitation. I look forward to it immensely."

The following day the two workers tracked me down to tell me that a visit that very night would be good timing. I knew why. It was that popular day that has people jumping for joy the world over… payday.

In northern Zimbabwe that would mean villages and compounds celebrating with Chibuku, the local beer, a sort of alcoholic mud that needs drinking before it turns to poison. Not being a huge fan of the toxic potion, that evening I bought six bottles of lager, then took off down the dirt track that wound for a kilometre from the lodge to the compound, to where the native labourers were housed, tucked far out of sight, away from the guests and their bubbling plunge pools.

It didn't take long to reach, but having never been there before

I stopped at a distance, taking it in: there were around a dozen breeze block huts, a shared water pump, a communal fire, some wooden benches, and a handful of animated chickens. No power line. No phone line. It was a glimpse of how the other half lived; but not wanting to ruin the evening – something I'm more than adept at achieving – I decided not to comment, instead focusing on the night ahead.

Once in the compound, I was surrounded by children playing games, women cooking dinner, as their husbands milled about in overalls and gumboots, sharing stories of the day. They teased and laughed. They ate and drank. It could have been any post-work catch up, anywhere on Earth.

As the last rays of ruby sunlight streaked the sky, the community disappeared indoors, leaving me to sip beer, and poke the fire. Some twenty minutes later, as darkness took hold, they re-emerged. My jaw dropped. I was treated to an unexpected sight, something I'd only previously seen in *National Geographic* magazines and GCSE textbooks, something from a time before the arrival of the European: before me was a fully kitted out African tribe, covered in animal hide from head to toe, feathers bristling on high, brandishing shields and spears. It was a colourful, powerful throwback to a way of life they clearly didn't want to forget.

Then the penny dropped.

In an instant I could see why they'd hark back to 'the good old days'. No more punching-in for an unappreciative boss, forced to watch the other half enjoy the fruits of their labour. No more donning blue overalls earning pennies to work land that once belonged to their ancestors. And of course they'd hate the fact that I – a tenuous link to the coloniser – earned more than they did, especially at the age of eighteen, *especially* given my limited safari knowledge.

I'd be livid.

Maybe it was the giant joint being passed around, but in that warm, hazy campfire moment I reached a state of champagne socialist enlightenment, and then, like every other champagne socialist, I decided it was far too serious for polite conversation, so buried the 'good old days' topic forever.

After several more tokes, and a few slugs of Chibuku, my head was spinning, as I danced around the community fire, singing songs, mimicking ancient war dances. Sadly I looked like a drunk uncle 'bopping' at a family wedding, but bridges were being built, friendships being formed… and that's where it goes blank… the following morning I was sore headed, fuzzy-mouthed, but ecstatic about my trippy night dancing to the African beat.

Until I was summoned for my first ever 'strike one' chat.

And it hit me for six.

"Where were you last night?" demanded Mr Douglas.

He'd collared me as I was walking through the grounds, bleary eyed, nauseous, en route to meet a group of guests for their intro-ductory safari chat. Unaware there was a problem, I told him I'd been at the compound celebrating payday with my fellow employ-ees. I thought he'd see it as company bonding, and maybe even be impressed at my efforts to learn about the land, its traditions, and people, but nothing could have been further from his mind.

"Go down there again and you're out," he barked, before marching off.

I stood there, frozen. If I'd been a cartoon character I'd have been suspended in mid-air, head extended from my torso, limbs taut at every angle.

Number two reality: Beware the Boss.

Without knowing it, I'd broken one of his cardinal rules: you don't socialise with the native population. He never said it in those words, but the implication was clear: *mix at your peril*. From a working point of view I'd been given my first official warning. From a personal point of view I'd seen behind the curtain, into the backward men-tality of a land modernity forgot. The reprimand was also a lesson in how a job's 'dos and don'ts' can spill into your private life; it was simple, but sad – in order to keep my job, I'd need to toe the line.

Following the compound incident I became one-tracked, focused on guiding. I threw myself into the job, becoming mentally and physically stronger. And after just seven weeks I began to notice something unusual. Something unprecedented. I was looking 'toned'. I didn't even know I had the requisite muscles to be toned; I knew they were likely enough there, but they'd always failed to overcome their apparent shyness, hiding behind a stubborn layer of donuts and fish fingers.

With the physical change came a new confidence. I felt manly, even when wearing short shorts, knee-high socks, and moccasin shoes. I looked like a member of the Village People who'd collided with a rugby-playing Eskimo. Yet I wore the uniform with pride, rolling up my sleeves to a level last seen on American sailors in '50s musicals. Smokes tucked in. Dancing with a mop.

Yes, I was *that* manly.

And I loved it; the 'Africa bug' had bitten... hard.

That's not a terrifying parasite that swims up your urethra, killing you from the inside (which, by the way, does exist in parts of the continent), but a term anyone who knows Africa will recognise; it's the inevitable love visitors develop for that rugged, spacious land, and its vibrant wildlife.

I'd been bitten, no doubt, but there were several times when that love wobbled, and one time in particular when it was shaken to the bone, due to a request for me to feed an unusual lump of meat to the reserve's voracious leopard.

The strangest day of my life in Africa was when a racecourse in Harare dropped off a dead horse for feed, and the job of throwing the deceased animal's head into the leopard enclosure was given to me. By the time you're into your sixth attempt to lob a forty-kilo horse's head over a sixteen-foot fence you think differently about a nice day at the races. You're also adept at ignoring the pool of vomit you've coughed up, the horse's eye swinging from its decomposing head, and the 200-pound leopard agitating behind its chain-link fence.

Once done, I returned to my room, took a long shower, and shelved the experience. It was part of the job, and as long as I could do the job I'd flown there to do, while avoiding Mr Douglas, the working world suited me just fine. I'd do whatever they asked of me, and I'd do it with a smile.

But just as I was feeling settled at Tusker Game Reserve, developing a mature approach to the workplace, becoming knowledgeable in the animals and terrain, unbeknown to me a fax would soon arrive with the power to change everything.

And as my eighth week in the job came to a close, that fax was being penned in a first floor flat in distant, darkest London.

Back in 1996, in the farming communities of Zimbabwe, communications were more akin to the 1950s than the latter end of the 20th century. Local farms shared one telephone connection called a 'party line', which meant that rather than pick up the phone and dial someone, you'd pick up the phone and there'd be a neighbour speaking, whose conversation you'd have to interrupt.

"Alright Bob," you'd say, "Can I make a call?"

"No problem, just give me five minutes," would be the usual answer.

I had no mobile phone – they were rare in those days – and even if I'd had one, connections were terrible; there certainly wasn't 3G, 4G, or broadband. The 'party line' was the only way to connect to the outside world, but we weren't allowed to make phone calls, so contact with home was done via a fax machine, which, for those of you born after 1990, effectively sends copies of paperwork down the phone line. You feed a sheet in one end, it's digitised, and seconds later printed out by a similar machine thousands of miles away.

Faxes had to be routed through Mr Douglas's office, usually sent by his staff in the middle of the night when the 'party line' was less busy. Every few days I'd write a page or two to friends or family, telling them how I'd been hit by an elephant or bitten by a hyena, and they'd send something back. Standard stuff. Messages for my eyes would be dropped off at the staff bungalow, waiting for me to read at the end of my shift. There was a charm to it, like taking photos on film, travelling an ocean by boat, or wearing a suit for the sake of wearing a suit.

What I didn't realise was that the fax machine was right beside Mr Douglas's desk, and – far more importantly – that he read every outgoing and incoming message, top to bottom...

"Get back to the lodge right now!!" barked the ageing boss.

On a bright, fresh morning I heard those words and feared the worst. You don't need to be an expert in the working world to know that a shouted order doesn't lead to an unexpected bonus.

At the time I was forking out hay from the back of a pickup truck. It was 7am; already warm. The peak of dry season; dew long since burnt off. Dung beetles went about their business. Zebra waited to feed. Dust hung in the air. But my peaceful morning was interrupted by Mr Douglas careening to a halt alongside me, just long enough for him to deliver his unambiguous order.

I threw my gear into the pickup and followed him to the lodge, driving through air turned dense by his aggressive acceleration. He stopped outside the staff bungalow, and climbed out, arms folded, foot tapping.

"What the hell is this?" he demanded of me, thrusting a piece of rolled up fax paper into my hands.

I took it, unrolled it, and began to read. As the large man paced in circles I saw that it was a fax from a friend in London writing to say, 'Hi, hope you're well. Hope you're meeting loads of great people. Sounds like you're loving Africa. It must be a fun experience. Great that you're now a trained guide. And how amazing it is that you've slept with the boss's wife six times, and he still doesn't know...'

I stopped.

I'm no genius, but I was fairly certain where the problem lay.

"What the hell is this, Charles?" he said again, which of course sounded more like, "Wat de hell is dis, Chars?" in his utilitarian Zimbabwe accent.

There are times in life when you know that whatever you say just won't cut it. Instinctively I knew I'd never again lead a safari drive at Tusker Game Reserve, or sip sundowners overlooking the lodge's watering hole, or even lob another horse's head to their ravenous leopard. Nonetheless, I tried saving the moment. My first job couldn't end due to a fax suggesting I'd had sex with a woman fifty-five years my senior, who was, no offence to Mrs Douglas, not exactly my type.

"Er…" I stammered, "it, it, it's got nothing to do with me. It's a joke. Not a good one, but it's just a joke."

"I judge a man by his friends, Charles, and your friends are fucking idiots. You had something to do with this, and even if you didn't, I would still judge you by your friends."

Seems fair, I thought.

"Go pack your bags. You have one hour, then my driver will pick you up, bring you to see me for your final salary, then take you to Harare," he added, so ending my African dream in two simple sentences.

With that he jumped back into his car and sped off, taking the troublesome fax with him. Part of me wanted to cry, part of me wanted to laugh, yet my angst was focused on my idiotic friend who'd penned a fax that would compel the other guides to believe I had a thing for the much, *much* older lady.

True to his word, one hour later a driver showed up. *This is actually happening.* I was in shock. On seeing the car, disbelief that I could be dismissed in such a way sunk in, but when you're working illegally there's little you can do. I grabbed my bag, and was soon being driven from the reserve, past the eland, kudu, waterbuck, and wildebeest, past the impalas and zebra, past the farm workers, past the leopard and lion. I took it all in, one last time.

Soon enough we were on the drive to the boss's house, somewhere I'd rarely visited, but was damn sure I'd now remember.

A twenty-foot chain-link fence topped with barbed wire surrounded his immaculate lawn, swimming pool, and three-storey colonial house. We parked. I approached the gate. An elderly guard manned the entry point. On the other side was a fearsome Rhodesian ridgeback.

I eyed the dog, aware the staff avoided it. The guard pushed open the gate. I walked in. The dog looked up. The guard closed the gate behind me. The dog started in my direction. I paused. Fearing the worst I turned to the guard, who smiled, and then said the most poignant line I'd ever heard:

"He won't attack. You're white."

In five words he'd summed up Zimbabwe's deep-rooted divide, yet before I could dwell on the moment my former employer was beckoning me into his house to collect my severance pay. I meekly followed, patting the mini-horse as it slobbered over my legs. And then, as I climbed on to the wooden porch, lo and behold, the subject of my supposed lust wandered outside; it was none other than the irresistible septuagenarian, Mrs Douglas.

"Hello, Mrs Douglas, do you know why I'm here?" I asked.

"Oh yes," she replied.

"So can you tell your husband it's not true? It's rubbish. This is…"

I stopped, knowing my next words would underscore my teenage years.

"…so unfair."

"Yes, but what Mr Douglas says goes, so that's all there is to it."

I knew there was no point in trying further.

The pair of them deserve each other and they can go to hell, my mind ranted, *they've ruined my life!* And then, like the teenager I was, I held out my hand to accept a wad of cash from an authoritarian figure, head down, eyes to the floor. I left their house without giving any further line of defence, climbed into the waiting car, and with a heavy heart asked to be driven to Harare.

As the arched sign over the game reserve diminished in our

wake, disappearing into the folds of a mirage, it seemed an unlikely way to be spending my mid-morning, but life can be like that. A three-year relationship can end in a throwaway comment. A technological advance can wipe out a decades-old industry. A single decision can lead to disaster, or heroics.

A person's qualities, they say, are judged not by how you behave on an average day, but by how you pick yourself up after a fall; how you cope with a bad situation and make the most of it.

I needed to make the most of a bad situation.

But first, it was time to take stock.

JOB ONE: SAFARI GUIDE

Lessons learnt:

- Government bureaucracy can be incredible in its futility. If needs be, assess the system, and work out how to beat it
- Discussing salaries is not the done thing
- A job's 'dos and don'ts' can spill over into your private life
- Your boss will probably be a pain, whatever you do, wherever you go
- Everyone should work an outdoors job, at least once
- It's harsh to judge a man by his friends… but maybe fair
- Never shag the boss's wife, even if it's not true. And I promise it's not. Yet even though I've asserted my innocence over the years, people still think I have a thing for the much, *much* older lady

CHAPTER TWO

Harare: unemployed, 5140 miles from home.

Decisive action was needed, but my first step was the same one all boys – and many men – take in times of trouble: I called the mother.

"I want his name!"

She was livid, demanding to know who'd sent the fax, on the warpath for whoever had screwed up her little boy's African adventure. Not wanting blood on my hands I gave her a fake name, so saving the world from a brutal incident of maternal revenge, and then, once the mood had calmed a touch, I told her I hoped to stay in Zimbabwe, that I'd given myself a week to find a new job, and that if I failed, she'd need to expect me back in London far sooner than initially planned.

My return flight wasn't due to depart for three months so needed bringing forward, as I prepped for the likelihood of an early exit. In those simple, analogue times, otherwise known as 'The Pre-Internet Age', that meant communicating with Air France's regional office… *in person*. I tracked it down in Harare's drab, medium-rise central business district, an area strewn with street hawkers flogging a factory load of textiles, elephant carvings, and giraffe statuettes.

A grey block housed the airline's operation, and once inside I found a musky travel centre, time-warped, sun-bleached posters printed eons earlier promoting Paris, Lyon, and the French Riviera. '70s beige and brown held fort, strip lights belching a uniform neutrality. Cutting through the dust-laden air, I approached the counter, unfolded my papers, and asked the blue-and-white scarfed agent if my ticket could be changed to depart seven days later, with the option of a further change, if needed.

The woman behind the counter listened to my request and responded with a distinctly French shrug, even though she was native Zimbabwean. I wondered if it was requisite for the job. As she tapped away with apparent disinterest, I mused on the idea of Air France making her suffer through months of Parisian training.

"Next week we do the boff, the zut alors, the shrug, and if you succeed you will learn ze 'wrong directions for Englishman' routine. Study, femme, study!"

Clearly having scored full marks, she tapped, twiddled, shuffled, and shrugged, eventually sliding over a set of updated tickets, before turning back to polish her long, purple nails.

It was now or never.

I had seven days to find a new job, with dwindling cash, and no work permit. At least my first safari job had left me with a decent grounding in taking tours, the confidence to talk to guests, and a clear understanding of Zimbabwean rural life... surely that was enough to open a door or two?

Slam!

Slam!

Slam!

I grimaced, gripping my 'safari company hit list' tighter than a drowning man clutching flotsam. It was all I had as I pounded the uneven streets, a man on a mission. There were about twenty businesses to visit, and – determined to try them all – I marched into every one, invited or not. Unfortunately safari operators in Zimbabwe are less numerous than hotels in London, or brothels in Amsterdam, so I was soon running short, as I continued hearing the same answers:

"We're not hiring."

"It's not the right time."

"You have no work papers."

"We heard you shagged the boss's wife."

With two days left until my return flight, out of options, I slumped back to my hostel hoping to fall into a state of happy delirium with the help of a dozen beers and some idle banter. On entering the backpackers' retreat I was surprised to see two of my ex-colleagues sitting on bar stools, decked out in their short shorts and khaki shirt uniforms. I waved, smiling, but was on edge, unsure what they wanted.

"Bru, we've got good news," said Martin, grinning broadly.

"Oh yeah, what's that?" I asked.

"Mr Douglas has received another fax from your mate in England," said Lee, a tall, fair Zimbabwean in his late-twenties.

"Great, what now?"

"It's an apology."

I'd told my fax-writing friend in London about the carnage his first missive had caused, ranting about how he'd ruined my time in Zimbabwe, but I hadn't expected him to send an apology.

"Really?"

"Mr Douglas wants to offer you your job back. Everything as it was. He apologises for going off the handle and would like for you to return," said Martin, playing the part of the good news messenger, expecting me to leap from my seat in fervent joy.

Except I didn't.

What I said next surprised even myself.

"You can tell Mr Douglas…" I started, "…well, you can tell Mr Douglas… you can tell him to take his job and stick it up his fucking arse," was my eloquent response.

The guides thought I was joking.

"Yeah, sure. So you want to get your things?"

"I'm serious," I replied. "He thinks I want to work for him now I've seen how he treats people? Now I've seen what he's like? No way."

Martin gawped at me as though I'd spat on his grandmother's grave.

"It's a no. Thanks, but no thanks," I added, reiterating my stance in a slightly more polite, professional way.

Saying "no" was an instinctive reaction to a messy situation.

Even though I knew I could have cancelled my flight and headed back with them that very afternoon, it would never have been the same. The dynamics had changed between Mr Douglas and myself, and I knew the job could never be as it once was. Maybe I'm too proud, maybe I was still angry about being fired, but I stand by the decision.

That ship had sailed.

The two guides, perplexed by my response, headed back to the park, jaws dragging. Before leaving they wished me well on my return to the UK, justifiably believing my time in Zimbabwe to be finished, having seen me all but seal my fate.

But fate was about to turn my way.

For an oyster came a-knocking.

"Pack your bags!"

"Eh?"

"Get up, man. Pack your bags!"

"Eh?"

It was six in the morning, as the first rays of an African dawn broke through the odour of my male-only dormitory, one day before I was due to fly home. By that stage in my brief job hunt, with nothing on the table, I'd prepped myself for the embarrassment of an early return, had vaguely planned to punch my fax-sending friend, after which I hoped to blend back into London life, memories of my African adventure fading to nostalgic pulp.

The person kicking me out of bed had other ideas.

"Come on, lazy, I've gotta get going."

Her name was Kat Mason. I'd met her three days previously when she'd told me her lodge, Shute Safari Ranch, had no work available. But things had changed. The good news was that a job had come open; the bad news was that she'd decided to tell me by pulling me out of a beautiful, beer-induced sleep at six in the morning.

"What the…" I stuttered, bleary-eyed, half-naked.

27

"I need a guide. Are you interested?"

"Er… yes," was my confused, instinctive response.

"Pack your bags. We're heading to the lodge."

Needing no more incentive I jumped out of bed, brushed teeth, packed bag, and was ready to leave in ten minutes, something most of my friends would say is beyond my skill set. Turns out, all it takes is the fear of failure.

Once on the road the reality of the situation dawned on me, like a hippie stumbling into a marijuana plantation – slowly at first, followed by the world's biggest grin. The oyster theory was alive and well in southern Africa. I was to work at one of the biggest private ranches in the country. It was a miracle, a reprieve for my battered pride, and a last-minute escape from clichéd quips like, "you'll get back on the horse," said with a slight squeeze of the shoulder, a patronising glint in the eye; but instead of facing such blatant *Schadenfreude*, I was sitting in a Toyota pickup truck beside a perfect stranger, en route to guide safaris on her famed ranch located about 100km north-west of Zimbabwe's capital. Set within some of Africa's most lush and bountiful lands, it was blessed with every species of animal, insect, flora, and fauna that tourists love to see.

To my amazement my desperate search for work, along with Kat's employment needs, had collided to save me. It was a lesson in how luck and timing can determine your career path, often being just as crucial as education and talent. Sometimes you plot a course and set sail; other times you go where the wind blows, and the wind that day was blowing me towards stunning waters.

We rolled into the ranch an hour later, the world's biggest grin still slapped across my mug. The property spread out in all directions, was four times the size of Tusker Game Reserve, boasted five more Land Rovers, and could accommodate twice the number of tourists. I dumped my bags, called the French Zimbabwean to change my flight – I could swear I heard her shrug down the line – and then I lay on my bed, amused by the chaotic nature of life.

The uniform would again be shockingly short shorts, so again I'd feel like a member of the Village People, but I wasn't complaining. I'd been given a second chance to wear them with pride. And so with short shorts on it was time to learn the lay of the land, where to find the buffalo, rhino, hippo, and elephant, and how to mix the lodge's speciality sundowner cocktail.

In my varied, choppy and – some might say – disastrous career, those days at Shute Safari Ranch stand out as some of the happiest and most satisfying, and therefore there's not much to comment on.

I could reminisce about a British Airways cabin crew arriving, skinny dipping and leaving, without me seeing a glimpse of their glorious pool time; or I could wax lyrical about an enraged rhino trapping me in a damaged vehicle for two hours, finally being freed by passing workers scaring off the confused bully. Those are memorable tales from a positive experience, an experience I relished having been saved from an early return home, so my main take-away was simple:

Appreciate it when times are good.

My employer treated me well, and in return I worked hard, and did a good job. It's the way it should be, and I can only hope they saw it the same way. I look back on my time there with a sepia-tinted fondness that filmmakers use to identify the 1930s, and that's more than enough.

In fact, it's ideal.

Enjoying it, the days merged into one; I lost track of time.

Christmas arrived, barely noticed; it was just another day, another safari, but as I dragged myself from bed I felt a change in the air. It was the second time in as many days that I'd felt it, the first being as I drove through the outer reaches of the ranch, not a soul in sight, and glimpsed an African image I'd dreamed of seeing: two giraffes strolling across an open veld (grassland) towards a thorny acacia tree, sun setting behind them, the entire scene tinged in a golden-red richness.

I'm unsure why I wanted to see this vision of Africa, but it was in me, as clear as a marketing poster for a national park, or a still from *The Lion King*. Déjà vu. I scrambled for my camera, unable to believe what I was seeing, couldn't find it, looked again, then stopped, sinking into my seat. I took a deep breath, realising the moment was just for me. Forget the camera, forget sharing; this was mine and mine alone. I can still recall that image, as clear as any photograph, and it's mine to enjoy, my perfect African vista.

But from that moment on, something changed.

It wasn't all that noticeable at first, just an unidentifiable itch, a gnawing thought, yet before long it had resolved into an unavoidable desire, as clear as parental advice on narcotics. It was a simple realisation, but it was the truth:

I'd got the T-shirt. I'd done it.

It was fait accompli.

Whatever I'd come to Africa to achieve had been achieved; it was time to move on. I'd taken a hundred safaris, and that was enough for a boy who'd arrived to experience Africa, not become a permanent resident of Africa. Having learned every facet of animal weight, feeding habits, mating practices, nocturnal behaviour, and more, having seen my 'giraffes at sunset' vista, having swatted a million mosquitos, I knew I'd been a safari guide long enough.

I told the Mason family I was ready to head home, and we agreed on a late-January departure date. Itchy feet had forced my travel plans. Little did I realise it would be the first in a long line of 'itchy feet' decisions, catapulting my career in unpredictable directions throughout my twenties and thirties.

But, I reasoned, *a man's gotta do what a man's gotta do*.

After all, the oyster theory permits it.

JOB TWO: SAFARI GUIDE, TAKE II

Lessons learnt:

- Knock on every door and be tenacious. It's not until you've tried every option that you can resort to self-pitying drinks at a hostel bar

- Stand by your guns; be wary of knee-jerk employers
- The fear of failure is a powerful force
- Sometimes you set sail, plotting a course, but other times the wind blows, and you go with it. Pray it leads to stunning waters
- Never wander off when randy cabin crew are in the vicinity
- Recognise when the going is good, and enjoy it
- Even the best jobs can become monotonous
- There's no stopping determinedly itchy feet

CHAPTER THREE

When the sky clouds over, and those little ovals become streaked with spray, you know your jet's reached the verdant shores of the British Isles. And so it was in late-January 1997 when a trained, semi-toned (slightly less fat), English safari guide arrived from Zimbabwe via Johannesburg and Paris.

I'd survived my first brush with work, but spending five months on safari was hardly career-building stuff. It was little more than a working holiday, a soft introduction to the working world, and a real introduction to the wider world. Like most Brits I'd holidayed as a child, but combining work and travel had opened my eyes to a new way of experiencing foreign lands. You get a far better picture of life overseas once you've been quizzed about your salary, disciplined for visiting a compound, bullied by a rhino, and fired for sleeping with the boss's wife.

Ready to travel some more, back home I threw myself into planning another overseas trip, but not to work, instead to back-pack SE Asia, as I sought to maximise my free time before university and the rat race clogged my calendar. A clichéd route was booked in, travelling from Vietnam to Bali, where I'd be living on $10 a day, meeting backpackers from around the world, while growing hair longer and greasier than a 1980s thrash metal band.

That may be, but this isn't a story about extended holidays; it's about career. Lessons learned on the backpacking trails of Asia are best gleaned by going there and getting your own T-shirt. Yet there's one aspect of that trip that stayed with me long after my hemp-woven Aladdin pants had turned to ash, a peculiarity that helped me better understand what I wanted from the working world, unwittingly fuelled by a group of people I'd meet time and again on those hedonistic trails:

The eternal traveller.

They were found on the beaches of Vietnam, Bali, and Thailand, and I instantly liked them, as they talked of choosing to check out, of beating the system, of living the good life. They were utterly different to anyone I knew. Mostly Westerners, young and old, they shared the same trait of swimming against the current. It was obvious they'd stay overseas for as long as possible, on the open road, or rooted to a beach, yet although they were seemingly content, I knew I could never join their gang, for something was missing.

It was something intangible, something they seemed to lack, something that made their lifestyle unsuited to my future. At the time I didn't know what it was, but I could sense its need; years later, it's as clear as day:

They were lacking... purpose.

That's the fundamental driver that keeps people creating, working and developing, giving them fuel to live and thrive. And that friendly, hirsute crowd were lacking purpose, or at least any purpose society deems useful, which made their lifestyle distinctly unpalatable. I could never live their way because it didn't fit with what I was subconsciously seeking.

Henry David Thoreau said, "Success usually comes to those who are too busy to be looking for it." That's a strong reason to stay busy, as is this from Lord Byron: "The busy have no time for tears," which is somewhat more depressing and less inspirational, but Byron's sad message is backed by Kim Cattrall, an actress best known for playing sordid Samantha in *Sex and the City*, who adds contemporary weight: "Since doing the show I've been so busy that I've not really had time to mope." And that, as they say, is case closed.

Find purpose. Stay busy. Don't mope.

On returning from Asia, remembering those eternal travellers, I was a little wiser about what *not* to do, but none the wiser as to what *would* keep me as mope-free as Ms Cattrall. All I knew was that I wanted to be busy and productive, so I figured that it was time to test the water.

Before university began I'd take on two stints of work experience, which I assumed would clear up what I should be doing with my days on Earth. It seemed simple: *I'll dip my toe in the working world, see what it's about, and know what to do. Parents, teachers, they over-complicate it. Bandits. Nah, I'll be fine. I've got this career shit wrapped up, in the bag. It'll be sorted by uni, nuff said...*

Of course, doooood. Teenagers believe so much to be black and white, yet some kids *do* fall into career paths that easily.

Would I be one of them?

It was time to pick a path, and the line of work I chose to experience was one I was convinced would suit me, partly because several of my teachers had suggested it, but mostly because it matched my interests. I'd always liked the industry, had always enjoyed its products, so assumed working on the inside would be just as enjoyable as leafing through its inky pages.

And with that in mind, I set my sights on exploring the competitive, oft-derided, always feared world of British news journalism.

THE DISCOVERY OF PURPOSE

Lessons learnt:

- Pre-university travel is the ultimate nirvana
- The eternal traveller is seemingly content, but it's not for everyone
- Purpose is key (even if you're not aware of it)
- Lord Byron was a bit of a downer
- At some point, you need to pick a path

CHAPTER FOUR

Work experience. What was I thinking?

The term sent shivers down my spine. This was no way to end a year off. Reality should have been on hold, waiting post-university, not crashing into my nineteenth year joining other unwelcomed guests, in particular the zit that overtook my entire chin for a month – 'moon chin' will never be forgotten – and a spell of bronchitis that denied me junk food for three weeks.

And now work experience, the cherry on the cake. But it was time, so I drew up a shortlist, placed calls, and waited to see which way the wind would blow. Fortunately seeking work experience is significantly easier than securing an actual job, so it didn't take long before I was offered two weeks at *The Cambridge Telegraph*, where I'd be witnessing the daily grind of regional news, joining staffers at the coal face of community journalism.

I'd wanted to test the water; this was as wet as I could get.

Journalism had been suggested at school, not only by the faculty, but also by a careers evaluation test using a two-bit super-computer to analyse hundreds of assorted multiple-choice answers. Admittedly suggesting a media career wasn't a bad shout, but the super-computer also advised being a 'prison officer', which I'm disappointed to report has yet to bear fruit.

As a lifelong career-flipper I expect I'll eventually add 'prison officer' to my CV, presumably to be tried after divorce, or diagnosis of erectile dysfunction, those being the most pertinent times to release pent-up anger – and where better than on Britain's convict population? Or maybe I've been watching too much reality TV, have misjudged prison management and, following these comments, should permanently strike off a future career in the UK penal system.

Super-computer aside, the long-standing wisdom in career planning is that for those adept at English studies (and little else) journalism is the right path. If you're good at English and Maths, follow Maths. If you're good at English and French, follow French. If you're amazing at English, have a devil's tail and an uncanny ability to eat human flesh, become a lawyer.

I was plain old good at English, so journalism it was. I'm sure I once had the potential to enter the legal world – flesh-eating aside – but when I later learned that lawyers are some of the most depressed people in the UK I wasn't disappointed to have missed out. Besides, law firms would have discovered that at a young age I'd once helped an old lady to cross a road, thereby marking me out as permanently unsuited to the legal profession.

Too much lawyer bashing? Admittedly lawyers do receive a tonne of bad press, but so do journalists, who write the press, yet are paid a fraction of the rate for their services, so who's the real loser? That should be clear to all, but the finer details of postgraduate salaries aren't a priority for work experience grunts, so I carried on towards journalism, lured in by its creative temptations.

Trying newspaper work is like buying a slice of pizza in Leicester Square. You want it to be delicious, but deep down you're wary, concerned about hygiene, flavour, and grease overdosing. Similarly, reporting is a popular career choice, with journalists able to shape opinion while flexing their creative muscles, but it's a greasy temptation, for below that shiny surface lurk the distasteful, even poisonous twosome of bottom feeder pay and torturous hours.

There are pros and cons to every job, but at the outset it's the pros people focus on, prompting English graduates to seek journalism for a living, hoping one day to win 'Journalist of the Year', possibly having uncovered government corruption or corporate crime. The low pay, they assume, will pale into comparison to such a worthy career, as they defend the rights of the people, of their esteemed, trusting readers. They reason that reporters are the

Fourth Estate, watching the watchers; the downsides are irrelevant to such a position in society.

And I too believed in these pro points, so eagerly awaited my chance to put them to the test. With a mission at my side, I left London, pushing into the English countryside, heading towards the colleges of Cambridge and their terrifyingly intelligent kids. Yet they weren't the destination; I was aiming for a bland industrial estate on the outskirts of the city, where I'd be shadowing journalists and challenging the truth at the headquarters of *The Cambridge Telegraph*.

Walls covered in historic headlines. Photos of major events. A calendar years out of date. The newspaper's interior looked just as Hollywood had promised, minus the shouting, arguing, and necking of blood pressure pills.

The receptionist pointed me towards the editor, a plainly dressed man in his mid-50s, who was studying the previous day's edition. I thrust out my hand, but he barely registered me, even though I'd arrived on time, shoes polished, pen and pad primed. Nowadays I know why. Interns can add to, rather than aid, a workload. "Sit there, look, and learn," was his simple command; in other words, keep quiet, observe, and stay out the way. His reporters, clearly over-worked, were also unwilling to enlist the new kid, who'd likely ask a thousand questions, further delaying their scramble to meet deadlines, yet I couldn't complain; from the off, I was doing what I was there to do: 'experience work', watching journalists hit the phones, take notes, select images, write stories, and chase down leads.

And then, at the start of day three, as I began to fidget and count ceiling tiles, I was brought into the fold, tasked with one of the most common assignments on any newspaper worldwide.

"Take a look at this page, read it carefully, and note any errors. The dead don't care, but the living don't like mistakes," said the editor, giving me my morbid chore. I nodded enthusiastically, the sage words of my mother ringing in my ears: "Whatever they ask you to do, do it, do it well, and smile about doing it."

I grinned the grin of politicians grasping for last-minute votes on suburban doorsteps, then settled into my task with as much vigour as could be mustered, proofreading obituaries of the region's recently deceased.

Sitting there, staring at a page that summarised the lives of people I'd never know, I suspected a love for journalism wasn't going to flow from my time in Cambridgeshire; but I wanted it to flow, I truly did, so I carefully checked every date, name, motto, and farewell message left to the good, dead people of the county, while angling for a speedy move to the news desk.

That's where the real power lies, I reckoned, but when I was finally rewarded with a news assignment, it was to write up one of the biggest stereotypes in regional journalism – and it did little to increase my fervour for the profession. It was a story I never thought I'd see, let alone research on a two-week stint of work experience. It was the ultimate cliché: FIREMAN SAVES CAT IN TREE.

I'd say you couldn't make it up, but you could, and people would think you were being unimaginative. I don't have to. That was literally the story I was told to research. Maybe it was an industry joke, or bad timing, but for my first ever article I found myself interviewing the 'victims' of a cat-stuck-in-a-tree incident. There had literally been a cat. Stuck in a tree. And it had been rescued. By a fireman.

Clichéd it may have been, but this was regional news. Get the angle, do the interview, write the piece, hook the reader, and keep them buying. It's a proven business formula – one that's worked for centuries – and it was now my turn to write an editorial piece, joining this refined process.

But where should I start? Was the victim the cat, the fireman, the cat's owner, or the bemused newspaper intern? Was I really writing about a cat in a tree? Was this really the reward for proofreading a hundred RIPs? I sat bolt upright, stared at the computer screen, and I hope it's brazenly obvious what I thought:

Flee, young man, flee! shouted à la Doc Brown in *Back to the Future*.

Regional journalism had shown its true colours, failing to grasp my attention, let alone my love. It had been tedious, even depressing work that I was keen to avoid... but I wasn't free of it yet.

After several more days reporting on similarly ground-breaking news I left Cambridge for another stint of work experience, this time in a niche environment, based far closer to home. I was switching to a financially focused magazine, giving journalism one more shot, so it was out of the provinces and back to the capital. Next stop: the much-revered *Blackfriars Teller* magazine, located in the hothouse environment of the City of London.

Scratch regional journalism. Balls to that. Totally dull. This is where it's at, in the City. This must be where journalism gets interesting, working in Britain's financial district, surrounded by blazer-clad traders, public school bankers, barrow boy dealers, and Eurotrash Hedgefunders. This is where Britain makes its cash, so why be anywhere else?

That was my thinking, but there was one hitch: my knowledge of the City was non-existent. For starters, it goes to show how little I knew about the Square Mile that I'd term anyone a 'Eurotrash Hedgefunder'.

Work experience 'Take II' opened my eyes to a corner of the British capital I'd never previously explored: the Square Mile, Planet Earth's financial hub. Medieval lanes, modern towers, tiny shops, bustling cafés, and an aggressive atmosphere permeate the tightly packed area that generates almost ten per cent of Britain's annual wealth. It's a centre of business that began with the Romans, was developed by traders and merchants, decimated by the Great Fire of London, and is now home to tens of thousands of bankers, stockbrokers, and traders, along with specialist media outlets reporting on their daily efforts to turn piles of money into ever greater piles of money. It's a world in which greed is good, trading is gambling, salaries make eyes water, and where the hungry of Europe fight for a place at the most rewarding of top tables.

Watching that gold-plated table is the Fourth Estate, reporting and investigating financial stories for the world's business pages. It should have been an exciting world to enter, chasing the trades of the day, focusing on the hottest brokers of the year, but alas… it wasn't.

Within a day I knew the supposedly exciting reputation of the City of London (or the Square Mile) wasn't to be found in an office proofreading finance articles. Europe's wealthiest may have been all around, but when you're working for free spotting errors that would bore an economics professor, you're never going to 'get the call' – that is if journalists can, or do, 'get the call'.

It was an introduction to the true nature of the City; it's not all Gordon Gekkos and Alan Sugars. The glamour of the finance community, of shouting traders and dodgy brokers, is a tiny part of a far more pragmatic machine. The reality is the careful, steady analysis of numbers, patterns, people, preferences, disasters, opportunities, upturns, downturns, and more, which lead to predictions, which lead to gambles, which lead to profits and losses. That's the finance game summed up in one line; unfortunately I had to endure a far more detailed introduction.

How to steer an intern away from journalism in one easy step: tell him to proofread the whole of your financial rag, while ignoring him for the entirety of his two-week stint. After a week of such tedium I was fantasising about the long drop, drowning in a bath of my own urine, or undertaking an American-style machine gun rampage. Sadly I fear heights, can't produce enough urine, and don't have access to American gun stores. Instead, I did what all Brits do in times of peril; I went to the pub and moaned to my friends.

It goes without saying that I ran from journalism, ran as fast as my little legs could carry me, sure in the fact that I never wanted to write another word, proofread another page, or edit another article, for any publication, ever again. Repetitive, mundane work wasn't to be part of my future.

Years on, I now know I experienced the crummy end of the industry, never meeting any of those wise, friendly, mentor types who take a few minutes to show you a small window into the best of their world. Maybe if I had, I'd have loved it. Who knows? You can never look back with regret, as long as you choose your moves wisely, having sized up the best information to hand.

And as far as I knew I *did* have the best information to hand, gleaned from four weeks spent inside two bastions of the industry. It was enough. I'd keep my options open, searching for a better fit. University was just around the corner, with its wise lecturers and inspirational guidance, so I assumed the answers I'd need to the working world were mere months away.

It's like, obvious, given a bit of time. University's all about preparing us for the future, so, like, what's the big issue?

Soon enough I knew I'd be surrounded by the sharpest of minds, driven to excel, to thrive in a first-rate establishment of British higher education, leading to a universally-respected degree, and a top-tier job at a top flight company.

And that's *exactly* what happened.

Yeah, sure it was.

WORK EXPERIENCE

Lessons learnt:

- A zit that covers your entire chin will never be forgotten
- Two-bit super-computers are hit-and-miss, but your gut instinct will tell you what to ignore, and what to follow
- Below the shiny surface of journalism lurk the distasteful, even poisonous twosome of bottom feeder pay and torturous hours
- Spend a few days reading obituaries; it'll seem as though every human has led the most angelic of lives
- Finance news remarkably provokes both homicidal *and* suicidal instincts
- It's a good thing I can't produce large amounts of urine
- Journalism was absolutely, 100%, not for me

CHAPTER FIVE

Alcohol makes me sexy. The police are on your side. Chicken tikka masala was invented in the UK. Heinz ketchup is British. Universities provide halls accommodation to all first year students.

Most of you will know that none of those statements are entirely accurate. Alcohol *can* make you sexy, but only to your own ego; the police *are* on your side, until you annoy the wrong officer; chicken tikka masala is (of course) *Indian* cuisine, but tweaked for the British palate; universities *can* provide accommodation, but only if you apply on time; and lastly – odd one out – Heinz ketchup is *fully* American, not even a teeny, tiny bit British.

Unfortunately several weeks from the start of university I knew none of this, believing all those statements to be true. Within a month I'd realise the inaccuracy of one in particular, but none the wiser I wasted away the last of my summer days, blissfully unaware that the University of the West of England in Bristol – where I was to study for three years – offers student accommodation, if you apply on time, the cut-off point usually being in early-June.

And so, as other students diligently filled out forms, I was in Cambridge reporting on cats up trees. As other students chose halls of residence, I was proofreading financial pages. As other students were awarded accommodation, I was soaking up the sun. And as other students were preparing to move into uni digs, I was feet up, watching *Buffy the Vampire Slayer…* until a friend casually asked where I planned to live in Bristol.

"Uni halls, of course," came back my response.

"Nice, which one?"

"I dunno, whatever they assign me."

"But… you should know by now."

"How?"

"By getting the paperwork back from the application form you filled out."

"What application form?"

I'm sure you can see what happened next.

Panic. Unrestrained, overt panic.

Flash forward three minutes:

"Hello, is that the University of the West of England?"

"Yes…"

"Can I speak to someone regarding student accommodation please?"

Flash forward five minutes:

"Yeah… hi Mum… we need to chat about Bristol… there's been a slight glitch…" But not even the best of mothers can conjure up a room in a halls of residence, a week before term starts, at a 27,000-student university.

That door had firmly shut.

Thud, thud, thud, thud, thud, thud.

The regular rhythm meant it could only be one thing: my housemate and his girlfriend were at it again. It was so loud I felt part of their love-making, just not a willing part. I groaned, glaring again at my new surroundings: four feet by seven, the room was barely big enough for a mattress, but it was mine, my new home, and ongoing third party love shack.

Having confirmed there was no way I could get into a halls of residence, a mad search had begun for somewhere – anywhere – to live. An old friend was studying in the year ahead, and he had what he honestly termed a 'broom cupboard' going spare. With no other option I jumped at it, but the reality of living in a 'broom cupboard' soon hit me, and was hitting me hard, hitting me in the head, hitting me over and over, hitting me with every thrust the libidinous man in the next door room could pound into his willing partner.

At least one of us was into it.

University had started with a literal bump; even so, I was excited to shift into higher education, a step I was sure would lead to solid future in a successful career. But that academic idealism faded fast, as within weeks I discovered that some universities have a mass production mentality, churning out degree-awarded students, yet failing to connect with the individual; and it appeared the University of the West of England (UWE) fell squarely into that category.

To know why, we need to go back a few years.

Once known as Bristol Polytechnic, UWE became a university after a change in the law. For those of you not familiar with the scintillating world of UK higher education, here's a politics-light round up:

It's 1992 and the Tory government is firmly in power, and has been for thirteen years. Maggie was pushed out two years back, so cricket bore John Major is leading the Conservatives, turning Westminster grey with his bland but safe approach to leadership. In a moment of unusually leftist thinking the government decides the university system is too elitist, so resolves to tackle the problem. The Further and Higher Education Act 1992 is brought in, and overnight around thirty polytechnics – essentially professional training institutions – are turned into universities in the vague, albeit aspirational hope that more people from varied backgrounds will achieve degree-level qualifications.

What happened was rather more than the government bargained for, as every Tom, Rick and Barry could now attend university, leading to a massive increase in people exercising their right to free education. For most it was an opportunity to expand their horizons, but some went into what the red tops termed 'Mickey Mouse Courses', which popped up to cater to soaring demand, targeting students unable to gain – or unwilling to seek – places on mainstream subjects.

Golf Course Management, Surf Science, and a module that

saw students analysing the football culture of David Beckham all drew media attention. You might as well study 'Wooden Slat Stack Management' (how to use a ladder) or 'Plastic Profit Science' (how to juggle credit cards), both of which are useful in the real world, but tend to be learnt the hard way.

An English degree, on the other hand, is a respected choice, although I have no idea why; the studies I did could have been passed by a sixteen-year-old. In fact, sixteen-year-old me would have done much better than university me, likely walking away with a higher grade than my 2:2 result (a fifty to sixty per cent score). Sixteen-year-old me would probably have got a first (over seventy per cent), due to drinking less booze, and being far more disciplined.

Not so during my uni days, where discipline meant only smoking a joint *after* midday. It's a surprise I even managed a 2:2, having missed several exams, half my lectures, and most of my tutorials. But I did, and ever since have been able to flaunt a British university degree that's useful worldwide.

Times they are a changing, though. Coasting to a degree these days is as popular as VHS tapes and the Filofax, as students have to fork over ever increasing amounts for higher education. The 1992 polytechnic switch led to university funding spread thin, running on fumes, with the obvious outcome being an end to free degree-level education. The first students to stump up tuition fees were enrolled in courses from 1998, charged £1,000 a year, but that rose to £3,000 in 2004, and jumped up to a top rate of £9,000 a year from 2012.

Although unpopular, it was all the government could do to keep the lights on in campuses and colleges, but it means students now rack up stratospheric levels of debt for their degree, averaging over £50,000 (once you factor in living expenses). Facing that kind of bill it's no surprise most millennial kids study damn hard to ensure they're first in line for a highly paid job on graduation. How different in '97, when university was free, and the only pressure students faced was respecting the etiquette of the 'pot circle' – 'puff, puff, pass… puff, puff, pass…'

Many times I've looked back on those hazy days and thought I should have ploughed through a course in Business Studies, leading to a profitable career in something dull but comfortable, that being the usual deal struck between high earners and dreary companies. Instead I studied English Literature, a course I thought would include Shakespeare, Keats, Wordsworth, Byron, Milton, and other legends of the 'Lit Pop' scene; yet the powers that educate had other ideas, focusing my studies on niche American literature, the analysis of an Australian soap opera, and a drama module that saw me pretend to be a lily pad as other students mimicked frogs, leaping over me, presumably thrilled at the realisation they were leap-frogging towards an internationally-respected qualification.

Lacking interest in most of my curriculum I considered quitting, but without a plan I stuck with it, and thank God I did. Having sprawled out as a lily pad on the grimy floor of a Bristol gymnasium in order to pass a year-two drama module, I've been able to apply for jobs that only accept degree-level applicants.

That's the way the world spins.

It's better for a young person to spend three years at university being leap-frogged by stoners, than it is to leave school and enter the workforce. Attitudes to studying may have matured, yet I'm still amazed that employers put almost any degree above relevant, working life experience. That you can regurgitate information in an exam hall should be of little comfort to corporate shareholders, but that's how the game works.

Be the lily pad, get the qualification, and leap ahead.

And so that's what I did, right to the end of my last exam, after which I bolted for the motorway before anyone had donned a gown, or thrown a mortarboard within an inch of me. I had no interest in celebrating such an odd use of my time. University was over, evaporating in a redundant blur, but the highlights are still clear:

A casino membership used for free sandwiches, afternoons spent playing Mario Kart, a lecture devoted to watching *Neighbours*, half my course missed; yet through it all, one degree earned, and one boy – supposedly – ready to hit the working world as an educated, useful member of society… nay, as an adult, a participant, a man, *dammit*, a man.

According to family, teachers, professors, civilisation, and the British government, I was ready to enter the workforce.

Gulp.

BIG GULP.

UNIVERSITY: AN EASY LEAP AHEAD

Lessons learnt:

- Alcohol doesn't make you sexy. Ever
- Universities, like all organisations, require research
- Overhearing the next-door lothario never gets pleasurable
- Don't screw up 'pot circle' etiquette: it's 'puff, puff, pass…'
- Lying flat, pretending to be a lily pad, puts you in better standing than those without degrees. But you'll still need to answer *the ultimate question*

CHAPTER SIX

Gulp-*ish*, that is to say.

Even though I was still to answer the ultimate question, and as terrifying as the real world is, following graduation I felt buoyed. I'd earned something nobody could take away from me, and it boosted my confidence tenfold: *I have a degree! I'm invincible! I'm coming to shake shit up. I can do whatever I want to do!*

It's at times like this that people pray you'll walk into a street lamp or a sharp bayonet, several times over.

But the world had never looked more inviting. A degree had added extra struts, support beams, and deep foundations to my ingrained oyster theory. I'd been told that success began with a degree, and with one now adorning my CV I assumed doors should crack open, just a little, just a bit, just enough.

Yet before I got close to those proverbial doors, there was something that demanded serious attention: *the ultimate question.*

Even though I thought doors would crack ajar, I still didn't know what doors to approach. As a reluctant student I'd barely thought about the future. It had seemed a distant prospect, tomorrow's problem, but of course many of my peers *had* been planning, having chosen studies connected to their intended paths – it's called Golf Course Management for a reason.

Ironically the group not heading in any obvious direction were those students who'd taken 'respected' humanities degrees – English, History, Philosophy, History of Art, et al. – leaving many of us to share the same thought:

Oh, shit.

But whether a humanities or science graduate, or the future manager of St Andrews Golf Club, all of us shared one common trait: we were completely unprepared for the real world. That's because real life demands a plethora of skills that schools and universities fail to provide, a dismal realisation that left me wondering: *How is it that after thirteen years of primary, secondary, and tertiary education, I'm still unprepared for adulthood?*

I've thought long and hard about this, about what skills are needed, and it all comes down to what Mr Average Graduate will face during his average life, as he faces average problems that require average solutions, so let's break it down:

Mr Average Graduate, let's call him Mr AG, will need a place to live. He'll need knowledge of tenancy agreements, basic law, basic plumbing, basic electrics, dealing with bills, local government, and how to avoid being ripped off.

How is Mr AG going to know what to say when Mr AP (Average Plumber) tells him the 'decarbunculator' on his 'redondabit' at the back of his ten-year-old boiler needs replacing for £550, plus VAT, for four hours' work? Does he have the ability to say, "You're having a laugh, mate; that part only costs £3.99 from any hardware store."

Of course Mr AG can't.

He hasn't got a clue.

Lucky for him that's the landlord's job, but Mr AG will need a job to pay his rent. At this point interview skills, job-hunting tips, and workplace etiquette would come in handy. What if he needs to drive to his job? Can he avoid being conned into buying a car that's worth ten per cent of its advertised price? And once bought, should he not have basic mechanic skills so that Mr AM (Average Mechanic) can't rip him off in the same way as Mr AP?

Maybe Mr AG wants to save some money as he earns in his new job. Should he understand finance, or be open to crooks conning him into investing in dodgy schemes, or taking out high-interest loans to support his twenty-something lifestyle? Maybe he'd like to conserve cash and cook at home; shouldn't he have a working knowledge of culinary skills, and basic money management?

There's more, much more, but I won't go on. The facts are

so obvious it's depressing. Educators need to think about this, but instead they'll keep on pumping out poorly prepared graduates.

I have a theory as to why it's set up this way: it props up the economy. If people saved money it wouldn't enter the system, so with Mr AG wasting his salary the economy wins, businesses win, and by the time Mr AG has learned the hard way he's broke, in debt, paying it back forever, steeped in loathing, ready to rip off the next generation. Genius.

Of course it *is* important to inspire and amaze the young with arts and culture, languages, and history, but a balance can be found. If it isn't, millions more AGs will enter the real world without a clue as to how to avoid its pitfalls.

I carefully considered my skill-set in light of Mr AG, and quickly realised my buoyed confidence to have been vastly misjudged. I threw out the arrogance, deleted, *I'm invincible!* from my thoughts, and eyed up my next step with reassessed pragmatism. I was just another AG, entering the world with a banal humanities degree, barely able to look after myself, let alone offer useful skills to Britain's demanding employers. On top of which, I didn't want to work in journalism, *so what the hell would I do with an English Literature degree?*

The GULP returned.

BIG GULP.

But there was no going back.

It was time to answer the question.

THE UNIVERSITY OF LIFE

Lessons learnt:

- A degree will boost your confidence
- Golf Course Management is clearly a subject to be revered (and studied)
- Mr AG has problems with plumbers, mechanics, finance, and cooking. Let's face it, he's got issues

- Have a plan going into higher education, as it'll be twice as hard to mould one at the back end of your studies

CHAPTER SEVEN

Choice. It can be paralysing.

Like a Las Vegas diner eyeing up a lavish buffet, unable to choose what to devour, picking a career can also result in salivary paralysis. There are simply hundreds of options to consider, but there's one group that has nothing to contemplate, at least not for several years:

Military-funded students.

Those that secure a place on the Army Undergraduate Bursary scheme are locked into a three-year deal to fight for Queen and country, leaving no question as to what they'll do post-university. Sometimes I regret not signing up, especially on those wish-I-had-a-gun-in-my-hand type days, as semi-automatics are provided to all, even on Mondays. Yes, you may end up dying in a firefight for a cause that some git in Westminster thought important, but don't focus on the negatives; think about your job security, and soon enough you'll sleep like a baby (once the enemy stops shelling your Forward Operating Base).

Of course the army being a dependable step is nothing new; it's been a recommended career choice for centuries. From medieval times to the end of Victoria's reign it was the approved destination for the gentry, but they weren't alone, as all strata of society had expected careers – or 'work and duty' – slapped on them from birth, governed by a system that's been forged over millennia.

To grasp how the working world came to be what it is today, you need to go back through the annals of time, all the way back to those free-thinking, 100m-sprint-in-the-buff-and-celebrate-with-a-boy Ancient Greeks. They had a relaxed attitude to career, instead weighting their time towards developing the body and mind (which was possibly made easier by the use of slaves to do society's hard graft).

Centuries later Jews then Christians would turn that attitude on its head, promoting the need for hard work, the faithful required to toil long hours in order to be free of the sin of sloth, thereby drawing close to their Almighty. Within a thousand years this idea of hard work and pleasing God had become enshrined in Western civilisation. That the Church used the idea to control its subjects, preaching piety through labour – while demanding you fill its coffers – isn't up for debate. Landlords, nobles, and monarchs also loved the idea, taking as much as the masses could stomach. When the serfs were pushed too far they'd revolt, as in France, 1789, inspired, some say, by the American War of Independence, or in Russia, 1917, inspired, most agree, by the need for slightly tastier potatoes.

On the other hand, British serfs sucked up their society-imposed 'career choice' of pig farmer or turnip harvester without much ruckus. The Magna Carta of 1215 began the lengthy process of enshrining citizen rights into law, as did the development of a strong parliament, backed by the Bill of Rights in 1689, leaving the average Briton (in theory) somewhat protected, but power still lay in the hands of the aristocracy, and their fellow land owners.

The Church promoted the natural order of career – meaning you'd follow what you were born into – and monarchs followed the church's edict. Even when England drifted into Protestantism (around the 1530s), the divine order of work was kept. It was believed, or it was useful for those in power to believe, that God chose a place for you on this planet, so it would be irreligious to go against His decisions. 'How dare you want to be a court jester, you're born to be a turnip farmer,' was the general idea, updated now to, 'How dare you want to be a computer programmer, you're supposed to be a Starbucks barista.'

The idea of working for yourself, not the landlord, started to take root in the 16th century via John Calvin's teachings, who broke from the Catholic Church to preach, in part, about individualism. But he also spoke about not spending your hard-earned money on enjoyable pastimes, which is possibly why his followers aren't seen on street corners the world over.

Things were improving, slowly, yet it wasn't until the Age of Enlightenment in the 18th century that it was no longer seen as irreligious for people to pull themselves out of poverty – it was seen as progress. The roots of our modern-day career culture were taking hold.

Things moved faster following the Industrial Revolution of the late 1800s and early 1900s, as people flooded the cities, searching for a slice of prosperity, possibly even happiness, something the United States of America had in 1776 shockingly proclaimed as an acceptable ambition. It's of no surprise that millions of Europeans left for America, but many more were drawn to their nearest factory, attracted by any job, as long as it paid more than working the land.

These weren't yet career choices, but lifestyle choices of people seeking to improve their lot. It wasn't until the middle of the 20th century that actively choosing a career would become the norm, not the exception.

After World War II, the old system finally began to fade, as a new world emerged, and with it, opportunities for all. As the West screamed for a wobbly-legged American in the '50s, an English pop foursome in the '60s, bell-bottomed fashion in the '70s, and a "yee-hee!" youngest brother of five in the '80s, a career revolution was reshaping the workplace. Education was still a barrier for many, but career choices were becoming more widespread, more accessible.

And as choices grew, so glass ceilings and social mobility barriers were smashed. The first female stockbrokers were seen in London in the '70s; and a decade later non-private school 'barrow boy' traders arrived, relying on street smarts, showing City chiefs how to make even bigger piles of profit.

The masses took over the media – so long, 'Mr Well-Spoken BBC announcer' – and as the jobs market was shaken up in sectors as diverse as banking, media, property, medicine, and hospitality, so the economy itself changed, the UK developing into a service-led sector, partly driven by a need to adapt, as British manufacturing struggled to compete with foreign goods and labour.

In every country you'll still find the 'it was better in the old days' brigade, but there are few who could claim that Western society, even global society, has failed to make huge advances over the past 150 years, improving the lives of millions.

Leaving university at the start of the new millennium was therefore nothing to complain about. Opportunities, even for a humanities graduate, were for the taking, but I still had to tackle that inescapable problem:

The ultimate question.

In trying to answer it I took a step back, carefully sizing up the buffet, assessing every option suitable to my skills and interests: publishing, property, catering, communications, hospitality, travel, recruitment, marketing, politics, policing, aviation, finance, photography, sales... I considered them all.

There were pros and cons to each one, but a decision was needed, *now*. I felt under pressure, rattled, a state only worsened every time somebody asked me where I planned to work... *choose, dammit, choose...* but there was too much on my shortlist, too much choice... *how the hell do people do this?* Not knowing, I took one last look, listened to my rumbling gut, and decided to behave like a Las Vegas diner. Dinner plate at the ready, I stepped forward...

...and lurched at the most succulent item on the table.

HOW WORK TO LIVE, BECAME LIVE TO WORK

Lessons learnt:
- Choice can be paralysing
- If you have wish-I-had-a-gun-in-my-hand type days, avoid the army
- Don't blame the nearest Jew or Christian for your fourteen-hour workday. It almost certainly isn't their fault

- Russian serfs will do anything for slightly tastier potatoes
- Leaving university at the start of the new millennium was far from a bad time to enter the working world
- If in doubt, think like a Las Vegas diner – listen to your gut instinct

CHAPTER EIGHT

I blame my sister. Well, to be accurate, I blame a friend of hers. Okay, to be 100% accurate, I blame her friend's fantastic job.

In the summer of 2000 Mel Pritchard was a movie locations scout, tasked with travelling the world in search of stunning backdrops. After uni, back in London, I found myself in a pub garden, in the midst of an innocuous conversation with Mel and my sister, talking over the usual subjects: family, travel, jobs, what Mel was doing, along with my own lack of work and direction.

As the chat lingered over my career uncertainty, Mel began to ask me about my interests and ambitions. It seemed routine, polite, sociable, so I'd never have expected that a brief answer to one of Mel's brief questions would soon see my life take a sharp, unexpected turn.

The proverbial 'succulent item' was about to be eyed.

Yet in many ways what was to unfold had been brewing for years, the seeds having been sown from a young and mischievous age.

Growing up in London there was an overpriced multiplex cinema within minutes from home. On quiet, wet afternoons I'd go there, pay for one movie, but watch two, even three, timing it just right, jumping from screen to screen. It was a military operation, guided by a copy of the *Evening Standard*. There was no better way to escape the tedium of teenhood than to hop from sci-fi epic, to teen comedy, to action-adventure romp, leaving the cinema after dark, bleary-eyed, and skittish of the authorities – a sort of 'Dracula: Young Ticket Evader', if you will.

I never thought of going to the cinema as a shared outing, and still regularly visit on my own, often late at night, relishing a quiet auditorium. Without the popcorn-munching, smartphone-shining, seat-kicking cacophony, it's film enjoyed the way it's meant to be. I can remember my first eighteen-rated movie, *The Running Man*, not watched in a multiplex, but with subtitles in a French bar; I can remember my first cinematic walk out, *Honey, I Shrunk The Kids*, to go see *Indiana Jones and The Last Crusade*, and I fondly remember watching *Kindergarten Cop*, but now realise it as a low point in Arnie's career.

And so, following a lifetime of cinematic escapism – needing a silver screen high at least once a month – it's of little surprise that the 'succulent item' I was drawn to was the alluring world of movie production.

All I needed was a shove in the right direction, which brings us to that innocuous conversation with Mel, who after a few minutes of career chat could see I was enamoured with her tales of far-flung film locations, leading to her brief question, and my even briefer answer:

"Would you be interested in work on a film shoot?" she asked me.

"Yes."

The answer took milliseconds.

Work's needed. I love cinema. What's to consider?

Mel left, promising to update me within a few days, and as promised, a few days later she called with news: I was green-lit.

She'd found an opening.

I was to get a taste of life within the thick of the film industry, but this was no cushy, latte-fuelled, Soho office job.

Not in the slightest.

"What's the soup of the day, mate?" asked the hairy grip.

I wanted to smack him.

The temperature was oppressive: 50° Celsius inside, 35° out. I wiped glutinous wads of sweat from my forehead, trying, failing, to stop them from dropping into the very soup he was asking about — a rather bland French onion mix, imbued with subtle traces of catering hand odour.

July 2000. Bologna, Italy.

Since my conversation with Mel things had moved fast. I'd jumped at the chance to work on a film shoot, and work on a film shoot was exactly what I'd got. There are times in life when you jump at something and, as the task, challenge, or job becomes clearer, little voices in your head question your original intent. As French onion soup splattered over my apron, the hairy grip shrugging a look of weary discontent, I knew I was in the midst of one of those moments.

It's hard to say exactly how I ended up serving soup in Italy, but I'm sure telling my mother about a "fantastic opportunity" — without knowing the relevant details — was probably a factor. Once the mothers are on board, pushing for victory, your part in the process is over.

As initial details trickled in, it became clear that Mel had lined me up to work for a month on a TV shoot in Italy — which sounded incredible — as part of the catering team, which sounded, well, slightly less incredible. I'd hoped at least to be a production assistant, but it was what it was.

I focused on the highlights: a month in Italy. On a TV shoot. Paid.

Surely it *was* a 'fantastic opportunity'?

By the time I'd doled out my eighty-sixth bowl of soup from the rear of a blisteringly hot catering truck for the twelfth day running, I'd firmly erased the word 'fantastic' from how I was to ever describe the experience. It was an opportunity, merely an opportunity, *and that was final.*

The 'opportunity' I was experiencing was the filming of Italian scenes for a one-off drama called *Torn Between*, a story about an air hostess with romantic entanglements across Europe. The plot didn't concern me in the least; the process of filming it did, yet it was impossible to sneak on set, the infernal catering job demanding every waking moment, serving food from the back of a 1960s con-verted Leyland lorry, a gurning lump the size of a coach, similar in ability and age to the one last seen dangling off a cliff at the end of *The Italian Job*.

Owned by a softly spoken Welsh couple, it had been fitted with a professional kitchen, adding significant weight, yet was still pow-ered by its original 1960s engine, meaning a toddler could beat it in a downhill dash. Needless to say, air-conditioning didn't feature, neither did a cassette deck. It was that old. But its owners loved it, so it was dragged across Europe, a Trojan donkey torturing all inside, including me, its latest soup-serving grunt.

But despite being anchored to the catering corner, little by little I was seeing the players, learning the game.

The average film set has dozens of crew, cast, and hangers-on to feed, numbering around 50–150 on any given day, depending on what's being shot, ranging from a one-person, one-location set-up, to hundreds of actors and extras populating a crowded city scene. As the providers of human fuel we were therefore an inte-gral department, always parked within reach, yet always just out of earshot.

Whenever you see a film crew, try this:

Look away from the main event, where the looky-loos are try-ing to catch a glimpse of the stars, and turn instead to the most quiet, practical corner of the entire location. That's where you'll find the catering team, tucked away like cabling behind a TV, nec-essary but unseen.

Caterers are the first to arrive on set in the morning, and the last to leave at night. They work within hot, sticky, enclosed condi-tions that only lunatics would enjoy. They also produce surprisingly edible food from their cramped kitchens, but good meal or bad, it all needs clearing away – a duty that no one enjoys; a duty that landed squarely at my feet.

Washing dishes has to be one of the most tedious, insipid tasks known to mankind. The chore has led to flatmates falling out, families failing to talk, couples arguing, even divorce; I'm sure that in Viking times doing the dishes led to all-out war, followed by bondage to the victors' sinks.

And in modern times, that acrimonious job was assigned to Gianni, an Italian catering assistant, and myself, tasked with washing up mountains of soiled plates, bowls, and cutlery after each and every meal. I'd love to say that as we attacked those dish buckets Gianni and I would spend hours conversing wisely about Italian cuisine, history, opera, art, and architecture, but I'd be lying.

"Arseeeenal," said Gianni, a tall, bearded man in his late-twenties.

"Yes, Arsenal," I replied, "multa bene."

"Si, multa bene!" he shouted.

"Chel-y-sea."

"Yes, Chelsea," I replied, "multa bene."

"Si, multa bene! …Man-chist-rrrrr Un-eeeee-ted…"

"Yes, Manchester United… multa bene."

The gripping 'do-you-recognise-the-incredibly-famous-English-football-club' conversation could have been better, but it was all we had, so I'd let it roll on while gazing over the stunning streets, piazzas, and buildings of one of Italy's most celebrated cities. Yet even with such a setting, the gripping conversation would eventually break me. After two hours I'd need a time-out.

I'd need a smoke.

On film sets there aren't many ways for a catering assistant to make friends – most people are too busy adjusting things, or learning lines – but through an old vice (I've now thankfully dropped) I discovered a way to build bridges. Shoots can be prolific for smoking due to the amount of downtime many of the crew need to fill during takes, when the actors, director, sound, and camera teams are busy making movie magic, but most others are on standby. During those quiet moments I'd try sneaking over to the smoking gang, usually gathered near the colossal 'gennie' (generator) trucks, to share my duty-free cigarettes, and strike up a conversation.

At that point in my brief, soup-stained career I knew nothing about film production departments, so would ask the smokers to explain the duties and terminology each crewmember was assigned. 'Best boy' has to be a favourite term, along with 'gaffer', both of whom work in the lighting department. Then there's the first, second, third assistant camera, loader, first, second, third assistant director, riggers, sparks, dolly grip, director of photography, boom operator, lead man, sound mixer, props master, and so it goes on.

It's a strange and daunting world to the uninitiated, but soon enough it's just sound, lighting, wardrobe, make-up, props, camera team, director's team, all given specific terms or nicknames that relate to a technical skill, such as a 'spark' being someone who deals with electricity, and... *too late...*

"Charlie!!! Stub it out and get over here!!"

Bollocks, back to the catering team... yet another meal to prepare. There's *always* another meal to prepare. It's a dependable feature of life as a catering assistant. Early tea, breakfast, late tea, coffee break, lunch, tea break, high tea, and dinner in a continuous, forgettable cycle of food purchase, preparation, cooking, serving, clearing, washing up, and repeating.

It's the same every day.

But in Italy there was one, unforgettable, exception.

Just over three weeks into the job, after we'd finished serving lunch from a tree-shaded corner of a marble quarry about 40km outside of Bologna, something caught my eye. Something unusual. I glanced up from my dish bucket to notice a new, particularly distinct member of the crew.

You couldn't miss him.

Sharp pinstriped suit. Handkerchief flowing from top pocket. Bright white teeth. Polished black brogues. The man was welcomed by every person, in every corner of the set. Even the director fawned over him.

Who is this mystery man?

I grabbed my trusty pack of cigarettes, and raced to the smoking gang, found loitering by a pile of rough-cut rocks in the shade of a JCB.

"Geoff, er, who's the new guy?" I asked, trying to be nonchalant.

"Which one?" replied Geoff.

I took a drag, sucked in, and blew out slowly, eager not to seem eager.

"The, er, that guy, the one just, you know, that guy…"

Geoff searched the scene.

"Yeah, not sure, mate. Where am I looking?"

"The guy in the pinstriped suit!" I blurted out.

"Alright son, calm down, calm down," said Geoff.

"So?" I nagged.

"You've got an eye, mate, that's the top dog."

"From the Beeb?"

"Don't be daft. That's the producer. The boss."

"So what's the producer do? How come he gets to swan about?"

Geoff paused, à la *X-Factor*, teasing my intrigue.

His answer would set my eyes alight with ambition.

"He finds the script, gets the cash together, gets the heads of department hired, gets the ball rolling, and then comes on set, has everyone gush over him, and takes all the profit," he finally said, somewhat summing up the complex work of a producer in one digestible sentence.

But it was a sentence that clicked. I watched the producer go from person to person, drink in hand, munching on a wad of beef fillet, and at that moment a cathartic peace took hold, soothed by the knowledge that I'd found my answer.

It was standing right in front of me, in a pinstriped suit.

My search was over.

I wanted to be the man, the man in the suit, the man in charge of the whole damn show. I *had* to be that man. It was a done deal:

One day, somewhere, somehow, I'd see 'film producer' on my CV.

With that thought in mind, watching the producer being driven away in the back of a German auto, I tingled at the prospect of my newfound prize, excited at the prospect of what lay ahead.

A week later the first assistant director called out, "That's a wrap everyone!" – the Italian scenes for *Torn Between* were 'in the can'. Lights and cameras were packed away, equipment trucks returned to their owners, and the crew settled in for one last night of debauchery before flying out the next day.

The catering department wasn't to have quite such a fun departure. Our vehicles had come from the UK, and had to be returned to the UK. The drive from Bologna to London is about 1,500km, with the ever-efficient Google Maps estimating the journey to take 14h 38min, yet for reasons best known to Google it doesn't use the average speed of a 1960s Leyland truck for its calculations.

Following a minor alteration to the classic GCSE equation of DST (distance = speed x time), our journey would actually take the best part of forty hours, not including three overnight stops en route. To make matters worse I wasn't even driving the Leyland; I was in charge of a modern Mercedes van, but had to follow just behind the slothful truck for the entire trip, in case of breakdown. It was tantamount to entering Usain Bolt into an egg-and-spoon race.

Four days after the rest of the crew had arrived home, our catering convoy crawled on to the M25, London's clogged ring road, completing the last leg of the slowest pan-European journey since Hannibal woke one morning and struck fear into the eyes of his generals with the little-documented phrase:

"Horses are for girls; I need elephants."

On my European road trip I'd learnt how to have a conversation with myself, sing all of the French Top Ten, and pinch my inner thigh to stay awake, but while useful, these aren't CV-worthy skills.

I'd arranged with the boss to split off at a Tube station in outer London, so was dropped off at the end of the Metropolitan line, waving farewell to the vintage catering unit, and my time serving soup. Unsurprisingly, being free of the convoy wasn't the saddest of moments, yet I was immensely thankful for the experience, as it had put me on a path I now thoroughly believed in.

I thought back to Italy, focusing on the revelation – on the pin-striped producer – and I felt myself tingle once more.

No doubt about it.

The ultimate question had been answered.

JOB THREE: LOCATIONS CATERING ASSISANT

Lessons learnt:
- Grab hold of whatever opportunities come your way
- Once the mothers are on board, your part in the process is over
- Sweat goes completely unnoticed in French onion soup
- There are some benefits to smoking (but not many)
- Minion jobs can lead to revelations, but finding the answer is just the start

CHAPTER NINE

This was it. Game on.

I was focused. I had a plan.

And yet… well, kids will be kids…

As keen as I was to chase the producer goal, I found myself distracted, torn between my newfound path and a long-held desire to work in a distant place I'd loved for over fifteen years.

The love began in 1984, a year of fictional dystopia, but also the year of my first visit to the spectacular mountains of southern France. The trip inspired a lifelong passion for sub-zero villages and bone-crunching winter sports, a passion that only grew stronger when *vin chaud* was thrown into the mix. And that passion was why my embryonic advances into the British film industry were put on hold, replaced instead by hedonistic research into the Alpine ski season.

The rationale was that it had to be enjoyed sooner rather than later, otherwise career would take hold and there'd be no opportunity until retirement, which isn't the apex moment to live at 1500-metres above sea level. Post-sixty-five your body won't survive five consecutive months skidding on snow, surrounded by twenty-something boarders named Josh, who'll force you to buy tequila slammers as they brag about 'backside 180s' they pulled on a 'gnarly kicker' built by their mate, Josh.

You really, really won't appreciate it.

It was now or never.

My film career, barely able to flap its wings, was put on ice until winter had passed, at which point it would be thawed out, leaving it years to fly, perhaps to even soar. Without analysing the decision further, I plunged into the abundant array of winter vacancies on offer, researching companies that require an immense task force to oversee everything from a five-star chalet to a zero-star apartment.

Every winter, snow enthusiasts descend on the Alps (including about a million Britons), and looking after their every need is a youthful army of 'seasonnaires', comprising drivers, guides, cooks, cleaners, nannies, managers, and more. Tour companies hire them in their droves, relying on the same cross-cut of able-bodied staff; the same train 'em fast, get 'em working approach; the same work 'em hard, replace 'em annually attitude; the same jobs in the same set-ups catering to the same needs, servicing everyone from a penny-pinching Pyrenees snowboarder, to a Jacuzzi-wallowing St Moritz skier.

For a young man with safari experience – i.e. time spent behind the wheel – the obvious goal was a driving job. I was tempted by ski guiding, but knew I'd rarely get mountain time without a group of slow (or drunk) tourists five feet behind me. Bartending also appealed – it seemed glamorous – but who wants to clock off at 4am? Working in a ski hire shop required better French than my grades allowed. Working in a chalet involved too much client interaction. It had to be driving, so I dove in with an application to a chalet company in Meribel, a Brit-friendly resort known for its youthful nightlife and plentiful slopes. It ticked all the boxes.

Within days, I'd been invited to interview.

Dogs lay on wooden floorboards. Large windows flooded the converted barn in late-summer rays. Death-defying ski posters hung on walls. At a rustic table covered in chalet brochures, we spoke.

"Do you have a driving licence?"

"Yes."

"Are you aware that drink-driving is illegal, even in France?"

"Yes."

"*Parlez-vous un petit peux Francais?*"

"Bah oui, oignon, boeuf, baguette, orrrni-orrrni-orrrni-hon, garage, bicyclette, ou est le syndicat d'initiative, deux bierres…"

"You're hired."

When the job's to drive a van in a ski resort few questions are needed. It was 'interview light', conducted in a British way, with tea and biscuits, a discreet background check, inoffensive small talk, and a firm handshake.

I'd survived my first face-to-face interview, albeit not to run the United Nations, but it was still a proud moment. I left the meeting impatient to start work in a region offering some of the finest skiing on Earth.

"Is it grass skiing then?" asked the observant nanny from 'up north'. I groaned, partly through exhaustion, partly through disappointment. She was spot on. The resort looked better suited to lawn bowls.

It was early December as our staff coach finished its sixteen-hour journey from London, rolling into Meribel on a hot afternoon, not a snowflake in sight. Nestled in the heart of Les Trois Vallées – the largest ski area in the world – the resort was experiencing its warmest start to winter in years. In barely two weeks' time our first punters were due to arrive, and if the status quo persisted we'd need to expect supremely miserable faces.

Management were upbeat: "Fear not, the snow always comes! Just settle in and learn the ropes."

Praying the white stuff would arrive, I turned to explore our staff accommodation. All the nannies, drivers, maintenance men, and office staff – i.e. anyone not running their own chalet – were housed in a crumbling, ramshackle building that would make a Tokyo hostel seem spacious. I'd later discover this to be the norm for the ski industry, but on first appearance the word 'disappointed' registered from deep within.

I was to spend the next five months sharing a bedroom the size of a postage stamp with two fully-grown men, three wardrobes, three bedside cabinets, one table, and a radiator at the foot of my bed. Living in a bitterly cold environment I thought the last point a godsend, but how wrong I was, for a radiator may keep you warm, but it may – and will – be used to dry heaps of malodorous, sweat-caked clothing, the stench of which will permeate even the deepest of deep sleeps.

Cheap French beer will mask the problem, I assumed. It was a solid plan, a youthful plan… a foolish plan.

"Listen up, don't go out drinking, then do the bread drop," said Vicky, the manager of the driving team, a few hours into training.

"What's the bread drop?" I asked.

Two of the other drivers flicked that all-knowing look indicative of dire news ahead. One of them piped up:

"It's when you get up at 5.30am, drive to the bakery, pick up baguettes for all of our twenty-five chalets, then drive to each of them, dropping off the correct quantity of bread at each kitchen. That's why you don't roll out of bed at 5am, having gone to bed pissed at 2.30am. It's called drink driving, Charrr-leeeee."

Was the passive aggressive use of 'Charlie' really necessary? I felt a fresh adversary cropping up, much like the theatrical one I'd had at school some six years earlier. I'd missed having a nemesis, but couldn't afford to cultivate a fresh one, the need to settle into my job taking justifiable precedence.

"Cool. Got it. No boozing before the bread drop," I said.

But I could see it didn't wash; I was making enemies, not impressing the do-gooder, appearing too keen to the rest. I pinched my inner thigh, reminding myself to shut up. I never make a good first impression. Some people need to be slow cooked rather than flash fried. I'm a Beef Wellington.

Having taken in the crucial news about the 'bread drop' and drink driving, it was to be a poor start to the job when a week later I failed to heed my colleague's wise words. I blame Josh, the maintenance man, who convinced me that a few "cheeky Christmas drinks" were a good idea. Call anything cheeky and apparently it's acceptable. I expect Lenin called his revolution 'cheeky' to rally comrades to his cause: "Come brethren, we have cheeky uprising, cheeky slaying, then cheeky vodka, and cheeky Big Mac on way home…"

Knowing I had the 'bread drop' to undertake the next morning I was careful to control the night, right up until Josh suggested "cheeky tequila shots" at midnight, followed by several more... followed by the inevitable stumble home at 2.35am-3.35am... exactly when is unclear.

What happened next is not.

Beep-beep-beep... 5.30am... *snooze.*
Beep-beep-beep... 5.45am... *snooze.*
Beep-beep-beep... 6am... *snooze.*
6.14am: "Charlie, fer fook's sake ger' up, man."

It was my new Geordie friend and fellow driver, Matt, also my wingman for the 'bread drop' that morning, clearly unhappy at my comatose state and snooze button usage. He shook me hard. I woke fully, realised I'd missed our 5.45am start, but even worse was unable to help with driving duties, for legal reasons, combined with basic life preservation.

Fortunately Matt was a dab hand at the job having done it five winters straight, so he took control of the wheel, demanding I deliver baguettes to each kitchen, ensuring I suffer as God and tequila intended. Behind schedule, the chalet staff opened fire at every stop. When you have staff whining that breakfast can't be served due to missing baguettes, so guests will be late for ski lessons, kids won't be ready for nursery, and cleaning rounds will be delayed, you realise just how incredibly loud and unattractive chalet girls are at sunrise – no wait, that wasn't the lesson – it was that you're part of a system relying on every cog to work.

Just like on a film shoot, if you mess up, everyone messes up.

Keeping staff onside is one thing, but they're teddy bears compared to the people you're there to serve, the people who fuel the Alpine economy – the dreaded punters. They're just so... what's the word? *Irritating.* Being asked to return to a chalet by a middle-aged man, one who's perfectly capable of holding down a FTSE 100 job, but can't remember his gloves, hat, or ski pass when departing for a day on a mountain isn't only tedious, but mildly depressing.

Regardless, you have to smile. It didn't come naturally, but a perfect grin is integral to the hospitality industry, so I had to try. Millions of women know the trick I had to perfect, and millions have perfected it well: the ancient art of faking it. And so I practised fake smiling at families with screaming brats, at thirty-somethings with relationship strife, and at dejected grandparents left to trawl the shops; it became second nature, and once mastered – with snowflakes finally falling – I was all set to enjoy the season to its inevitable conclusion.

Life in the mountains rolled on, week after week, a cyclical world to which you quickly adapt. Without twenty-four-hour news, or broadband Wi-Fi, we were in a bubble; the weeks blended together, the only discernible change being the weather, lengthening days, and the arrival of fresh punters. Most people have experienced the repetitive nature of the working week, but nowhere is it more clear-cut than during a holiday season. On Saturdays the airport bus rolls into town, taking away glum faces, dropping off elated replacements, and the reset button is pushed; everyone goes back to first positions.

It's an Alpine version of *Groundhog Day*.

Prior to the winter season I'd hated routine, but happily fell into its grooves in southern France, and so, like thousands of 'seasonnaires' before me, I considered the prospect of extending such happiness into a lifelong career – could I avoid the rat race, instead staying in the mountains? And if so, how?

It should be of little surprise to those who've asked that question before me that I couldn't find a satisfactory answer. There's one major stumbling block that can't be overcome: what to do in the off-season?

Winter season staff are only needed from early December to late April, after which you're surplus to requirement. Sure, you could work the summer season, but yachts and villas can't replace mountains and chalets, leaving a seven-month gap between jobs.

It's the caveat that ends the dream, forcing snow-lovers out of seasonal work and into the cities, from where few emerge. It's why most people enjoy a one-off, once-in-a-lifetime experience, after which they become bankers, lawyers, estate agents, policemen... even film producers.

It was a conclusive result. This was it; therefore I had to make the most of my time at altitude, relishing every day, so it was with a heavy heart when the final weeks rolled in, heralded by softer snow, warmer temperatures, and increasing chatter about what to do next.

As the last punters rolled out of town I gazed at the awesome beauty of the towering peaks, promising to return, knowing it to be empty rhetoric.

Departure was a one-way ticket to the real world.

Out of patience, a pinstriped goal was thawing fast.

JOB FOUR: ALPINE VAN DRIVER

Lessons learnt:

- Working the winter season can't wait until retirement
- Nannies from 'up north' have a delightfully succinct way of putting things
- Tequila, driving, snow, and baguettes should never be mixed
- Don't annoy a chalet girl at sunrise
- If smiling is part of the job, learn to smile, learn to fake it
- 'What to do in the off-season' is a deal-breaker
- You can only delay the real world for so long...

CHAPTER TEN

Yin and yang. Positive and negative. Good and bad.

These terms were to hang over my head for the next few months as life unfolded in a balanced, frustratingly even way.

Spring, 2001. Back in London the economy was reeling from the dot-com bust, investors licking wounds, as others shook heads, tut-tutted, and reassessed plans of becoming Internet billionaires; but the economy creaked on, tech failings or not, so I threw myself into a vigorous job hunt, determined to see the producer dream take flight, convinced its wings could soon be flapping.

I had a university degree to hand, and a clear goal to mind; surely nothing else was needed? Almost nothing, except for the fact that employers need to be picking up what you're throwing down – and that means getting noticed. It's not easy, especially not when you're relying on the same scattershot approach as everyone else, indiscriminately pumping out CVs, praying your bachelor's degree and 'love of film noir' will mark you out as supposedly employable.

But the odds are never in your favour.

And that's when I started to feel the negatives and positives, the yin and the yang, as I crashed through a chaotic job hunt, teased with promise, offered hope, knocked back, and told to try again.

Without contacts you're at the mercy of a brutal system, an exhaustive numbers game that can destroy even the most head-strong of employment-seeker. Contacts are key; they're the fastest way to getting your CV into the right hands. That's true in all fields, and the film industry is no different. Yet even after a month working on a TV shoot in Italy I still had no useful contacts, as I still hadn't learnt the crucial art of networking; that tried and tested system of hoarding business cards, contacting those con-nections, and then easing open any potential doors as subtly, but determinedly, as possible.

I was therefore on my own, in need of a break, but it was proving elusive. As the weeks rolled by, my resolve weakened, rattled by reply after reply of the same generic response to my request for employment.

If you don't know the wording, it looks like this:

Dear _____,

Thank you for contacting Another Average Film Co.

We regret to inform you that we have nothing at the moment, but we will keep your CV on file, and will contact you should a suitable position become available.

Yours,
Mr Average Person
HR Automaton

Even though I'd always expect the above response, I'd still hope for more. Every time an email or (in the old days) a letter arrived I couldn't help but get a tingling of hope that this one would be different. I'd put away doubting thoughts that said, "If they'd wanted you, they'd have called you," instead telling myself it would be an offer to interview; then the inevitable rejection would appear, followed by its ever-present shadow, dejection.

I'd rather receive no response. It's like asking to buy a girl a drink, but rather than her pretending not to hear you, she leans in, tells you to piss off, adding she'll keep your offer in mind, and should no one else meet with her approval she may, possibly, come back to you later.

Some rejection letters even offer a reason as to why you're not acceptable: 'Your experience is not equal to the job you've applied for', being a regular excuse. I could fill in the nightclub equivalent to such feedback, but I'm sure you can combine the words, 'experience', 'too small', and, 'not coming home with me, love', in your own particular fashion.

I have a file at home filled with hundreds of such letters. It should be of no surprise that I never heard of any 'suitable position' coming available, which – if I were to be cynical – might indicate my letter was never kept on file, in the same way that I'd never expect nightclub girl to return with the news, "You're in, mate, everyone else is far uglier than you." And if she were to tell me that I'd likely decide not to buy her a drink (but there's no guarantee).

In this joyless way, weeks of research, letters, hope, and heartache wore on, yet just as I was about to lose patience with unemployment, becoming ever more despondent, the postman delivered a piece of mail that caught my eye. Yes, a postman. Delivering mail. For a job hunt. It sounds bizarre to me too. I opened it, read it, raised an eyebrow, put on fresh underwear, and left the flat, for the note within demanded exertive consideration.

A Soho-based company called GSS Films needed a production assistant. That much was a thumbs-up. They were looking for someone to start immediately. Also a thumbs-up. The job was an unpaid position… *wait… what?* Far from a thumbs-up, it had me pacing the streets, considering the pros and cons.

Without knowing it I was assessing the Achilles heel of starter jobs, especially in the film world. The issue is that creative companies 'employ' a huge number of people in unpaid positions, teasing them with the promise of paid work once a period of free graft has been completed. That inexact 'free period' may last a while. A long while. I've known people to work unpaid positions for twelve months or more. That's illegal. In fact, it's almost tantamount to slave labour, and I say 'almost' as I don't believe any unpaid grunt has ever been worked to death assisting film producers in London or LA… but I could be wrong.

An unpaid stint should last four weeks at most, after which payment should be received. That's not to say the pay will be any good, or even close to good, but it should at least cover a bedroom, travel, a sandwich at lunch, and a pint on a Friday. At least the employee then feels part of the organisation, albeit a poorly paid part.

Some sectors are known to treat interns well, especially finance, government, accounting, law, and IT, but the creative industries are famous for exploiting the system – and those that can afford to play along.

This recruitment ruse typically results in a high number of kids from wealthier backgrounds entering creative companies, since unpaid work needs to be supported. Employers therefore miss out on hundreds of people who could potentially have thrived in their exciting spheres, but are forced into paid jobs in other fields in order to put food on the table.

Fortunately for penny-pinching MDs and CEOs there are thousands of youngsters able to take on unpaid stints, justifying their free labour to mum and dad with promises of, "Purrrr-lease, it won't last long," forcing parents to Google the company whose payroll they're about to fund, fully in the knowledge the greased-up exec topping the 'About Us' page is about to take their retirement fund for a ride.

Having mulled it over, aware of the pros and cons, I knew there were only two factors to consider: my inbox was empty; these guys were interested. That was it. *Pay or no pay, for God's sake, take the interview.* And so, like every other media grunt with supportive parents, I shelved my concerns, promising my mother that, "I'll receive a salary before long, *if I even get the job.*"

Spying its next victim, the film industry licked its lips.

On a cloudless, late-spring day I walked towards the Soho offices of GSS Films to interview for the most junior of junior roles. Disappointment at the job's lack of pay was shelved, replaced with anticipation that this could be the start of an ascent to pinstriped status. All that lay in my path was the interview, and so as my destination loomed ahead, I paused, breathing deep.

After weeks of Sisyphean job-hunting I was within feet of rolling the rock to the top of the mountain, of completing the task. This was it. I stepped inside the modern office block, rode the lift to the third floor, signed in at reception, met the fifty-something boss, and received an offer for tea or coffee.

I declined, so we began.

"Are you able to type fast, read fast, and listen well?"

"Yes."

"Are you aware there's no salary for this role?"

"Yes."

"Do you speak a bit of media lingo?"

"Of course, BAFTA, dah-rling, starlet, you're going places, show me the money, where's the bar with the overpriced cocktails, two cappuccinos…"

"You're hired. Start Monday."

Barely ten minutes after entering the office, I was back on the streets, elated at the fast result; yet dragging on me was an instinctive response that kicks in when anything seems too easy: that defensive trio of disbelief, mistrust, and fear. I walked for half an hour, separating the positive and negative reactions. I knew they were taking liberties, but also knew there was no better way to enter the film industry, so in theory there was nothing to mistrust or fear.

This is how things are done.

I accepted it was a done deal. I could stop worrying and start working. Although the job was unpaid, the interviewer had assured me it would turn into a paid position, "at some point, once budgets allowed," which sounded promising.

Surely they wouldn't lie to my face?

Once on the payroll, I'd be underway. It was then only a matter of time before I'd rise to the top of GSS Films, accepting BAFTA awards along the way, hobnobbing with London's creative elite, laughing at how we all started in unpaid gigs, "And look at where we are today" "And isn't that bloody hilarious?" as we'd jump in stretch limos, disappearing to secret after-parties, guffawing at the little people, squeezing each other's buttocks, and…

…uh-oh, a mere modicum of success had gone to my head. Later that day I may have even practised an Oscar acceptance speech in front of the mirror, but I can't be sure what I was accepting, as there is no 'Best Producer' award. These fantasies lose clarity fast; I was probably just trying to impress Jessica Alba.

Either way, I was still buzzing when I returned to GSS Films the following Monday, ready to start my first official day as a tiny cog in the behemoth machine of the global entertainment industry.

"Mine's a grande mocha, no cream, with chocolate dusting, and an extra shot; here's a fiver, don't forget the change."

It's a standard demand in many lines of work, maybe less so in coal mining and trawler fishing, but especially so in the media. I grimaced, then remembered the 'fake smile' I'd perfected in the French Alps, so beamed a smarmy grin, took the five-pound note, and departed to buy coffee for the fifth time that day.

It's part of the job, I'd tell myself. *Stick it out, and soon enough they'll bring you into the fold. Patience and a smile, that's all you need.*

Other than the ubiquitous coffee run I was given a desk to watch. And papers to shuffle. I wanted to do more, but had to be careful. When starting out in any new job there's a fine line between being the keen guy and being the irritating keeno. You need to play it carefully, offering to help where possible without becoming an irritant. If you push too hard they'll give you something time-consuming and tedious to tie you up for hours.

I knew I'd achieved 'keeno status' when asked to hole-punch and bind forty scripts that had mistakenly arrived unbound from the printers. It was a mindless task, one of a thousand interchangeable chores that production grunts undertake on a daily basis, so I rattled through it, before finding a quiet corner to read the story I'd just been binding. It was a low budget romantic-comedy, minus the laughs. Cinema needs no more of those, so I'm relieved to report it disappeared into the recycling bin, never to be seen again.

Mind-numbing chores aside, scripts were crossing my desk, which could only mean one thing: I was on the inside. It was a thrill to be part of a busy production team, watching seasoned producers steer their ship, eying up opportunities, planning productions, talking ticket sales. I'd see them meet financiers, script editors, actors, and casting agents, some of which I could overhear, some of which I was invited to join, even if it was just to take latte orders; but so be it, I was an active cog, close to a hive of cinematic profit-plotting.

After three weeks I'd settled into my dogsbody role, had learned the ropes, and was on first name terms with the barista at Starbucks, so found it disappointing when a senior producer announced the office was to close for two weeks for a minor expansion and redecoration. Never one to look a gift horse in the mouth I concluded that a fortnight's downtime, with a job locked in, was no bad thing.

Not only was my career on track, I'd managed to uphold the oyster theory, work a winter in France, return to the UK, enter the film industry, and now stood on the first rung of my career ladder, ready to ascend.

I'd come to believe anything was possible.

Two weeks later, three pounds heavier, I returned to work. On entry, a quizzical look from Crispin, the office manager, should have been flagged, but I ignored it, continuing on into the newly-expanded office. I stood in its centre, looking around. A wall clock ticked loud. Something seemed off.

Heads began to rise.

Something was definitely off.

What was it? The team began to stare, some with that pitiful look younger people exhibit when trying to explain Wi-Fi speeds to senior citizens.

No one said anything.

Then I saw the area where my desk had previously been stationed. It wasn't where it had been two weeks earlier. It was gone. In its place was a wide archway leading to a new, rather plush extension.

I turned. Those pitiful looks were now exaggerated, like a

crowd at a basketball game on seeing a woman say "no" to a public wedding proposal. "Sucker!" shouts a voice from the cheap seats.

Sucker indeed.

I should have left, enough had been communicated without the need for dialogue, but I had to double-check, just in case there really was an elderly person in the room trying to understand Wi-Fi speeds. I knew it was wishful thinking, but the question still tumbled from my mouth:

"Um, so, where's my desk?" I asked, trying to stay upbeat, but giving away my fear in that trembling tone that's hard to hide.

"Sorry, Charlie, but there's no room for you now, I'm afraid… er… since the redecoration," said Crispin.

"I see," I said, not seeing at all.

It was the last thing I'd expected to hear. Tell me I'm shit. Tell me I smell. Tell me I scare the ladies. Don't tell me you have no space. You've just extended the fucking office! It was the worst excuse since Bill Clinton justified smoking marijuana by saying, "I didn't inhale."

There was nothing left to do. I could have fought it. I could have pointed out the glaring flaw in Crispin's reasoning. I could have asked why I was being replaced by an archway, but there was no point.

It felt as though the entire office was on the verge of cracking up, so clearly the polite course of action would be to leave the room, letting them have their laugh. I opened my mouth to say something, but couldn't be bothered, so turned around like a good little Englishman, and walked out without saying another word.

The episode was a wake-up call as to how companies can treat unpaid staffers, but also a heads-up that I'd need to shine brighter at my next opportunity. I trudged into the street, bewildered at how fast my day had crashed. In a matter of minutes I'd been knocked off the ladder, lied to my face, and left to start over.

If ever there was a time for a mid-morning pint, this was it.

Five pints later I stumbled out of Soho, without direction,

mumbling about how 'Crispin' sounds rather like a savoury snack. Drooling slightly, I eyed a McDonald's... *Christ, no, was it really possible? Already?*

Beer, angst, and comfort food.

"Welcome home," purred unemployment. "Welcome home."

JOB FIVE: PRODUCTION ASSISTANT, TAKE I

Lessons learnt:

- Employers need to be picking up what you're throwing down
- Learn how to network, exchange business cards, and create connections
- Unpaid work is the Achilles heel of starter jobs, especially in the media
- If someone gives you a dumb excuse, say something – don't be an English gent, be an English bulldog
- Trust nobody in the corporate world (which is an awful lesson to learn, but a necessary one nonetheless)
- It hurts to discover that you're less employable than masonry

CHAPTER ELEVEN

Even though it was only an unpaid dogsbody role, losing to an archway still drew blood – just a bit – and the subsequent 'woe-is-me' call list was as predictable as it was necessary:

"Don't worry, sweetheart. Something better will come along. The important thing is to start looking as soon as possible."

The mother.

"Fuck it and fuck them. You'll be all right. We're going down The Imperial. Come drown your miseries."

The friends.

"Yep, that's a shame, a real shame. Pay your tab."

The barman.

"All hope is lost, I tells ya! Lost for good! You'll never get another opportunity like that ever again. Ever agaaaaiiinnnn…"

Me.

It was back to square one, back to staring down the abyss, back to daytime TV, and back to pumping out CVs. I took one look at my mailing list, sighed, thought better of it, and escaped into an Australian soap. The hunt could wait, at least a week; at least until I'd had time to guzzle down a dozen pizzas, thereby becoming depressed about being unemployed *and* overweight. Sometimes you need to hit rock bottom before rising up the other side.

And then, a week into bemoaning my situation, wallowing in crass self pity, the type that saw me consider the most hideous move of all, applying to be a Foxtons estate agent, I received a phone call I wasn't expecting…

…but desperately needed.

It was karma, calling long distance from New York City.

If you're imagining a Buddha-like character sitting on a cushion in Times Square, you're in for a modicum of disappointment.

Karma – or the re-balancing of positive and negative (according to how I saw it) – came in the slightly less divine form of Nick, an old friend at the end of a Manhattan night out, abusing his 'cell' by drunk-dialling the UK.

Having listened to a detailed, "She wasn't keen, but her model friend was," report of his last few hours, the conversation swung to me, woken at 7.35am, there being a five-hour time difference between downtown New York and suburban south London. I immediately told him my recent tale of archway woe, to which Nick gave the most unprecedented of replies.

Having heard the usual, "You'll find something better," and the other classic, "It's their loss," both of which are charming, but throwaway sentiments, he was the first person able to smack a smile back on my lacklustre face.

"Do you know what a second assistant director does?" he asked.

"Not a clue," I replied.

"Don't worry, you'll learn on the job."

"Excuse me?"

"Don't worry about it, just get yourself to New York."

"Er, sure."

The line went dead.

Karma had other Brits to wake.

I'd apparently reduced my all-time fastest interview to eight seconds; I didn't know what the job entailed, yet was somehow already on the payroll.

I stared at my mobile, looked at the brooding skies of London, and whispered a word of thanks to the inebriated rainmaker in Midtown Manhattan. Winds were blowing westward. The dream was alive and well, reinvigorated by a far-flung friend racking up a three-figure phone bill.

I reassessed the morning. At approximately 7.42am I'd become part of the crew on *Best Served Hot*, a feature-length movie Nick was directing, scheduled to start production in late September. It was a significant improvement to my expected day of microwave meals and quiz show repeats.

I prayed Nick would remember the conversation when he woke, but to be safe I raced to an Internet cafe, emailing him the bare bones of our chat. I embellished on how much he'd pleaded with me to, *"Get out here as soon as possible, as I really need you!"* – making it clear there was no going back, that I was about to book a flight, and would be ready to depart within days.

Email sent, my itchy feet trembled at the prospect of exploring the Gotham-esque wonder that is New York City. I sat back, carefully considering what I'd so far learned about the working world, and concluded I'd need to tackle this opportunity with level-headed maturity, impressing from day one.

"Yeeeehaaaaaaa!!!" I shouted from a cab at 3am.

Bollocks to maturity, I was in New York City, dammit, a place I'd ached to see for years, a place I'd just arrived at, out the blue, within a week's notice; and I was now cruising down Second Avenue, hanging from a yellow cab, hunting for a twenty-four-hour restaurant to fuel my American burger lust.

In the Big Apple such desire can be easily sated, even at the darkest of the night. After just a dozen blocks we pulled up outside a facade of neon lighting, the bright colours luring me into a traditional booth-and-bar-stool diner, celeb photos on walls, '50s jukebox touting for singles. Once I'd placed my order, the chef flipped and fried, a one-man operation tending to his jet-lagged client.

"Order up, bacon double cheeseburger," shouted the 200-pound, paper-hatted grease monkey. I stared at the shimmering dish, part confused, part ecstatic.

"That's two burgers."

"Yah. Bacon *double* cheeseburger, man, that's what-chya ordered," he barked, wiping grease-sweat from his furrowed brow.

The serving was immense, in the way that only Americans are able to create (and justify); my eyes lit with glee, as my heart groaned at the impending delivery. I'd arrived in fast food heaven, a land where you receive double what you expect, at half the cost. Ketchup at the ready, I loosened my belt.

Burgers digesting, I hailed another cab and cruised on, gawping out the window, tongue lolloping, mesmerised by the high-rise landscape. Manhattan is an island that amazes on first sight, the downsides trickling through later, much like the city's irate traffic during its interminable rush hour.

On night one, though, it's an unquestionable delight.

Soon enough I'd fall for the gritty Bronx and Brooklyn accents, as much as the Fifth Avenue princesses and SoHo fashionistas. It's a place where being told, "Yo, buddy, move out da fackin' way!" as a truck reverses into you, isn't considered rude or inconsiderate, it's local vernacular. It pulls no punches.

As my stomach struggled to process its double burger injection I knew I'd found a home away from home. Next up was to find my literal home away from home, a room Nick had arranged at his friend's duplex apartment on East 91st Street (in an area that was, in 2001, somewhere between up-and-coming, yuppie, and family-friendly, as per property sales lingo).

Waking the Texan owner at 4am wasn't ideal, yet with true American hospitality he greeted me warmly – "A cup of tea for my Eng-er-land guest?" – then showed me his spare room. It was classic NYC living: small, basic, and not all mine. I'd be sharing a dogleg basement with Joe, a six-foot-six, fast-talking Italian-American, the two of us sleeping on mattresses at either end of the unfurnished, white-tiled, windowless space. Even with the dogleg layout there was little privacy; snores, grunts, and groans bounced around, there being no curtain, screen, or opaque slice of crack den sheeting.

But not even moans, groans, and the trapped odours of two unhygienic men could dampen my reserve. I was in New York to be part of Nick's film.

Nothing else mattered.

It was the required mentality, as from day one Nick put me to work, and at the start of production that meant script revisions. Although I had vast, drive-a-bus-through-them gaps in my industry knowledge, it doesn't take a genius to grasp the basics, especially not the basics of script revision.

The task is bound by a few simple rules: every script page, depending on content, will cost the production a certain amount of money to turn into cinematic footage, from a few hundred dollars for an ultra-low-budget movie featuring unknown actors in cheap locations, rising to millions of dollars per page for a studio blockbuster about inter-planetary destruction starring Hollywood's biggest names. But whether independent or studio, producers will always want to minimise costs, beginning with unnecessary pages never being shot in the first place.

Rule one: reduce, reduce, reduce.

That was our task for the 160-page screenplay that was the initial rough draft of *Best Served Hot*. Most scripts are around 90 to 110 pages, with one page equalling about one minute of screen time. Our 160 pages therefore needed drastic thinning. The structure was in place, but superfluous scenes, action, and dialogue had to be cut, otherwise thousands of dollars would be wasted filming material that would only see the cutting room floor.

Rule two: if in doubt, cut it out.

Movies are made three times. First, a writer types it as a script; second, hundreds of cast and crew shoot it during production; and third, a pasty-faced editor sits in a darkened room crafting the finished version. Each step needs to be completed with the finished product in mind, so our script revisions needed to be as tight as possible. My red pen went to work.

While the script was being fine-tuned, actors needed lining up. Nick had already cast three of the male leads, one to be played by my basement-dwelling roommate, Joe, another by Nick himself, and a third by an Englishman called Martin – our 'man candy' – but there were six more lead characters to cast, along with half a dozen supporting roles.

We'd need to track down New York's finest out of work actors, and convince them to work on a feature-length film, for free, promising just a DVD of the finished product as payment. We prayed we'd at least find a few passable actors for the main roles, and assumed anyone else would be played by students, friends, or people grabbed off the street; yet little did we know that we'd vastly underestimated the hunger of New York's acting community.

Instead of needing to pray, we were answering prayers.

The postal worker stared at us with that look that's reserved for constipated people relieving themselves for the first time in three days.

"You the film guys?"

"Sure, guess so," we replied.

"Thank God! Your post's blocking the passage. Over here," he exhaled, as he waddled off in his regulation dark blue shorts and light blue shirt of the US Postal Service (USPS). We exchanged befuddled glances. He led us into a secure area within the post office, then pointed out a dozen boxes stacked high with Manila envelopes.

"They're for you guys," he wheezed.

"Which ones?" I asked.

"All of them, man."

I was silenced, in shock. There must have been over a thousand envelopes. I thought our PO Box would see minor traffic, twenty or thirty replies, but nothing close to the number heaped beside by the panting mailman.

To have received such a phenomenal stash would suggest we'd peppered every acting school in the Greater New York area. Not so. One small, innocuous ad placed five days earlier in *Backstage* magazine – 'the actor's resource' – was all it had taken. The ad read: Casting for Spike, early 30s, and three female leads, late 20s, for comedy feature film shooting in Sept/Oct/Nov. No pay, no agents, DVD for reel, send headshot to PO BOX 555, 10012 NY, NY.

That was it. We'd later learn that it's unheard of for a feature film to audition without using agents – their job being to sift gold from dirt – so the acting community had been thrown into a frenzy over our open audition.

The film they were looking to star in was part romcom, part gross-out comedy, based on four men trying to find love in the Big Apple. It had a naughty, adult edge, but could still be watched by the fifteen-rated crowd. Of course, these days teens switch between hundreds of websites every hour, able to see smut on each of them, so what's a little fetishism between friends?

We eyed the mailboxes, made a quick calculation, flagged down three cabs, and began loading. The USPS staffer was elated, clearly having dodged a bullet at being forced to shift them himself. We threw him a tip, sped to the apartment, dumped boxes, and debated how to proceed.

Potentially within arm's length of our cast, it was impossible not to open a few envelopes at random, checking out the headshots within. The range of abilities, ages, and looks was overwhelming. On the back of each headshot – usually a black and white photo of the auditioning actor – there's a CV that lists where the actor studied, what TV, commercials, theatre, or film they've been in, and what special abilities they have. Everyone had eclectic skills to brag about. I perused a handful, impressed, but we had over a thousand to open; a systematic approach was needed.

Minutes later, boxes circled around us, we decided the best course of action would be to take turns reading aloud each applicant's highlights, and then take a vote on who to keep and who to leave. The four of us – Joe, Nick, Martin, and myself – knew in general what we wanted, but faced a casting quandary:

What do you look for in an actor's headshot? How do you know if you're casting the next Rick Moranis or Mark Hamill? How do you know if you're passing on the next Johnny Depp or Robert De Niro?

There's no easy way.

It's why casting agents have a prominent credit at the start of every film; this job takes skill, instinct, and experience. We had none of that, so assumed we'd best discuss each headshot in depth, knowing we didn't want to miss out on a potential star. The first candidates were pulled from their envelopes.

"This one's a Stanislavski method actor."

"This guy's been in every Shakespeare play ever made, along with a recurring part in *Friends*."

"This chick can swallow swords."

"This guy went to RADA."

"This woman went to NYU Tisch."

"Will we need a juggler in Act Three?"

Ever so slowly the Yes, No, and Maybe piles grew, but at an agonising pace, so much so that after an hour we'd barely vetted twenty headshots. There wasn't time for this type of fastidious behaviour; it would take a week to go through every envelope. We had a film to make, rehearsals to begin, locations to book.

A new tack was needed.

Without debate, the four of us knew exactly what to do: keep it simple, keep it male, revert to being seventeen. Positions were shuffled, the other three acting as judges, myself as gameshow host.

"Yes, no, or maybe?" I'd ask, sweeping the headshot round for all to see.

"No!"

The No pile grew larger.

It was that easy. If the majority liked the actor based on looks, the headshot would go in the Yes pile, vice versa for the No pile. If it was a Maybe result I'd read out the actor's attributes – theatre/TV/film work, Spanish-speaker, sword-swallower, etc. – and cast the deciding vote.

Within thirty minutes we'd motored through a hundred head-shots. I was beginning to rethink my praise for casting agents. *If this is all they do in backstreet Hollywood offices, it's lucky they get a passable mention anywhere in the credits, let alone alongside the director, producer, and lead actors.*

After a day of paper cuts, and shallow choices, we'd sifted through every headshot. The No pile lined the walls. The Yes pile held about 150 actors, all of whom we'd need to audition. The following morning we got to work, calling every actor on the Yes list, locking in audition times for the following week. Some were elated to get the call, some surprised, but for most it was just another audition, another attempt at beating unfavourable odds in a dog-eat-dog city.

With actors booked, and a studio space lined up, I looked forward to the next step of the production process – our 'star finder' auditions – due to begin at 9.30am the following Tuesday.

As the owner of a video camera I was to be in charge of recording duties, leaving Joe, Nick, and Martin to take turns performing opposite each hopeful. Everything was in place to meet New York's voracious acting community, find the talent to match our film, offer roles, and leap into rehearsals.

We were confident, all eyes on the prize.

Little could stop us now.

As is the way with time and patience, so Tuesday rolled around; it was heralded by a shrill alarm, set early to guarantee a punctual arrival. Within seconds of the alarm going off, Joe and I had risen from our respective mattresses, eager not to be the weak link in this crucial day. Video camera, charger, tapes, headshots, notepads, scripts, and our casting schedule were dumped into a bag, and then lugged to the local subway station.

Outside, the morning was sunny, crystal clear. People went about their business, sipping coffee, rollerblading, begging for quarters.

I ignored the lot, focused only on the day ahead.

At the same time as we were walking the half-dozen blocks to the subway station, around the world, from California to the Carolinas, from Norway to New Zealand, in schools, prisons, bars, and cafés, people were tuning into pictures of an implausible event unfolding at the southernmost point of Manhattan. Yet we were oblivious to the breaking news, oblivious to our proximity to what was fast becoming the most unforgettable morning in modern American history.

After a five-minute walk we arrived at the Lexington Avenue & 86th Street station, at which point Joe received an unexpected call. It was his mother; and she immediately asked him a rather bizarre question: "Did you boys know that a small plane has hit one of the World Trade Center towers?"

The time was 8.53am – September 11th, 2001 – seven minutes after American Airlines Flight 11 had struck the World Trade Center's North Tower.

No, we didn't know.

Once she'd hung up, Joe filled me in, telling me that she seemed concerned, but that it sounded like an accident. She had the TV news on, but it was unclear what had taken place.

"Just be careful," she'd told him.

Assuming they were the kind words of a concerned mother we let them drift by. It seemed unlikely, unreal. And even if it was real, there wasn't enough detail for us to alter plans, so we waited for a 4/5/6 train to whisk us downtown.

Once aboard, nothing seemed out of the ordinary. People sat quietly, avoiding eye contact, reading newspapers, twitching at music players. On exiting the station at Union Square there was nothing to suggest the unimaginable events unfolding just a short distance away. It seemed as normal as New York could ever be; yet while we'd been travelling downtown, the day's horror had doubled.

At 9.03am United Airlines Flight 175 had smashed into the WTC South Tower, killing all sixty-five on board, and hundreds more inside the skyscraper. Many of those murdered had witnessed the fate of the North Tower, but hadn't fled, having been told by their building-wide PA system that the South Tower was secure.

The crisis was seventeen minutes old.

It was already the worst ever terrorism event on US soil.

Two-point-four miles north of the carnage, the streets were at peace. It was 9.12am as we crossed Union Square. Sirens could be heard in the distance, police cars raced downtown, but sirens could always be heard in New York City, emergency vehicles always sped through the streets. That there were more sirens than usual should have been noted, but we were fixated on meeting our future stars.

The journey to the studio facility took less than five uneventful minutes, walking on a few streets south. Once there, we entered the building and headed straight to our first-floor audition room. Inside the simple, white-washed space sat Nick and Martin, who'd taken an early cab, leaving them also in the dark as to the day's astonishing events.

Four men, two miles from tragedy, completely unaware as to the crimes taking place on their very doorstep.

As we discussed the day's audition schedule – preparing to put thirty actors through their paces – at 9.17am the FAA closed all of New York City's airports. At the same time, news networks began to reference the plane strikes as terrorist acts, and then, at 9.21am, Manhattan went into total lock-down, traffic barred from the borough's jugular network of bridges and tunnels.

We were under siege, but in an era before smartphones and Twitter updates, the four of us laid out scripts, stacked chairs, and drank coffee.

Yet the day was about to reveal itself, as we began to question where the actors were that we'd scheduled in. There should have been three or four people anxiously awaiting their turn, but just one woman sat patiently, her audition not due for another half-hour. Having spent a full day carefully choosing our potential cast, followed by frustrating hours juggling their schedules, it was a massive let-down that only one person had deigned to show up.

It's so unprofessional, I thought, unaware that as the clock ticked past 9.30am, President George W Bush was on-air, telling the nation, "Today we've had a national tragedy. Two airplanes have crashed into the World Trade Center in an apparent terrorist attack on our country..."

There was no one else to audition, so we called in the waiting hopeful, an actress from New Jersey. Her face was contorted in amazement.

Not the good sort of amazement.

"Are you guys really doing this today?" she asked.

But without stipulating the reason for her amazement – that she knew of the attacks and couldn't believe these callous filmmakers were continuing with their auditions on such a day – and without any of us asking her to explain her apparent incredulity, we answered:

"Yes, of course."

She looked nonplussed, then proceeded with her audition, delivering lines in a clipped, hurried fashion. It was over fast, after which she rushed off with barely a farewell, leaving the four of us alone, hoping the rest of our applicants wouldn't be quite so keen to depart. Was it something we'd said? Had someone broken wind? It was a bad start, but these were open auditions; you take the rough with the smooth.

Things would improve.

We checked the passage. It was empty. Four hearts sank. Twenty chairs waited to be filled. I assumed it was part of the creative process, so shrugged, closing the door. We waited for a polite knock.

It wasn't to be.

"We're under attack!!!"

The flamboyant studio director burst in, finally hooking us into the 9/11 news cycle, alerting us to its chaos and carnage.

"The Pentagon's been hit!!!" he shrieked.

It was 9.57am, twenty minutes after the headquarters of the US military had been smashed into by American Airlines Flight

77, killing all sixty-four on board, taking the lives of a further 125 on the ground. As the fortress burnt, the most dire of precautions were taken: the White House and US Capitol were evacuated, while America's entire airspace was shut down, flights forced to land at their nearest airport.

The studio director had been searching his cavernous building to find anyone still at work, arriving at our room to see us feet up, wondering when our actors would show. Phones had been checked a thousand times, but mobile connections were jammed, overloaded by the city's eight million residents checking on loved ones. Known as a 'mass call event', the cellular network had crashed in minutes.

On seeing our incredulous reaction to his Pentagon news, he asked if we knew of the attacks that had taken place a mere stone's throw away.

Blank faces prompted a fast update.

What he told us seemed absurd, possibly anti-Bush propaganda. I was confused. Anything seemed more likely than the outrageous events he was describing. *This didn't happen in America.* There was only one way to find out for ourselves, so we ran from the studio, down the passage, through the fire exit, racing a few blocks west to where you could normally see the Twin Towers standing proud at the south end of Manhattan Island.

Not that day.

We were greeted with the strangest of sights; instead of two gleaming, 110-storey skyscrapers, smoke billowed, because at 9.59am – minutes before we'd dashed out – the South Tower had suddenly collapsed, crumbling in around fifteen seconds. Witnessed by a shocked global audience, the resulting debris mushroomed out, engulfing the North Tower, leaving many to believe an explosion had brought down both towers.

The immense scale of the attacks instantly sunk in, as did the changed atmosphere on the streets. The volume of sirens was palpable. Now we noticed it. Cop cars shot downtown, followed by ambulances and fire trucks. The day's madness stunned us, bolted to the block corner, speechless, and tense.

"It's the end of the world!" shouted one wide-eyed lunatic, but this was no time for theatrics. New Yorkers from all backgrounds shouted back, "Shut the fuck up, asshole!"

As we took in the corrupted scene, far to the south in a quiet field in Pennsylvania a fourth hijacked plane came crashing down, unobserved by anyone except for livestock. Flight 93 was thought to be heading for the White House or US Capitol, but as the story goes, on learning of the fate of the three other planes via phone and text, passengers on board fought back, forcing the terrorists to abandon their course, instead crashing into farmland in Somerset County at 10.03am, saving unknown hundreds in Washington DC.

The demise of Flight 93 was unknown at the time; not even the US Air Force or Vice President knew, Dick Cheney ordering fighter jets to engage the aircraft 10–15 minutes after it had crash-landed. Presumed to be flying low and off-radar it was deemed a top priority, with warplanes sent to a location based on expected trajectory and speed. They found nothing.

It wasn't until a half-hour later that reports emerged of a fourth downed plane; and it would take far longer to piece together the courageous acts that led to its destruction in a rural community approximately 160 miles north-west of DC, rather than on the south lawn of the President's home.

In downtown Manhattan, my instinct was to follow George W Bush and head into hiding. I'm not ashamed to say so. It was a terrifying day, not only because of the attacks that had taken place, but also because of what else might unfold. What other horrors lay in wait? How many more planes had been hijacked? Could there be other types of attack?

Four shell-shocked wannabe filmmakers needed a plan. First up, we rushed back to the audition studio, debating options. There were two options: one was uptown, back to the apartment and relative safety; the other was downtown, towards the biggest attack on US soil since Pearl Harbor.

The decision was made. It didn't go my way.

The plan was to go downtown. I could have left the others, I could have gone uptown, but there was an inquisitiveness to witness the scene for myself. The 'flee instinct' was beaten back, so we exited the building, back into the clear sunshine of that tragic September day, and began to wind our way through the streets, heading towards what would eventually become known as Ground Zero.

Due to a lack of traffic, an eerie quiet had settled over the streets. Nobody had anywhere to be. Public transport had shut down. You couldn't leave the island. There were only pedestrians, mostly moving uptown, away from the crisis.

From time to time the quiet was broken by the sound of transistor radios and TV sets. People were gathered in shocked groups around cars, outside shops, sitting in restaurants, and on apartment steps, following the news. On every TV the image of United Airlines Flight 175 smashing into the South Tower played over and over again, inter-cut with live shots of the burning North Tower, and the inferno destroying a full side of the Pentagon.

As we walked near New York University (NYU), about twenty blocks north of the World Trade Center, the next act of devastation befell the city. Due to the high buildings around us we didn't see it, but at 10.28am the North Tower could hold out no longer, imploding like its sister twenty-nine minutes earlier, sending a giant shot of smoke and concrete far into the sky.

We may not have seen the tower fall, but we were about to witness its aftermath. Four blocks south of NYU, the visceral reality of 9/11 revealed itself. On turning a corner, our line of sight along the next street was no more, filled instead with an impenetrable dust cloud that expanded between and above the buildings, blanketing all. The dark mass crept toward us, its energy dissipating as it fanned out from Ground Zero. And then, from deep within, a cop car appeared, covered in debris, red and blues spinning in vain.

After the cop car, came the people.

Office workers emerged, slowly shuffling, seeking refuge. One man, covered in grey powder, used a handkerchief to stop the bleeding from his forehead; a lady, uninjured, cleaned herself off, stepping carefully into the daylight. Her elegant, suited attire was a reminder that this was no war zone. It was a regular Tuesday, a regular office day. Paramedics tended to those in need. Those not wounded just stood there, in shock, staring at the cloud from where they'd come.

We moved on, arriving at Canal Street, where police had established a perimeter. There was no going further south. We were back on one of the city's busiest thoroughfares, joining the masses as they crowded around car stereos, praying that everyone had been rescued, seeking assurances the day could get no worse.

The mood was defiant. The attacks had brought New Yorkers together, sharing information, supporting strangers. It reminded me of history classes, of how the Nazi Blitz on London had strengthened the resolve of the people. Tyrants and terrorists rarely win, but they can draw blood trying. And that morning Osama bin Laden had drawn blood. Casualties were mounting, as fire crews searched for survivors in the rubble, but there were few to be found.

The imploding towers had left nowhere to hide.

It was time to leave. Trained professionals were doing what they could; if we weren't part of the solution, we were part of the problem. There was no need for us to be downtown. We pointed our way north, seeking sanctuary.

Alongside tens of thousands of New Yorkers – native and visitor alike – we began the hike uptown to sit tight and wait for news. Mobile phones were still out of service, and with communications switched off, New York went mute.

We hit Second Avenue – the very avenue that two weeks previously I'd gawped at on arrival – and joined a sombre mass of shell-shocked people shuffling their way home, filling the avenue's width. From time to time they'd gaze back at the billowing smoke to check the day was no illusion.

But in the distance, smoke still rose into the September blue.

Around a third of the way to 91st Street we passed Mount Sinai Beth Israel hospital where a queue of hundreds of people had formed to give blood. At that point in the day it was assumed that thousands of injured victims would need treatment; no one expected there would be so few survivors.

We joined the line, but on hearing our accents a nurse explained that because we were British we couldn't give blood. We threw her quizzical glances. *What's wrong with our blood?* She told us that we were barred from donating due to a UK-specific problem called mad cow disease. Our blood was therefore not acceptable in the United States. Amazed, we said nothing, nodded at the bizarre rationale and left, knowing it was a minor issue compared to the intense anguish others were enduring that day. Our group rejoined the tide of humanity proceeding north.

Block after block after block, on we went.

We couldn't, and wouldn't, complain about the march, but when we finally arrived at 91st Street, surrounded by a thinned-out crowd, it was noted the walk had taken almost two hours.

With nothing else to do, we took to plastic chairs in the back-yard, talking over the day, the expected military response, and of course what had happened to friends, and friends of friends, who might be missing. That was a conversation that would tail off, reaching its miserable conclusion over the coming days and weeks.

Not wanting to breach the trust of friends who lost friends, or to misuse the names of those that died that day, I won't go into detail about who passed away on 9/11, suffice to say that I pray those killed now rest in peace.

Following September 11th, like many businesses in New York, the production of *Best Served Hot* was put on hold. In fact, life was put on hold.

It gave us time to think.

For one of the producers, thought turned to action; she returned to Arizona, not comfortable in post-9/11 New York. I too contemplated home. Manhattan was a sombre, increasingly bitter place to be. Many Americans closed ranks, shutting out even their closest ally, the British.

That's not to say friends shut us out, but strangers were less open, with one New Yorker telling me, "You wouldn't understand. You've never been through something like this."

"Well, not exactly," I replied, "but London suffered IRA attacks during most of my childhood."

The argument fell on deaf ears: "It's not the same thing." Not wanting to be embroiled in a 'whose terrorist is worse' debate, I walked away.

On September 12th George W Bush told his cabinet the attacks "were more than acts of terror. They were acts of war." Talk of retaliation had begun, amidst a backdrop of FBI raids across the country, as government agencies sought answers, and culprits. A day later, twitchy authorities detained ten people at New York City airports, reportedly for reasons as disparate as boarding planes under false pretenses, and having taken flying lessons at the same schools as the 9/11 terrorists.

The arrests heightened nerves.

On September 15th the Bush administration again spoke of war, Colin Powell announcing that both Pakistan and Iran had closed their borders with Afghanistan, and that Pakistan was to allow America to use its territory as a staging post for a 'War on Terror' against the Taliban. The move prompted thousands of Afghans to head for the very borders that had just been closed.

On the same day, an Indian Sikh service station owner, an Egyptian Coptic Christian grocery store owner, and a Pakistani Sikh businessman were gunned down in Arizona, California, and Texas respectively, in what were assumed to be 9/11-related retribution attacks. The ignorant, revenge mentality would also see foreign taxi drivers openly abused on the streets of American cities.

And then – on September 18th – anthrax.

Media outlets in New York and Florida, then soon after two senators in Washington DC, were sent envelopes containing lethal anthrax spores, potentially sent by agents working for Osama bin Laden, Saddam Hussein, Colonel Gaddafi, or any other tyrant on Bush's 'axis of evil' hit list. In total five people died, but it wasn't until August 2008 that FBI investigators confirmed the culprit was actually Bruce Edwards Ivins, a US government bio-defence researcher.

The anthrax attacks further heightened the sense of a nation under siege. Evil was out there; America was scared. News outlets used generalised reporting to cover 'known unknowns', such as "anthrax probably sent by Osama bin Laden" or it was "the type of attack that Osama bin Laden is trying to achieve," leaving viewers in constant uncertainty as to the severity of the nation's terror threat. The media's guesswork and mind games hindered efforts to return to a normal way of life.

After two weeks of network news addiction, allowing it to terrify the crap out of me, I decided it was time to switch off the news… for good.

It was a decision that saved me from curling up on the floor, jumping at noises. US broadcasters had gone rogue. At a time when you'd think watching headline news to be a sensible activity, the reverse proved true. When they weren't being vague, they were being provocative, using hyped-up rhetoric and surreal imagery. Some bulletins even began with computer-generated graphics of fighter jets swooping in from left and right, leaving the words 'America at War' in their trail. And the tone of the programming was confrontational, bitter, vengeful. Anyone doubting the government or its military was un-American. Anyone not waving a flag was a terrorist. It was a good time to sell flags.

It was a good time to switch off the news.

The reality of the crisis was palpable enough without the

media's insanity. It was evident all around. On the streets. In bars. In cafés. The Big Apple was wounded. Once a Goliath, it had been brought to its knees, left to grieve its dead; but it wouldn't be allowed to grieve for long, for even though over 3,000 New Yorkers had been murdered within the city, President George W Bush decided it was time for Goliath – and the rest of America – to once again stand tall.

On September 20th he told Congress: "We will come together to take active steps that strengthen America's economy, and put our people back to work."

Whether or not New York was ready to re-boot, there was nothing else to be done, so barely two weeks after the Twin Towers had been felled by passenger jets hijacked by al-Qaeda terrorists, the production of *Best Served Hot* was put back on track, as recommended by America's Commander in Chief. New Yorkers mostly agreed with Bush, knowing their city to be a machine of commerce; if the cogs stopped grinding, the terrorists had won.

It seemed to make sense, but I thought a day of mourning, or a procession, would have been appropriate. Families, survivors, and the city overall, needed to gather in remembrance, but instead its residents gathered on the subway, returning to work, showing 'the terrorists in their caves' they hadn't won the day. It seemed like deference to America's leaders, rather than defiance to the terrorists, but either way, the nine-to-five was back in play.

Irritated as I am to admit it, George W Bush was right.

We did need to get back to work. Sitting in apartments obsessing over the events of 9/11 only exacerbated the situation. New York needed to get busy; and so as the rest of the city kicked into gear, so did we, hitting the phones, rebooking our aborted audition process.

Of course restarting the job in no way meant forgetting the enormity of what had taken place on September 11th. The attack could be seen on every block; its wounds, still raw, impossible to miss.

Across the city the New York Fire Department held candlelit memorials for their 341 fallen colleagues; Union Square was home to hundreds of pictures of missing loved ones, families holding out hope they could still be found; and downtown, frenzied work was underway at Ground Zero, as bucket by bucket the rubble of the World Trade Center was examined for human remains.

The 9/11 aftermath rolled on, and would continue to do so for months and years to come.

It was far from an ideal environment within which to ignite my fledgling film career, but once new audition slots had been confirmed, the team's collective mood began to lift. We lined up the same studio space as before, and more or less the same actors – a handful had chosen to quit the Big Apple – scheduling them in for what we hoped would be a thorough audition process.

A few days later we returned to Union Square, igniting tense memories of that traumatic day. It was déjà vu, camera in hand, scripts at the ready, eager to meet actors. It was unsettling, feeling oddly disrespectful; but the show must go on. After walking the same short route, I arrived at our rented studio, praying the day would unfold in a most ordinary, predictable fashion.

Fortunately for all, it did.

We even had bums on seats, early hopefuls awaiting our arrival. Yet had the actors known the process they were about to face, they might have thought twice about coming, for this wasn't to be a traditional audition, partly because none of us had ever organised a traditional audition, but mostly because we wanted to be different; we wanted to do things in a memorable, unique way. And we wanted to laugh. We needed it. They needed it. We *all* needed it.

It's hard not to smile when I think of the role-play we asked our female contenders to try. Nothing too scandalous, I assure you; we asked them to try an improvised scene where they'd play the part of a prostitute hired by a boy's father to find out whether or not his son is gay.

Raise that shocked jaw off the floor.

We offered them the choice of a more vanilla part, if desired, but almost all of them took to the prostitute role, often with zeal. It later became clear that other auditions – perhaps unsurprisingly – didn't feature such a request, and it was therefore deemed exciting, different, a challenge to be conquered.

With camera rolling, our 'star search' began, and the good times were gently reawakened. It was okay to laugh again, and it was hard not to, as I watched one of my team play the part of a seemingly asexual boy, sitting on a chair pretending to watch TV, while an actress performed – to the best of her ability – tricks a hooker might use to grab his attention.

There are few better ways to spend an afternoon.

Yet there was method to our madness; for starters, the actors needed to be comfortable with a film that had a high content of sexual humour – think *American Pie* meets *Secretary* – along with the fact that we actually *did* need two actresses to play prostitutes in a scene where 'Spike' wakes hungover, unable to remember a thing, having blown his entire savings on their specialist company.

I found the audition process fascinating. To see people willing to flex their creative muscles to gain the approval of complete strangers was uplifting, yet terrifying. Filmmaking is so popular, its rewards so intoxicating, that it draws people in, like sailors to sirens, most of whom are left shattered on the rocks. And we were to meet many such sailors, drawn in by the opportunity of a speaking role in an independent film, looking for it to be their launchpad to Hollywood glamour.

Meeting these people, whittling down the Yes list, was fun at first, then demanding, the stress of selecting the right candidate proving just as much a test for us, as it was for the actors auditioning; but the task was done as expected, through perseverance, second and third round auditions, and a final call offering out roles. There were squeals of joy. It felt good.

Once the actors had been locked in, the audition team split

off into different departments, prepping for day one of principal photography (the first day of filming). From then on, Nick, Joe, and Martin were out of sight rehearsing scenes, while I was assigned to the senior producers, arranging locations, finding crew, booking equipment, scheduling shoot days, and sorting the myriad other items and permits the average shoot requires.

Clipboard in hand, it was time to make a movie.

Once principal photography had begun, my workload increased exponentially, rising to fifteen-hour days, six days a week.

Time disappeared in a whirlwind of odd-job errands, renting cameras, returning lights, collecting lunch, shuffling schedules, writing call sheets, finding wardrobe, clearing lunch, assisting continuity, buying film, and even assuming the part of 'stubbly video store man' where I had to deliver a one-worded line (that I managed to cock up three times in a row).

A fully-fledged film unit is an army on active duty. Your life is theirs. You march to their beat; you eat when you're told to eat; you sleep when you're told to sleep; you react to battles, help where possible, and follow orders. There's always something that needs doing, always someone who needs a hand. It's a tough existence, but by no means impossible.

In Italy I'd caught a glimpse of how a production team works, but my smoker's vantage point had been limited. I was now experiencing it in full, glorious, Technicolor reality, and was enticed in by its immersive, breakneck speed. It was thunderous, a rollercoaster on acid.

Hold on tight.

This ride is not for children.

And so I held on as tight as possible, and after eight weeks of lightning fast loop the loops we shuddered to a halt, as the last take of *Best Served Hot* seared a strip of 35mm film, leaving its eternal footprint. And then, for the second time in my career, I heard an assistant director shout:

"That's a wrap, guys!"

All scenes had been filmed, all lines recorded, all locations visited. On hearing those famous words I was relieved, saddened, exhausted… and bent double, hobbling towards the nearest hospital.

"What have you been eating?" asked the doctor.

"Burgers."

"No, I mean for the past few months," said the doc, eyes rolling.

"Yeah, burgers… and sushi," I replied, impressed with the fact that I'd managed to lose weight while existing on a diet of soft drinks, coffee, burgers, and sushi. It was a miracle I hadn't doubled in size.

The doctor had a different take:

"IBS. You've eaten your insides bad," was his professional opinion.

I looked at him, baffled.

"What on earth is IBS?"

He answered, telling me in detail about the causes and treatments for Irritable Bowel Syndrome, an illness that relates to your innards being unable to process what you're ingesting, the result being…

…another spasm warped my abdomen; I begged him for meds. As I grabbed my sides, expecting my innards to burst across the floor, he laconically explained that I'd been drinking too little water, had eaten too much junk, and would therefore battle IBS for the rest of my days.

Ah, balls, I thought, yet another medical issue to contend with. Add it to the teenage zits, corny toes, broken ankle, dry skin, dandruff, in-growing toenails, mild arthritis, and failing eyesight.

I felt like the genetic equivalent of the Russian military.

Pleased to have an explanation, I drifted from the hospital, having been instructed to eat fibrous foods, drink water, and keep doing so until the pain went away. To this day, I still get cramps if I eat too much junk food, reminding me of that dry doctor in New

York City, rolling his eyes in desperation at the young man who thought he could live on burgers and sushi.

It was time to leave town.

Best Served Hot had propelled me further into the film business than I could ever have hoped, but had also been responsible for a painful and embarrassing hospital visit, of which I've been reminded ever since.

And so on a freezing day in late autumn I boarded a London-bound flight, drinking date juice, beaming a smug sense of achievement.

Aside from IBS, good times lay ahead.

No, scratch that…

Great times lay ahead.

JOB SIX: SECOND ASSISTANT DIRECTOR

Lessons learnt:

- Sometimes you need to hit rock bottom before rising up the other side
- Consider all opportunities, even those offered via a drunk dial
- Try not to arrive in a city you've always wanted to visit two weeks before a world-changing, cataclysmic terror attack
- In times of strife, turn to Rudyard Kipling's poem, 'If'
- 'George W Bush was right' – words you never expect to see in print
- Don't live on burgers, sushi, and soft drinks for longer than a day
- And visit New York. The city loves tourists, serves literal double-burgers, and has a magnificent way with words

CHAPTER TWELVE

I'm so average, so very average.

Sitting on a double-decker bus, it was the thought I couldn't shake.

It didn't take long for the shine of New York to wear off, as I slotted back into London, February 2002, forlornly thinking of packed days in the Big Apple, now on a commuter bus, surrounded by a workforce moaning about property prices in Fulham and share prices in the City.

Europe's financial hub was in a post 9/11 downturn, and the West was back at war. The US, UK, and an armada of allies had boots on the ground in Afghanistan, tasked with wiping out al-Qaeda bases, taking out the Taliban, and capturing Osama bin Laden. As ever, the UK supported its American ally, returning to Afghanistan, a land where British soldiers had fought two conflicts in the 1800s, resulting in one loss, one draw; yet such precedence was shrugged off, the military presumably grasping at a 'third time lucky' strategy.

Many thought the invasion unnecessary, nothing but 9/11 revenge, prompting protest marches worldwide, the largest of which took place in London on November 18th 2001, as up to 100,000 people waved 'Stop the War' and 'Not in My Name' banners, sending a global message that did little to change the mindsets of No. 10 and the White House. American protesters held their biggest rally on April 20th 2002, with about 75,000 people marching up Pennsylvania Avenue to the United States Capitol, yet the mission in Afghanistan continued on regardless.

George W Bush was not for turning.

And so as the world debated the pros and cons of fighting the Taliban, I had my face in a stranger's armpit, crammed inside a

No. 9 bus, trundling towards my second stint as a production intern. Following another scattershot job hunt, I was now punching in at Film & General Productions (F&G), a Knightsbridge-based outfit famed for co-producing *Tea with Mussolini* – starring Cher, Maggie Smith, and Judi Dench – in 1999, that earned the team one BAFTA award, and one BAFTA nomination. That's not something you easily forget, so the gigantic *Tea with Mussolini* poster front and centre of the office was a justifiable reminder of the company's gong-scooping past.

But in 2002 F&G was producing something a tad different, a children's TV series called *The Queen's Nose*. The company also had about fifty scripts 'under option' – having bought the rights to turn them into films – that were piled high on shelves around the compact workplace. My boss, a middle-aged firebrand of the media industry, had noted early on that I'd studied English Literature at university, so assumed I'd have an eye for critiquing scripts; my first task therefore was to pore over every one of those optioned screenplays, meticulously reading them front to back, setting aside any that might have box office potential.

Taking a punt on a script is one of the most challenging aspects of the film industry; it's where you make or break a company, searching for a nugget of gold in a broad and rapid river, praying you'll come close to *The Full Monty* (budget: $3.5 million, worldwide revenue: $250+ million). Optioning scripts is where a producer's talents are tested. If you screw up and choose a dud, you'll never cast actors, never ponce about in a pinstriped suit, never harass your editor for an early version to show distributors, and never waltz on stage to receive an award for your 'project that revived the British film industry'.

As I started on F&G's scripts I knew I had to treat the pile with kid gloves, not just skim-read the first few pages like a literary agent blasting through unsolicited material. This was *solicited* material, an investment in the future; a tangible punt at recreating the success of *Tea with Mussolini*.

Blockbuster gold had to be there… somewhere.

After three weeks of late night reading, diligently noting the strengths and weaknesses of each script, carefully panning for that presumed gold, I was ready to deliver my verdict. The boss's question was obvious:

"So what did you think? Any gems?"

"Nope, except one," I replied, having decided after much deliberation that honesty would be respected. *No point in pretending a script has potential if it doesn't. No point in sugar-coating it.*

The look on her face didn't seem to agree.

"That's it? You're sure?" she asked wearily.

"Er, as I said, I liked one," I mumbled, now concerned I might not make it through the day, soon to be impaled on a *Tea with Mussolini* prop, with shouts of "We won a BAFTA, you little shit!!" ringing in my ears.

But there was nothing of the sort.

"Which one did you like, then?"

"This one, the one about the refugee group crossing a continent," I replied, thankful to be offering solid feedback.

She smiled, knowingly.

"Ah yes, that one. And how much did you think it would cost to produce?"

"Er, about fifty million, give or take."

"Not bad, not bad. We thought about forty-five… and that, my friend, is why it's not been made."

The conversation was over. She returned to her office, and I returned to my desk, proud to have completed the task, yet disappointed I hadn't uncovered a gem, or steered the company towards silver screen glory.

Instead, it was back to the current money-maker, the children's TV show. Although everyone may dream of the big-ticket project, bills need paying. A kid's show might not be glamorous, and it won't garner laurel wreathes naming festivals that adored your 'indie masterpiece', but it will generate income, and that makes it just as important as any other project, if not more so.

Pre-production work on *The Queen's Nose* – a show about a magical 50p coin – continued through the spring months, scripts piling up in different colours, as re-writes followed revisions. At the start of summer it was ready for production, so we packed up the office, moving to a temporary space in north London, joining forces with a freelance crew that had been assembled to shoot the series.

Our locations team had found a disused warehouse near to Smithfield Market – ancient scene of medieval fairs and public executions – that boasted broken windows and rickety stairs, but at four storeys high was spacious, and, thinking like a true pinstriped producer, crucially located by one of London's finest eateries.

Once the warehouse had been made safe, sets built, and the young cast primed for their initial scenes, principal photography was soon underway. While it was exciting to be back near a professional shoot, it also turned out to be deeply frustrating, the film unit located in a distant part of the building, my days spent at a quiet desk, shuffling paperwork, collecting coffee orders.

After my time on *Best Served Hot* it was a dose of reality, a window into how most people start out in film and TV. I should have relished the job, appreciating it for what it was, but after several weeks of trying to sneak on set, only to be told to return to the office, an unfamiliar irritation began to creep across me, and it was one I never expected to experience: I had *too little* work on my plate.

If you told fifteen-year-old Charlie that one day he'd be frustrated at having too little work to do, young Charlie would laugh in your face, after which he'd tell you to piss off back to the future, probably having wedgied you in the process; but there I was, bored and irate, knowing it wouldn't be long before I'd seek a better way to fill my time; and so when a colleague told me that a friend of hers at a commercials company was looking for junior staff, it was more than enough to agitate my eternally itchy feet.

"You sure it would be a good move?" I asked.

"It should be," she replied, telling me what she knew about the job: it was at a central London company with a large turnover of commercials, in need of an assistant to help process their workload. It sounded ideal: great location, interesting work… a good move.

But would it be a *good idea* at this stage in my career?

One of the toughest things in the rat race is to know when to leave one job for another, unsure if the next job will provide you with what you think you need, always aware that someone will say, "be careful what you wish for," if it unravels in your face. Much like my assessment of work experience years earlier, all you can do is weigh up the information to hand, and make your play.

I took a moment, eyeing up the office. It was another quiet day, in a dreary warehouse, removed from the action. I was learning nothing, achieving nothing. The decision seemed easy. The opportunity felt right.

My colleague set up the interview, and I set my sights on a return to Soho, hoping this time not to be replaced by an archway.

Men have hoped for less.

Not much less.

JOB SEVEN: PRODUCTION ASSISTANT, TAKE II

Lessons learnt:

- Even the military seems to believe in 'third time lucky'
- Armpit proximity is an unavoidable part of commuting
- Honesty might not endear you to the boss
- Producers may aim for BAFTAs, but daytime TV pays the bills
- It's hard not to associate boredom with stagnation

CHAPTER THIRTEEN

Alcohol.

It's a troublesomely fantastic invention. Over the years it's dragged many a good, and many a useless, man into the gutter. In the summer of 2002 I was somewhere between the two, taking strides towards a successful career, yet far from receiving a decent paycheque.

And then alcohol reared its head.

After leaving *The Queen's Nose*, and having successfully secured yet another bottom rung position, I began life at Round Point Commercials, based in the heart of Soho. Officially my new position was junior receptionist, but it could just as well have been production assistant, coffee brewer, paper shredder, or bin emptier. I'd stopped caring. They all boiled down to *dogsbody*. I just hoped that this time the job would be active, fulfilling, an engaging challenge.

Within days it was clear the new job would be none of the above. It was disturbingly similar to my last role, but with longer hours, more menial work, and a shamelessly despicable boss.

As a yellow cartoon man once famously said: "D'oh!"

Pointless questions over my decision to switch jobs were immediately asked, but the answer was always the same: I'd based the move on the best reasoning I'd had at the time. All I could do to cope with the failed switch was assume an attitude of 'no regrets', accepting what had taken place, hoping one day to rise up the ladder, keeping my eyes on the prize, not on the past.

At times like this it helps to have a distraction, and at Round Point Commercials I was blessed with the ultimate of distractions, one that's guaranteed to take your mind off anything, including terrible career decisions. It's a distraction that every wage slave falls foul of, whatever the industry, and it hit me hard:

The office infatuation.

My new job was made tolerable by working alongside the always sunny, friendly, and extremely attractive Dani, who'd come to work each morning like Mary Poppins on Vicodin. Some days she'd even arrive singing, "Let's go fly a kite, up to the highest height, let's go fly a kite…"

If most people had done that I'd have brought a shovel to work, dispatching of them as nature duly requires, but there was no faulting Dani. It was infatuation at first song. She was skilled, efficient, warm, but above all, extremely sexy. Yes, blonde. Yes, slim. Yes, it's stereotypical, but so be it. I was an average man falling for an above average woman. I was smitten.

Of course as the cosmos demands, there has to be a balance. There has to be good *and* bad. The yang to Dani's yin, the Vader to her Skywalker, the Newman to her Seinfeld, was Beatrice, my new overlord and boss.

While I can't blame all of my increased drinking on Beatrice – partly it was the weather, world politics, career frustration – I did feel compelled to seek out a few cold ones after every frightening encounter with her. And if those encounters were numerous, so too would be my end of day drinks. Fortunately Beatrice worked on the top floor, Dani and I on the ground floor, but every time I heard footsteps stomping downwards, I'd panic, dribble, and prepare for the worst. Sure enough, every time there'd be an unpleasant comment or ridiculous demand:

"Get off there, now!" she demanded one morning. I was perched on the arm of the reception sofa.

"Where should I sit?" I asked, looking around the reception area that had one chair, one desk, and one sofa, all of which I'd been banned from using.

"Just stand," she replied, before marching upstairs.

On most days Beatrice had meetings, at least that's what she claimed. I thought it more likely she was boiling newts and bat heads in a cauldron under the Tower of London. But while

Beatrice tended to her rituals, Dani and I could breathe easy, distracted by a classic characteristic of life in Soho: the local brothel. Yes, our friendly next-door neighbours offered certain pleasurable services, the recipients of which became the highlight of our day.

Every time a 'gentleman visitor' came a knockin' his bell-ringing could be heard in our reception area, prompting Dani and me to skid into the alley to see who was waiting. I'd always pray for a politician, but it was inevitably just another suited businessman, pausing to be let in, turning ever-so red on seeing the neighbour's staff rush outside, pretending to look for a lost delivery van.

Yet, as amusing as the brothel was, and a daily reminder of how eclectic Soho is, it wasn't enough. Beatrice always returned, every day threatening fresh gloom. Despite my 'no regrets' attitude, regret reared its head.

While I hate regret, and tried fighting its advances, I couldn't ignore the fact that my mood was sinking. And then, as if to accentuate my downtrodden state, Soho began to stink. I mean truly reek. During summer, after two weeks without rain, nightly lashings of piss and vomit took on a smell, even a life, of their own. And inspired by (or reacting to) the stench, I haunted the local pubs and bars, helping me forget my "don't sit there" tormentor.

It was only a matter of time before the situation unravelled.

After a late night just six weeks into the job, the inevitable happened: I woke on a friend's sofa at 10am, wrapped in a beach towel, still slurring, kebab meat crisp and even across my front. It was a washed up scene of drunken ineptitude that needed damage control, fast.

It's at this point the customary late-for-work options are processed.

Could I pull off sounding sick on the phone? Should I avoid the office, dealing with it the following day? Should I drop in, look unwell, and hope to be sent home? Should I 'man up' and face the day? If so, what excuse could I use for my tardiness? Would 'personal problems' be accepted? Should I put my arm in a sling?

Should I try bribing a doctor for a sick note? How about eating the dribbled doner kebab, thereby getting actual food poisoning? *Ooooooh, that might work...*

Before I'd finalised a plan, my phone rang.

It was Beatrice. My mobile warned me not to answer. (Literally, it had 'Don't Answer' saved to her number.) In a flash, a whole new plan came to mind, created by tiny particles of alcohol dancing a jig through my system.

"Hellooo?" said I, in a way that's meant to suggest you have no idea who's on the line, while the caller knows perfectly well you have their number, and are fully aware of who's calling.

"Where are you, Charlie? Why aren't you here?"

Pause. Deep breath.

"Say what?"

She growled.

"I said, WHERE ARE YOU?"

Another pause. Another deep breath.

"I'm not coming in. I, er, can't be arsed."

"What the hell do you mean? Get in here right now!!!"

Pause. Here it comes.

Big mistake? Too late now...

"Beatrice, you can take your crappy job and shove it up your arse!!"

"What?!" she screamed. "How dare…"

I'd hung up.

The alcohol had spoken, resigning on my behalf, yet I wasn't in anyway displeased. I sat back, stupidly content with how the day was unfolding.

Remarkably, and to give her some credit, Beatrice called back.

Satisfied with how I'd behaved the first time, and not wanting to break a finely-tuned machine, I answered accordingly:

"Hellooo?"

"Charlie, what the hell do you think…"

"Say what?"

"Charlie, get into the office and…"

I'd hung up again.

Unsurprisingly it was the last time I heard from Beatrice. My time at Round Point Commercials was over. Alcohol and frustration had scuttled my entry into Soho production, potentially blacklisting me for life. At the time I blamed the job, the boss, the general machinations of the creative industries, but in hindsight it was none other than myself who'd pushed the self-destruct button.

Having done so, I'd have to start again. I'd have to pick up the pieces; I'd have to reignite my career in yet another way.

Not that I was particularly bothered, not on the morning I'd resigned in one of the rudest ways known to mankind. Quite the opposite; I was content, tipsy, and keen to make the most of my newfound time.

So that's just what I did.

I took a long shower.

Heated a curry.

And watched eight straight hours of daytime TV.

JOB EIGHT: PRODUCTION ASSISTANT, TAKE III

Lessons learnt:

- Be as informed as possible about moving jobs, especially if you're resigning from a half-decent position to take on a similar (or potentially worse) role
- An office infatuation will see you turn a blind eye to office karaoke, office dolls, and office birthday whip-rounds for the guy you never met
- After two weeks without rain, Soho stinks
- Try to resign with style. Telling anyone to "shove it up their arse" is far from stylish… yet I still have trouble regretting my actions

CHAPTER FOURTEEN

Fuck, fuck, fuckity-fuck.

Fuckity, fuckity, fuckity, fuck.

It was a frenzied mantra, ignited by doubt. *Would I bounce back? What had I done? Did it matter? Was I on the right path?* Confused questions. Decreasing self-belief. And through it all, the mantra kicked on.

Fuck, fuck, fuckity-fuck.

Fuckity, fuckity, fuckity, fuck.

Those words are used to great effect at the start of Brit rom-com *Four Weddings and a Funeral,* so I have to allude to the hapless Charles, played by Hugh Grant, who sleeps through his alarm, leaving him offensively late for a wedding at which he's to be best man. Charles's tardy actions are a fitting analogy for my situation in mid-summer 2002, as Grant's character could have been a more reliable, thoughtful best man, just as I could have been a more reliable, competent junior receptionist. But neither of us came close.

Who the hell would take me now?

There was just one place to go; the place I'd always retreat to in times of need, that instinctive point of shelter: the long-suffering mother.

And I don't say 'long-suffering' to be prosaic.

She really has been truly, greatly, long-suffering.

It started soon after I discovered the brutal allure of the fairer sex, just when it was time to focus on those all-important end of school exams. Predictably weak results followed, as did maternal disappointment. Her boy was just an average student going to an average university. And now I'd added workplace failure to the list, because despite having notched *some* career success, I was sure the style of my recent resignation would wipe out all brownie points banked to date.

Anyone who's met my mother may be wondering why I went home if I was seeking a shoulder to cry on. She's a wonderful, supportive, strong, straight-talking woman, who'll help where possible, but soft words are not her forte. Clear, accurate, loving advice, a fine leg of lamb, redcurrant jelly, a roof over my head, and a kiss on the cheek are what I could expect, along with a smattering of tough love, a touch of truth, and a sensible session of forward planning.

Yet that was *all* I needed.

It's all any wayward child needs.

A shoulder to cry on isn't justified for a young man who's single-handedly imploded his career, or even for a young man who's inexplicably lost his job, as that's how the conversation was handled; I didn't have the heart to disappoint my mother with news of unemployment, *and* the likelihood I'd developed Tourette's syndrome.

And so as August clouds nourished the green pastures of southern England, I returned home to thrash out a plan to set things straight, to find a new route to success. I'd only been out of university for two years, so the situation was far from dire, but change was needed – and that meant one thing, and one thing only:

The contacts' book.

I was proud that I'd never yet asked a contact for career help. Yes, working on *Best Served Hot* had been through a contact, but not through asking a contact for help. The catering job had also been offered, not asked for; and my safari job had been found via a tip-off from a contact, but no more. Shades of grey, maybe, but I'm pleading 'not guilty'. I'd always been loath to ask for direct assistance, yet of course knew the hiring power that lay within a strong contacts' book.

Ask anyone who heads a FTSE 100 company whether they had a leg-up, and chances are the majority did. The 'I climbed from delivery boy to chairman of the board' stories are few and far between.

In the UK the 'you scratch my back I'll scratch yours' system even has a name, The Old Boys' Club, which specifically relates to people from private schools helping each other out, yet may as well be widened to include society as a whole, as nepotism is seen across the board. It's so rampant that in 2011 politicians argued about making the system fairer. The official verdict? Lib Dem leader Nick Clegg pushing for career progression to be less dependent on, "… who your father's friends are." The unofficial verdict? PM David Cameron saying, "I feel very relaxed about it." I.e. if it ain't broke, don't fix it.

And the system *is* fairer in the 21st century. Whereas in the distant past The Old Boys' Club could find you work, these days contacts will only get your foot in the door; it's up to you to secure a job by impressing the interviewer. Whatever your opinion on the subject of contacts/nepotism/The Old Boys' Club, it matters little, as the practice of helping those in your social and professional circles isn't going anywhere – it's human nature.

People help those they know.

And if that's the case, you may as well use whoever you can to maximise your chances. The person to your left and right will damn well do so, given half the chance, and don't you forget it. There's no guarantee it'll lead to anything, but there's a possibility it could help you beat the competition, rising faster in the savage environment of the modern-day workplace.

Yet knowing our family wasn't close to Steven Spielberg, Oliver Stone or, sadly, Scarlett Johannson, I was pessimistic about contacts being of use to me, but when my mother mentioned a film connection through an old family friend my attitude changed, quickly followed by my interest soaring when she told me where that connection was based.

The contact was in a city a long, *long* way from southern England, across the Atlantic, in a country that welcomes new blood by the bucket load.

Travel *and* career? Clearly the contacts' book was the key. A call was placed. An invite extended. And the wheels of change ground into motion.

I was bound for a city with a thriving film industry, towering mountains, glistening beaches, endless rivers, and millions of chilled-out people who apologise when you step on their toes.

It could only be… Vancouver.

The idea of a fresh start excited and terrified in equal measure. It reminds me of 2009's *Up In The Air*, in which George Clooney plays Ryan Bingham, whose job it is to fly around the United States firing people. When the sacking's done Clooney says to the miserable, now unemployed person: "Anybody who ever built an empire, or changed the world, sat where you are now. And it's because they sat there, that they were able to do it."

Irony reminds me of that quote, as my insolent departure from Round Point Commercials did not, in any way, lead me to start an empire or change the world, nothing of the sort – this book is testament to that – but it did lead to change, which in a tenuous way is what Ryan Bingham is advocating. It led me to cross eight time zones. It led to a new city. It led to a continent that's attracted tens of millions to its abundant opportunities.

Over the past five centuries of North American exploration, conquest, colonisation, settlement, and nation building, both Canada and the US have grown into wealthy, successful countries, fuelled by entrepreneurial immigrants and seemingly bottomless resources. Yet in America's case, having risen to become the world's wealthiest nation, it's a paradox that in the 21st century the average US worker is one of the most downtrodden in the West.

Case in point: while European employees have a legal requirement to four weeks off a year, the American worker has no such protection, meaning most receive the paltry average of just nine days paid leave per year, not including national holidays. That's even more surprising when you compare it to countries where US troops have led 'liberation' forces; in both Iraq and Afghanistan it's a legal requirement to give workers at least twenty paid days off a year, more than double what the average American employee enjoys.

Researching Internet chat rooms for opinions on US, UK, and Continental work ethics highlights how some Americans are vociferous in defence of their system, stating that 'hard work builds a nation', calling their European cousins lazy, work-shy, or overly-reliant on bloated state subsidies. European writers counter such mud-slinging by naming the pleasures of being free from the office, of not being slave to a corporate master, of working to live, not living to work. It's an ongoing debate, fuelled by the usual trolls, but both sides believe one point to be true: that the French work the least hours. Yet it's a false accusation, as according to the Organisation for Economic Co-operation and Development (OECD) the Danish take poll position, averaging just thirty-three hours worked per week.

Of course there's no need to let the French off too easily, especially as they're blessed with five more days off per year than the Danish, and love exercising their right to strike. The British, who also enjoy a good strike (but use the tactic far less often), think most nations across the English Channel lazy, yet it's an impression born from envy of their Continental lifestyle, rather than American-style fervour defending hard work and long hours. You'd be hard pressed to find a Briton who wouldn't support a campaign for more days off – additional time to comment on the weather, or moan about the progress of motorway roadworks? That's a no-brainer.

So why is all this important?

Because when it comes to mastering the 'oyster theory' – and to answering *the ultimate question* – it's crucial to understand work ethics around the world in order to know where you'd be most comfortable living.

Are you closer to the Australians or the French? What about the German, American, UAE, or Indian workplace? Or would the Chinese system suit you best? There are subtle differences to every continent and country, and it pays to know what separates them. Variations are widespread; most countries inhabit a middle ground, but a few operate on the periphery, taking work to the extreme.

And there's one nation in particular that's in the extreme of extremes, viewing workers as virtual corporate property: the economic, futuristic powerhouse that is Japan. The oyster theory would struggle to exist in the land of the rising sun, as the Japanese rarely move overseas, and foreigners are rarely seen in Japanese offices. Although corporate culture is evolving fast, many there still follow a traditional career path, starting at the bottom of a large corporation, working hard, devoting their life to it, and so retiring wealthy, having lived a most honourable life.

Also structured, but at the other end of the extreme, is France, where corporate toil was given a legal framework in 1998, capping the working week to thirty-five hours. That's just seven hours a day. After a two-hour lunch break you've barely got enough time to discuss Paris fashion and mock English cuisine.

The thirty-five-hour law was meant to spur greater job growth, in theory sharing finite labour among the population, but instead it created less productivity, higher unemployment, and an easy stick with which to poke the French. It's no wonder the economy stalled, forcing Paris to update the law in 2005, extending overtime rules, which – and no surprises here – led to widespread strikes.

The British work ethic is somewhere between the French and Japanese; citizens inhabit a middle ground, similar to their Aussie and Kiwi cousins, all of them seeing work as something to be taken seriously, but not too seriously. For a Brit, the Japanese approach is anathema, particularly when you consider that (according to the Japan Institute for Labour Policy and Training) the average Japanese worker is able to take eighteen days off a year, but uses less than half of them.

Such corporate devotion is traitorous to the Anglo-Saxon.

An Englishman will damn well have his two weeks in Spain, tense family Christmas, and mini-break in *The Daily Telegraph*'s 'must-visit European city of the year', much like an Australian won't give up BBQ and beach time, or a Kiwi won't forgo time off to fight orcs, or throw cursed rings into cauldrons of fire.

These three nations are in sync on the fundamentals. There's work. There's play. Both are to be respected equally.

I could go on, commenting on every nation from India to Nigeria, Argentina to Russia, but take it that each country is slightly different, depending on a variety of anthropological, historical, financial, political, and meteorological factors, to name but a few. One result is that we're left with stereotypes about workers around the world, such as that Spaniards need siestas, Gulf Arabs don't need to work, the British are a nation of shopkeepers, Indians work the hardest, Americans are corporate slaves, Germans are the most efficient, and so it goes on... all based on half-truths, none of it true to everyone, all of it true to someone.

I've met Americans happy to bum around the world. I've met French content with long days. I've met inefficient Germans (yes, they exist). And I've met Spaniards who deplore the siesta, as well as those who mourn its decline, but the afternoon snooze was bound to fade eventually, knocked off the corporate agenda by affordable air conditioning, increased labour competition, and global pressures on the speedy delivery of goods and services.

The diminished siesta is part of a bigger picture of workplace evolution; due to changes in technology, demographics, connectivity, competition, transportation, and thousands of other factors, industries have had to constantly develop and adapt, and they'll continue to do so. The norm today will be old news in a hundred years' time, probably due to machines taking human jobs, but possibly because millions of workers will be needed to make weapons in a war against genetically-engineered panda bears – frankly, who knows?

What we do know is that working styles vary greatly, having evolved over centuries. In the US it could be argued that the modern workplace can be traced back to the country's puritanical past – effectively blaming early English settlers for modern-day labour woes – but the Puritans *had* to invest every moment in hard work, as they fought to establish a productive life in a perilous land.

Over the centuries a first-rate nation emerged, offering opportunities to those willing to work hard; and the American Dream keeps that puritanical work ethic alive, as people toil long hours hoping one day to be able to afford a detached house, heated pool, and annual 'vay-cay in Cabo'.

Hope and hard work links modern-day Americans to those early settlers, and I too was willing to work hard, hoping for a fresh start in the New World, but not in the US, rather in Canada, a country with a similarly colonial background and entrepreneurial outlook, one that welcomes around 250,000 newcomers a year, with many of those settlers heading to Vancouver, a relaxed, melting-pot metropolis, kicking back on the coast of the expansive Pacific Northwest.

The New World had welcomed me once before, but this time it felt more exploratory, more pioneering, more distant. And so, less than a month after my shameful departure from Round Point Commercials, I boarded a jet to the far side of the world, fleeing failure… seeking opportunity.

Canada's westernmost province of British Columbia has a coastline totalling 27,000km, a small chunk of which wraps around its largest, most prosperous city. Home to more than two million people, Vancouver is the attractive, perpetually stoned youngster of a reserved and courteous family. It's the far-flung outpost of the world's second biggest country, a place where Mounties are cops, people slurp coffee in Tim Hortons, and where hockey is religion. That's ice hockey, not hockey where a ball bounces over grass. It's hockey where grown men chase a piece of rubber over frozen water, have a punch-up every three minutes, while referees stand by, and kids fight in the aisle.

Oh, Canada.

The country stretches almost 5,000km from Newfoundland in the east to British Columbia in the west, ending at Vancouver Island, a blob in the Pacific Ocean that's still four times the size of the United Kingdom. Put another way, there are 262 people per square kilometre in the UK, whereas you'll be sharing your square kilometre in Canada with just three other people, two of whom will be involved in a hockey-related punch-up.

It's hard to grasp how big the country is, until you take to the air, peering down from 35,000 feet, en route from London to Vancouver.

But first up, you reach the Arctic Circle:

"To your right, ladies and gentlemen, you'll see icebergs floating off the coast of Greenland," said the captain of the 747, as I was nibbling on the remains of a croissant, watching re-runs of *Friends*.

I glanced to my right, barely able to believe that at the same time as enjoying French food and American sitcom, I could be having a David Attenborough moment out the right side of a jumbo jet. I glanced down to see thousands of serene white and blue giants drifting off the frozen mass of Greenland, melting their way into southerly waters. It was a front row seat to one of nature's finest shows. Nothing could be as gripping as this, nothing except...

"Another beer, sir?"

Thank God. I was about to start fretting over polar bears. I returned to the screen. *Friends*, season five. Monica dates Chandler. Ross and Rachel marry in Vegas. It had its moments.

Outside, the landscape changed again.

We were over Canada.

And Canada was empty.

I realised I hadn't seen human habitation since Northern Ireland. There was only wilderness, barren, dark, foreboding wilderness. I considered what would happen if we crashed here, we'd be screwed, but then again you could slam into the world's largest mattress store and your chances of survival would be the same.

The wilds of Canada are the reason most Canadians live within a hundred miles of the US border. It's almost impossible to exist in the country's interior. It's too remote, too dangerous. If you were an Inuit hunter you might survive, even thrive, but most others would rather be at 35,000 feet, watching sitcoms.

Yes, Canada is *that* barren.

On we flew, over mile upon mile of emptiness, until the most amazing thing happened. Just when you think you'll never see a human again, that the planet has reverted to the Neolithic era, that your jet is the last remnant of civilisation, you swoop over the Coast Mountains, and the stunning city of Vancouver comes into view, skyscrapers clustered at its core, comforting you with the knowledge that fresh linen and a warm shower are within reach.

All will be well. Canada *is* inhabited.

Vancouver usually claims a 'Top Five' spot in polls ranking the world's most desirable cities in which to live, alongside the likes of Vienna, Zurich, and Sydney. On first impression it's easy to see why; natural beauty surrounds it on all sides, mountains to the east and north, beaches to the west and south, and an inlet at its centre, linked to the powerful Fraser River.

You can ski in the morning and sunbathe in the afternoon, which may sound like a tourist office tagline, but is genuinely possible.

Of course my reason for flying across the Canadian wilderness wasn't to ski or swim, it was to meet a 'contact' who could hopefully help re-boot my stunted career. As a family friend working in Vancouver's film, TV, and commercials industry, Yves was deemed the man able to kick me up a level.

It was a long shot – in both mileage and risk – but 'never shoot, never score' was the thinking; yet employing a career strategy that echoes drunken mating advice might be considered imprudent. Any doubt faded, though, once I saw Vancouver on the ground. It had an immediate effect. I'd expected a sleepy, forested outpost, but had instead landed into a flourishing cityscape, cradled by nature.

'Imprudent' was not the word.

Departing the airport, I soaked in my new surroundings. Late-summer sun warmed all, unhindered by cloud. Suburban streets, lined with pine trees, groomed lawns, and pristine 'sidewalks', exuded healthy living. Traffic, unclogged, advanced freely. Vancouver felt different to London, New York, or any other major city I'd visited, and it was obvious why: nobody was in a rush. Anywhere. People were happy to meander, stop, chat, let cars pull in, pull out, let pedestrians cross, let cyclists pedal safely. It was a city in second gear, and it seemed little interested in speeding up. It felt peaceful, comfortable in its own skin.

After twenty minutes the cab pulled up to a wooden-fronted, two-storey suburban home, similar to a thousand others. Yves, a tall, clean-shaven man in his late-thirties, greeted me warmly, welcoming me in. That night we talked Vancouver, film work, and opportunities; he said it was an ideal time to arrive, there being many productions in town, so the following day, jet-lagged, I rose early, ready to seek them out, ready to throw myself into anything available.

Anything at all.

From day one I scoured the local jobs market, assisted by Yves, looking for vacancies, willing to do whatever suited my experience. I was open to everything, anything, but there was nothing; absolutely bugger all.

Nothing suited me.

And I suited nothing.

It turns out – and don't fall off your seat when you read this – that you can't just turn up in a new city and expect to find work, even with the guidance of an experienced contact. Professional film and TV shoots in Vancouver, Hollywood, and around the world use things called 'skilled people', who are signed up to other things called 'unions'. Young men dropping in, on spec, untrained, looking for a career boost, aren't in high demand.

Bugger. Bugger.

Bugger. Bugger.

Trying to stay positive I told myself that things could have been worse. Yves lived in the beachside community of Kitsilano, a place where it's easy to forget your woes. It's a tree-lined network of two- and three-storey homes, popular with families, where children play in the streets, rollerblading, skipping, or smacking hockey balls. Yet their playtime pales in comparison to the area's adults, who are also outside, jogging, running, power-walking, or sweating through any other form of exertive activity, morning, noon, and night.

After a few days I realised I'd never been to a more energetic, sport-infused place, with the exception of a ski resort, which has the name of an activity helpfully slotted into its description. Vancouver, named after a British naval officer, has no such hint. There's nothing to suggest that almost everyone there is hard-wired to some form of healthy lifestyle.

Like all locals, Yves had his favourite sport, kayaking, but most of the time he needed to focus on work, spending long days on set, leaving at dawn, returning after dark. The intrusion of an English kid was doubtless far from his '2002 wish list', but he did what he could, inviting me on set, introducing me to the key players; yet locking down a job was up to me – as it should have been – which is where my 'never shoot, never score' mentality failed to find the net.

As in London, I hit the phones and surfed the web, but after five weeks I was demoralised, having realised the New World has just as many barriers as the Old, if not more. The oyster theory had run snapped shut.

It was a no-hoper, so rather than waste my time scanning job sites for the hundredth time, I slapped on Lycra, strolled to the beach, and trespassed into the outrageously trim jogging pack. *If you can't beat 'em, join 'em*, I thought, somehow forgetting my fitness level, gut wobble, and abhorrent smoking addiction. Soon enough, though, I found myself pounding the path, cheeks squeezed into a pair of unforgiving shorts, huffing and puffing the length of Kitsilano Beach.

Slowing to catch my breath – desperate for an excuse to stop – I took a moment out to reflect on my current situation. *What the hell am I doing?* I wondered; I was unemployed, without work papers, half a world from home, and, most depressingly of all, exhausted after a three-minute jog.

Reality dawned, and dawned fast.

I flopped on the grass, lit a cigarette, and took in the view. It didn't look good. Well, to be accurate, it looked stunning, but aside from the toned joggers, it didn't look good. I took a long drag, drawing disapproving looks. I barely noticed them, tormented by the fact my career was, a continent and an ocean away, little changed. I'd need a *new* new solution.

Things looked dire, but at least there was a sliver of hope, as I had a vague plan to turn the situation around, based on an idea that had been simmering for a week. Without any better option it was immediately promoted to premier choice: 'To be taken seriously (because nothing else is working)'.

The idea sprung from needing to maximise my time in Vancouver, as well as improve the skills section of my CV. It was clear I wouldn't find work in Canada, but I *could* sign up for training, giving myself a much-needed boost into the working world; and there was a respected training institution right there in that fair city that could be the answer to all my problems.

As I wheezed on down the beach path, I vowed my journey to the New World wouldn't go wasted. Yves had recommended investigating the Vancouver Film School, and it suddenly clicked into place as the most obvious solution; I didn't need more badly paid work. I needed skills.

Mastering the industry's production techniques, finances, creative and business nuances would be my best bet at getting ahead of the curve, at rising to be that pinstriped producer, at finally giving my acceptance speech to that pained and unappreciative Oscars audience.

There was nothing left to consider.

Two days later I was sat opposite the Head of Admissions of the Vancouver Film School (VFS), having completed a brief tour. Based in the city's downtown district it seemed a decent set-up, surrounded by bars, cafés, and even a Scientology branch where a rather friendly man had tried to lure me inside.

The tour featured class visits, popping into high-ceilinged studios, lights and rigging strewn across the floor, watching students set up props, load cameras, and figure out what cable popped into what outlet, as teaching assistants looked on, jumping in before expensive equipment blew a fuse. The open spaces of that aging building seemed a haven of creativity.

That said, having not seen inside any other film school I had no point of reference, but I thought VFS had what looked like modern kit, functioning lights, cameras that made impressive 'whirry' noises, classrooms with upright tables and chairs, wide passages, and solid floors, none of which I fell through. All that had to indicate something close to a top-end facility.

The bottom line was that information was being passed from teacher to student in a professional manner. What else was needed? Grill the faculty? Check the equipment? Study the fire escapes? Rubbish. They had happy-looking students. I was a wannabe happy-looking student. Sign me up.

"When can I start?" I asked the admissions manager, keen to escape my inactive slump.

"Well, the next class starts in a week's time, but I think it might be full. I'll just go check."

At this point my desire to study at VFS shifted from kind-of-wanting it, thinking it an easy get, to desperately wanting it, having discovered it might not be available. Like a child not caring about a toy until another child plays with it, I wanted to play with the toy. A tantrum loomed.

She returned, her face impossible to read.

"I have good news and bad news," she declared. That wasn't good. When someone says that, only bad news follows.

"The next class is full, but there's space in January."

"January?"

I peered at a group of film students milling in the autumnal air, looking at what I'd thought – for a brief moment – would be my next step, discussing directors, debating the virtues of Spielberg versus Kurosawa.

"It's only three months," she said. "What do you think?"

Sitting in an admissions office that couldn't admit me, the question hung in the air. Three months isn't long, but when in need of change, time ticks with a limp.

"Er… let me get back to you," I said, as unheard a familiar mantra rose:

Fuck, fuck, fuckity-fuck.

Fuckity, fuckity, fuckity, fuck.

NEW WORLD, OLD TROUBLE

Lessons learnt:

- A profanity-strewn mantra feels really *fucking* good
- Nepotism and The Old Boys' Club are human nature
- Canada is ridiculously big, but ridiculously empty
- It can't be stated any more clearly: DO YOUR RESEARCH. If going to a foreign country to look for work, research how that work will be secured
- Joggers in Vancouver don't respect the new guy stopping for a smoke
- Building on your skills is a great option to pursue, especially if all other paths have been tried (or self-detonated)

CHAPTER FIFTEEN

Another jet dipped its wings through the stubborn gloom, descending to disgorge its load; I gazed up, picturing those above, straightening seat backs, preparing to land at Europe's busiest hub.

Living under a London flight path meant a plane overhead every minute of every day, and in early 2003 each one provoked a quickened pulse, a panicked glance, as fresh terror swept the planet, dragging aviation back to the front pages.

Another jet cruised purposefully, Heathrow-bound.

I flinched, wondering if it might be the one carrying misery to Great Britain, misery not released by any cave-dwelling extremist, but rather SARS, an accidental contagion born on a farm in China's southerly Guangdong province some four months earlier. By mid-March it had been rampant, hitting cities across East Asia, before hopping the Pacific to take its toll on Toronto.

The respiratory disease was an unknown entity, so much so that on March 15th the World Health Organisation issued a rare global health alert, gifting news outlets a speculation frenzy: 'might the illness land at UK airports?' Seeing as most other miseries have affected the nation – mad cow, the plague, punks, Dracula, John Prescott – the odds were high.

I could have ignored the media, drawing on my post-9/11 experience, but I couldn't ignore the planes; they kept coming, and coming… an endless ribbon of high-speed risk. It seemed utter madness that people were allowed to fly into London from infected cities, yet what really baffled me was why other Londoners weren't cowering in their homes, staring at aircraft.

And then it hit me.

Most Londoners didn't share my obsession with SARS because they had regular lives. They had children, mortgages, debt, leaky pipes, sick parents, demanding bosses, and every other facet of human life that keeps people busy, stopping them from obsessing over a disease killing fewer people worldwide than car accidents, steep stairs, or dodgy takeaways.

Unlike the rest of London I *did* have time to plane-spot, being back in search of work; and with idle hands, plane-spotting flourished. *Really flourished.* I was fast becoming a dab hand at tailfin insignia. That I knew to call it 'tailfin insignia' was bad enough, but worse still, I'd considered binoculars.

Anorak status loomed.

I also knew to expect Concorde between 5pm and 5.15pm, an event I'd note every day, its din loud enough to drown out a Welsh choir. Decelerating through the clouds, Concorde carried thunder in its wake, so loud it suppressed the city, so beautiful you forgave it, and then the roar would subside, returning the streets to the purr of 4x4s, and the nattering of middle-aged mothers.

Christ, I needed a job.

Of course, this'll be of some confusion to those of you paying attention, as you'll have clocked that by this point in 2003 I should have been studying in Vancouver... but it wasn't to be. Once home, I'd reassessed, concluding I didn't need further training, that I had a semi-impressive CV, so should once again pester London's production companies, likely securing a job within weeks.

How naïve.

Even insane.

Albert Einstein famously said the definition of insanity is "doing the same thing over and over again and expecting different results." Without knowing it I was flirting with insanity, taking on the same web-based job hunt I'd tried before, this time expecting to find decent, well-paid work.

It was utter lunacy, but the decision was done.

And so the same recruitment sites were searched, the same cover letters penned, pinged out to the same employers, gatekeepers who'd get a second shot at binning my forgettable skillset. It was miserable, like sleeping with an ex you never enjoyed sleeping with in the first place: a pleasure-less, dull, mechanical screw, ending in pregnancy-related panic, and sober promises to never meet again.

Even so, I was sure I'd find work, as I'd convinced myself that – with enough determination – *anything is possible*.

A year later Adidas would launch its 'Impossible is Nothing' ad campaign, yet unbeknown to them I was ahead of the curve, living the motto, worshipping its inane message. To most people such lines are mere marketing ploys, not useful in the real world, but that's not the case for those under the influence of BCO – or Blind Career Obsession – as the men in white coats shall henceforth call the illness pushing me towards the front door of the local asylum.

BCO sufferers ignore reality, pursuing goals regardless of fact, regardless of deficiencies in training, experience, skills, talent, background, or contacts. Everything is ignored, as BCO takes command of the head, heart, and soul, leaving the patient almost incurable. It's an illness that's discussed in hushed, embarrassed tones, as it drags its victims to the brink of self-destruction.

The scene for BCO is set at a young age:

"Darling, remember that you can do anything you set your mind to," says the loving, but unrealistic parent.

"Anyfing?" asks the wide-eyed child.

"Anything, baby."

"Eben beebing a Hollywoo actwess?" asks the child, who happens to be the genetic equivalent of a doner kebab.

"Even being a Hollywood actress," replies the parent, so setting another youngster on course for a life of BCO.

Of course I wasn't trying to be the next Brad Pitt or George Clooney, nor did my mother tell me absurd untruths about my non-existent abilities, but that didn't stop BCO from taking hold, because it's not only instigated by unrealistic parents; its roots are everywhere, feeding on a society that tells *everyone* they can be *someone*. BCO is inspired in villages, towns, and cities on a daily basis, leading to millions blindly pursuing improbable careers.

Fear not, though, I'm not trying to be a destroyer of dreams – people should have lofty aspirations – but if the dream isn't working, or the facts are screaming out for goals to be reassessed, then it's time to wake-up, face the truth, and make some changes. I too needed to wake-up, not to shake my producer goal altogether, but to change tack to reach it in a more realistic way.

Yet blinded by obsession, I ploughed on, undertaking the same job hunt as before. How I wasn't carted off is a mystery.

Maybe I staved off complete lunacy by expanding my tactics – there was *some* method to my madness – because aside from applying to online listings, I tried other job-seeking strategies, quickly learning their pros and cons, quickly understanding my daily tolerance to the corporate rebuff.

The top tactics are, in no particular order:

Firstly, hitting the phones. Calling potential employers is worth a shot, but you have to get past the 'gatekeeper' (normally a secretary), who'll likely shut you down, telling you X/Y/Z excuse about so-and-so being busy, asking you to call back another time, preferably in a decade or two.

Secondly, you can try knocking on office doors for the face-to-face approach, but the gatekeepers this time will be security guards, doormen, and receptionists, who may take your CV and pass it on up, or may use it to balance a wobbly table. Your chances are low, partly because few people deal in hard copy CVs, but mostly because nobody likes random visits from the desperate and needy.

Thirdly, you can ask people you know in your chosen field to tell you when jobs become available in their sector. This is similar to using contacts, but it's asking them to report back what they hear on the grapevine. In theory they'll let you know of an opening, but beware they're not a) disorganised, or worse, b) looking for a change of job themselves, likely to use insider tips to their own advantage.

Fourthly, you can contact the human resources departments of companies you're keen to join. These gatekeepers are normally friendly types who'll tell you to send in your CV, but it's a lottery as to what happens next; perhaps it goes on file; far more likely it disappears into their dreaded 'deleted items' folder. Chances of a positive outcome are slim, and that's not taking into account the jaw-dropping ineptness of most HR departments. Approach at your peril.

Fifthly, you can (and should) move beyond the mundane, taking on the role of detective, searching for information that suggests when a company will be hiring, e.g. by reading industry magazines, keeping an ear to the ground, sizing up what companies are growing, what projects are being launched, who's in charge of those launches, and how you can contact those people. The 'Sherlock Approach' takes time and effort, but should eventually get your CV into the right hands at the right time, giving you much-needed 'edge'.

Beware, though, if tackled endlessly these tactics – particularly the Sherlock Approach – will be incredibly draining. You'll need thick skin.

This process pushes many to the edge.

Your hunt may take months. In a downturn, even longer. It may take so long you'll be sucked dry, on lower energy than a Goth teen coming off Prozac. Yet if empty, deflated, and depressed, it's important not to let the hunt destroy you, or those around you. There's only so much screen time anyone can endure, and we all know what most men resort to with a laptop, an Internet connection, and a moment of privacy. It's crucial therefore to pause your search and seek fresh air.

Don't do this half-heartedly.

Wallowing in pitiful boredom will fast become a drag on you, your family, and friends, so leave the house every day, for at least an hour. The good news is that there's a plethora of cheap ways to distract the unemployed, with my top escapist retreat being – no surprises here – a trip to the cinema. And because most of your fellow citizens are slaving away at the nine-to-five, enduring meetings about meetings, movie tickets are often sold at a daytime discount, meaning you can watch films on the cheap, surrounded by the pillars of your community: bored retirees, truant kids, petty criminals, and indolent students.

The fun doesn't stop there.

Government-tended parks are yours, bereft of lazy lovers and picnicking families, reserved for you and your limitless availability. In London, Tube trains are less busy in the middle of the day, filled with tourists trying to navigate the city, befuddled by signs reading, 'Way Out' instead of 'Exit', cracking truisms like, "Yo, Britney, didn't this nation invent En-er-glish?"

And where are those tourists going? To the city's museums and art galleries, paid for by the great British taxpayer. Yes, those very people unable to enjoy such bastions of culture, as they turn cogs in air-conditioned tombs, are paying for Billy-Bob, Hans, Juan, Yoko, and yourself to be entertained by the fruits of their labour.

Anyone shouting 'irony'?

Of course there's the small matter of you, the unemployed urchin, not receiving a monthly payslip, not being part of the system, so even as entertaining as these distractions are, they're just that, *distractions*. The majority of your time will be spent tackling the job hunt, eyes on a screen, phone at your ear.

And in spring 2003 my days were exactly that, attached to my mobile, knocking on doors, pestering contacts, scanning for vacancies, but by late-March I was running on empty, out of ideas. London's film companies had been approached; there was little interest. I needed to prep for a fail, so began exploring Plan B: boosting my skillset at the Vancouver Film School.

Preparing the way, I called the admissions advisor, who told me I had five weeks to decide whether I wanted to be part of their next class, starting in June. I told her I'd be in touch. The ideal situation was to find a job in London, but that window was closing fast. The countdown had begun.

I had just thirty-five days.

As a dank April morning tested my will to rise, I pushed back the covers, drew the thin curtains, and muttered for the nth time about buying blackout blinds. I shuffled the passage to our shoebox kitchen, slumped into a hard-backed chair, and opened my inbox. There was nothing new, except penis enlargement ads, and kind offers to invest in Nigeria.

I checked the news. SARS marched on. The day before, April 2nd, the World Health Organisation had recommended postponing all non-essential travel to Hong Kong and Guangdong province. Not planning to visit either, I snapped the screen shut, losing interest.

I turned to the fridge, hoping one of my flatmates had bought fresh milk, maybe a yoghurt – guilty, I'm the food-pinching guy – but it would have to wait, as in the distance my mobile rang loud. It was a Nokia 8310, a phone smaller than a pack of playing cards, yet still pimped with Snake II, an FM radio, and a battery that could last a week. I still miss it. Slovenly I followed the chirping and located the tiny machine. Not recognising the number on-screen I apprehensively pushed the answer button, assuming it to be a sales call.

"Hi-yaaa, is that Charlie?" said an upbeat voice.

"Er, yes, speaking," I replied, preparing for a deluge of information about loan offers and APR rates.

"This is Nick from Pathé Pictures. We've received your CV."

It's the call you wait for, but never think will come. When it does, you sit there, shell-shocked, murmuring "yes" to whatever's said. He told me about a vacancy on his team, and then asked if I'd like to come in for a chat.

"Yeah, yes, yes, yes, sure… I'll come in, whenever."

"Great, tomorrow morning at 9.30am?"

A bit early.

"Sure, sure, that's fine," I said.

I took down the address, hung up, and sat back, shaking. They were looking for someone to join their script development team, reading scripts, advising on scripts, preparing scripts for production. It was so horribly perfect I wanted to jump into a cold bath or throw myself through a window. A grand gesture of some sort was demanded by this potentially game-changing call.

And then the adrenaline wore off; I calmed down, stopped pacing the room, and took in a long, deep breath. It was an interview, not an employment contract. There was little need to throw myself through a second storey window. I had a cup of tea, and settled into an episode of *Antiques Roadshow*.

An actual paying job, I mused, as a pensioner faked pleasure at a weak valuation on a family heirloom. *A job where I'll work at something I like, being paid a decent wage to do it? Without doubt I'll screw this up*. It's one thing nailing an interview if you don't care about the job, or are numbed by its low pay, but a job you like that pays market rates?

I'd screw this up, for sure.

The London offices of Pathé Pictures – known for hit films such as *Chicken Run*, *The Iron Lady*, and *Slumdog Millionaire* – are tucked behind Oxford Street, hidden in a nondescript throughway. Although indistinct on the outside, inside I found a buzzing environment, alive with skinny-jeaned staff, walls of six-foot movie posters, attractive receptionists talking to even more attractive receptionists, and in the distance, Himalayan piles of dog-eared scripts.

Internally I was drooling. Externally I controlled it, keen not to frighten off this most rare of rare finds: a potential employer.

Much like going on a date with someone you really like, the interview you truly care about is harder than any other. Going on a date with someone you 'kind of like' means you'll seem disinterested, but interested enough to keep their attention, which of course is classic dating strategy for 'coffee at mine' success. Paradoxically, the date with the person you actually like can tank, ruined by nervousness, awkward quips, and lead balloons.

Quid pro quo, the date you're less interested in will be the one that goes well, far better than the date you actually care about.

It's a crazy world, but I didn't make the rules.

In the same vein, the interview you really care about will be the most challenging to succeed at, but you can't use dating tricks of feigning disinterest. Quite the contrary, you need to be as keen as the last person, more so than the next, without crossing the line into psychotic-and-unemployable. With this in mind, keen to seem keen, but not 'creepy keen', I steered a careful path through the Pathé interview, desperate to be the kind of person I thought they'd want to hire.

At the end of the conversation, things looked positive. I'd kept the drool internal, demonstrated I was capable of critiquing scripts, and had chatted freely with the interviewer, showing him I'd be an easy fit for the team.

I left flaunting a slight spring in my step, certain I had to be in the running, at least a shoo-in for a second interview. Confidence was high, the day was clear, and I was walking through central London at a time when I'd normally be muttering drivel about paper-thin curtains and blackout blinds.

Brimming with more nervous energy than an underage teen buying corner shop beer, I walked and walked, through the West End and Knightsbridge, past lunching ladies and bag-laden tourists, past office smokers and corporate gossips, past police officers in crisp white shirts and bullet-proof vests, past bustling hotels, blooming parks, boutique stores, and the great River Thames, pushing into London's suburban streets, returning home ready to walk some more.

Once indoors, my mobile rang. It was quickly answered. A familiar voice I'd left that very morning spoke, delivering the best news I could ever have heard…

…the script job at Pathé Pictures was mine.

The End.

As if.

There was no phone call, nothing of the sort.

Just silence. An intolerable void.

For some reason, gatekeepers forget what it's like to seek work, leaving potential employees waiting for information like commuters on a stalled train, stuck between stations, dying to know how long they'll be trapped.

And so the Pathé wait began.

At the two-week mark I was itching for news. Most job seekers will have experienced this scenario, when your patience has expired, leaving you frustrated, wondering if it's game over. In situations like this, emails going unanswered, there's only one course of action left to try: call and request an update.

It's an awful, pride-swallowing moment.

Digits were dialled.

"Oh, right, yeah, we were going to call you, Charlie," said the interviewer at Pathé. "Things got busy; we're still deciding on the job. Hold tight. We'll call you with an answer real soon."

The blasé riposte maddened me, but I had to take it as a positive. The game was in play. The train was trapped between stations, but at least the conductor had given his passengers a hint of hope.

How long should I wait now? How long is "real soon"? Two days? Two weeks? The guessing game was killing me, ruining my sleep, wrecking my days, but I decided to give it another week before placing a follow-up call.

Every morning I'd pray for word; every evening I'd fret. No call came. Days were counted off in weary submission. On it went – my hopes pinned on Pathé – until the dreaded moment arrived to once again punch digits.

The same cheery voice picked up.

"Yeah, hi Charlie, I was going to call you. Thing is we'd love to get you in, get someone started on this position, but we're waiting on final word from the head honchos. Shouldn't be much longer. Hang in there a tad longer."

I could barely contain myself.

Have I just been told the job's mine? Am I being lined up to start? Holy crap, is this actually happening? It sounded like I was close to being green-lit, but that awful phrase "hang in there" was itself hanging in the air, infuriating, indecisive, potentially destructive.

Again I gave it a week, now familiar with his modus operandi, assured that cogs were in motion. Through the week my anxiety rose, necessitating walks, jogs, and runs, as I dealt with the intensifying process, something that must have been a mere diary entry in his life, yet was the only entry in mine.

The week evaporated.

At the end of it, fingers unsteady, I again dialled the critical number. *Is the wait due to paperwork? Are others being told to "hang in there"? Has he forgotten about me? Why can't he communicate?!!*

It rang and rang, one time, two times, three, four, five... *why won't he answer the DAMN...* six... *where the hell is...* seven... *for Christ's...* eig...

"Hello, Pathé Pictures."

Deep breath.

"Hi, Nick, it's Charlie here, calling about the development vacancy."

"Ah, Charlie, sorry not to call you, been full on here."

"Sure, no problem," I said, trying to sound relaxed. "Just looking to see if you have any update about the job."

"Right, yes, about that..."

He paused.

There was something in his tone.

Reflexes tightened.

He started again, "The thing is..."

Oh no.

"Well, the thing is..."

No, no, no.

"... the thing is that we've been advised from head office about that vacancy and others, and..."

No, no, no, no, no, no.

"They've, er, well, they've said we can't take on any staff due to a hiring freeze. I'm really sorry, but there's going to be no movement on it for a while."

Deepest breath… ever.

Hold it together.

"A while?"

"Well, for good, I suppose. I'm really sorry not to have told you sooner."

"So…"

"That's it, I'm afraid. Good luck with everything."

Click, dzzzzzzzzz.

He'd hung up.

I stood there, mouth agape, thousand-yard stare.

Closure.

Shaking, I slumped to the floor. A welling I'd not experienced for more than a decade took hold, as weeks of pressure released in a crushing blow of negativity. Abject failure ripped air from my lungs freeing a long-forgotten childhood instinct. Large, woeful tears flooded my eyes. The enormous weight of expectation imploded, extreme hope turning to supreme despair.

I drew my knees around me, defeated once and for all. Curled up on the worn-out carpet of our light-deprived flat, crying into shaking hands, I let go. Minutes passed as I wallowed in the experience, not able to continue the battle, not wanting to halt the puerile reaction. I wept for the dream that wasn't to be.

And then, at long last, everything came clear.

I saw my BCO for what it was; I knew it had to end.

Everyone off, this train terminates here.

It takes a variety of blows to reduce men to tears, but I'd found my breaking point. Over the years I've faced many strange and trying situations – including having to wait over three hours for a Sunday evening pizza delivery – but this was the moment that demanded tears, where hope fled, where I sunk to the bottom, felled by rejection, revelling in self-pity.

It's a moment I hope to never, ever relive.

The madness had to end.

Once tears had dried, I assessed the situation. Clearly the job hunt was over. I'd been dealt my last hand; I'd come up bust. It was time to re-energise my career, along with the weakened oyster theory, using the last trump card available to me: the phone call to Vancouver.

As there was barely a day left on the five-week admissions window, I called immediately, locking in a spot on the upcoming June class. A plan that had been foolishly derailed months earlier was now back on track, venerated as my best and only option. And with it, hope re-emerged, invigorating tattered dreams.

Insanity cured, I stepped from the padded room. The masochistic dream of film lived on, but I'd now taken a decisive step towards becoming its master. Whether that was realistic or not was tomorrow's problem. For now, I'd shifted my angle of attack, yet even with fresh focus, I still felt aggrieved, even vengeful.

My own city had callously spat me out, but we weren't finished; this was merely half-time. You may have won the battle, but the war goes on…

London, you bitch, I'll be back.

DOWN AND OUT IN HAMMERSMITH & FULHAM:

Lessons learnt:

- Einstein was right; insanity *is* doing the same thing over and over, but expecting different results
- There's a certain irony to the working masses paying for government-funded venues that are mostly enjoyed by tourists
- If unemployed, get out of the house; your health requires it
- You're more likely to screw up the interview you truly care about

- Waiting for employment news is tantamount to white collar torture
- Slumping to the floor, tears flowing, might indicate a need for change
- Always have a trump card in reserve

CHAPTER SIXTEEN

Farewell.

    Drink.

    Chat.

    Drink.

    Sleep.

    Plunk. Plunk.

    Fizzzzzzzzzzzzzzzzz.

    Pack.

    Eat.

    Antacid.

    Heathrow.

    Wheels up.

    Greenland.

    Icebergs.

    Nothingness.

    Friends.

    Nothingness.

    More *Friends*.

    (Don't judge me.)

    More nothingness.

    Mountains.

    Wheels down.

    Vancouver.

"If you see a needle on the ground... Hey, HEY!! This is important... come on, listen up, if you see a needle on the ground... this area's full of addicts... whatever you do, don't pick up used needles..."

Day One, VFS, June 2003.

The shock and awe welcome speech forced twenty-two fresh-faced students to share disbelieving glances. We smirked at the sage advice, nobody wanting to seem too scared, or too flippant.

"I mean it," said the school's rake-thin, fifty-something principal, casting a stern 'don't-fuck-with-me' glare across the room.

The twenty-two went silent, likely questioning why they'd signed up to learn filmmaking surrounded by Canada's highest population of drug addicts, or why the faculty thought it necessary to advise against picking up used needles; there's obvious, then there's just plain dumb.

Maybe the message should have been that if you play with used needles you shouldn't be taking a twelve-month course in film production; you should instead be taking 'Common Sense 101: How To Be Human'. Much like being told to not stare at the sun, walk over thin ice, or tickle nightclub bouncers, there are some hazards that don't need warning signs.

Sitting on red velvet chairs in a dimly-lit screening room, the wide-eyed 'freshers' sized each other up, gauging reactions. Constituting Canadians, Americans, Koreans, Japanese, Chinese, an Iranian, a Filipino, a Brazilian, and me, the token Brit, we were the ultimate melting pot. Believing it best to look blasé about the school being in the drug-addled rump of Vancouver, I gave the group the traditional raised eyebrow of confident nonchalance, but the reality of the Downtown Eastside did actually demand consideration, for its alleys were filled with characters straight out of a George A Romero zombie flick.

But these zombies had souls.

Never before had I been so close to such a rejected stratum of society. Never before had I witnessed the forgotten and forsaken. Of course I'd seen substance abuse over the years, but dope-smoking students in university bedsits are as distant to inner city crack addicts, as *Downton Abbey* is to *Girls Gone Wild*.

Crack cocaine and heroin were the drugs of choice in the Downtown Eastside, and those caught in their evil spell were a bad hit from dead. Their only interest was the next high, fuelled by a need to stay in that altered state of mind for the rest of their pitiful days. It's tragic to see first-hand. Beneath the grimy skin, blackened teeth, waxy hair, and grubby clothes – if you look closely enough – you can see the person they once were, but that person is long gone.

There's nothing you can do but sidestep the victim, avoiding the needles. The government tries to help, offering safe infection sites, but the policy only keeps a lid on the crisis. The theory seemed to be that if you can't stop it, you should try to contain it, offering orderly, state-supervised highs. The initiative's motto might as well have been, 'Happy Junkies, Peaceful City', alongside a picture of a little girl skipping over a comatose man.

But the addicts are just one characteristic of the Downtown Eastside. The area also has a high profile, tourist-friendly side, historic Gastown, where in the 1860s Vancouver's first colonisers began chopping trees and planning streets. Dominated by the usual grid system of New World cities – lined with souvenir stores, red brick paving, and a steam-powered clock – Gastown's blocks have featured in numerous Hollywood productions, including *Paycheck*, *21 Jump Street*, and *Fifty Shades of Grey*, with their generic North American feel acting as ideal substitutes for US cities, real or imagined.

The distance between upmarket, tour guide-approved Gastown, and the area's needle-strewn alleys is a matter of a few wrong turns, so it was critical for us to master the good, the bad, and the ugly. Led by a VFS teaching assistant, our familiarisation tour was soon underway, my group obsessively noting the area's safe and unsafe streets, during which time we began to bond; and for the token Brit, that meant it was 'performing monkey' time:

"Say tomato."

"Tom-ah-toe."

"Say bastard."

"Baaarrr-stard."

"Say urinal."

"Ur-eye-nal."

"Say bath."

"Barrr-th."

"Say 'damn Yankee' in a gruff Gerald Butler voice."

"Grrrrrr…"

The accent strikes again.

I'm sure many Brits have experienced this in North America, where you're told the English accent is dynamite with the fairer sex, only to discover it's more a source of amusement, than it is any aphrodisiac. All you can do is pray something more entertaining comes along – a fat-kid viral video, a teenage hockey brawl – to draw the mob's attention elsewhere.

Fortunately, at VFS, that didn't take long.

Much like med students needing to understand the entire human body, so we needed to learn every detail of film production, from script to screen. It's a process that's child play in places, but as technical as surgery in others, with complex chemicals, software, electrics, design, and special effects all integral to creating the medium's unseen 'movie magic'.

And so a day after our drug addict welcome speech, beginner classes were underway, straight into the history of filmmaking, going back to the birth of an industry over 170 years ago. Movies can be traced to the 'phenakistoscope' and 'stroboscope', parlour tricks that created moving images through the use of animated drawings, such as a horse in motion viewed through slits in a spinning disk; little did anyone know those toys were sowing the seeds for a wondrous craft, leading to extraordinary scenes of make-believe, such as Kate Winslet appearing to be at the bow of a doomed ocean liner, cruising across the icy North Atlantic.

Revelling in the evolution of film, we rarely left the classroom, but I often found myself gazing out the window, as clear days and cool Pacific winds created an idyllic climate. Due to Vancouver's stunning summers, its American-style locations, and, most importantly, its production costs being significantly lower than those in

Los Angeles, the city has been luring shoots off its Californian rival for years, earning it the moniker, 'Hollywood North'. Summers are usually blue and radiant, and 2003 was no different, film units taking advantage of a stellar run of cloudless days, extending into one of the driest seasons on record.

But while the weather was a boon for filmmakers, in the wild expanses of the British Columbian interior a dry run meant forest fires, with crews placed on high alert to tackle outbreaks across the province. It was rapidly developing into a destructive season, but nobody knew just how lethal it would become, not the firemen, nor the authorities, and certainly not my class in downtown Vancouver, where it was business as usual, mastering the art of cutting film, lighting sets, recording sound, financing projects, directing actors, and learning every other skill, trick, and tip needed to create profit-making content.

I finally felt that progress was underway, as though I was taking firm, positive steps towards a successful future, that the elusive pinstriped dream was gradually coming into focus. One little doubt lingered, though; one small, niggling, awkward, prattish concern. It was a thought that had cropped up before I'd even started at VFS, but had been filed away – 'to be considered later' – as it would have stopped my Canadian move dead in the water.

The niggling thought went something like this: *I'm studying at a school 5,000 miles from home, which is a long, long way away, so here's the $64,000 question... will my credentials be recognised in the UK?*

As the irritating thought crawled from its pedantic bolthole I looked outside, at the distant mountains, at my new environment, and buried it fast. Even though I knew it would fester, waiting for its fifteen minutes of fame, I couldn't face it, not that day; it was far too fine for such glum considerations.

In fact, the weather was so fine that by late summer British Columbia's fire fighters weren't only on high alert, they were overworked, over-stretched, battling chaotic firestorms ripping apart the province.

One of the worst outbreaks was an intense fury hell-bent on destroying Kelowna, a city on the banks of the Okanagan Lake, almost 400km east of Vancouver. At the height of summer, punters usually fill lakeside bars and restaurants, spilling on to lawns and beaches, but the fire advancing on Kelowna was intent on pooping the party, as bone-dry tinder ignited like kerosene.

Across the province, news of the inferno consumed local media. As reports soared of homes reduced to ash – 238 were destroyed or damaged – of sofas and TVs burnt to a cinder, blowing in the breeze, the scale of the event surprised all. Fire fighters faced insurmountable odds, as the intense flames sucked in oxygen, whipping up winds, fuelling a monster of apocalyptic proportions. In downtown Vancouver we were glued to the TV, watching nature's extremes play out, humans unable to control a fraction of her force…

…and then, just like that, cool winds brought sweet rain, and a record-breaking fire season fizzled out, leaving tender memories seared into residents across the region. It was an abrupt end to a savage summer. Those not left homeless thanked God they'd been spared, helped accommodate the less fortunate, and prepped for the next climactic onslaught.

Umbrellas were dusted off.

Having been built over a temperate rainforest, the wet season wasn't to be taken lightly. As clouds swelled overhead, I was reminded of a conversation I'd endured at the start of summer, accosted by an ageing local at a bus stop.

"Are you used to rain?" he asked.

Oh God, I thought. *Here we go.*

"Of course I'm used to rain. I'm English," was the obvious retort.

"We don't do gentle English rain," the old timer replied. "Vancouver does *hard* rain." I began to weigh the pros and cons of walking. Too late, on he went: "It lasts for days, even weeks. It'll be raining as hard in the morning as it was when you went to bed. It'll make you wish for English rain."

"Yeah, gotchya. I'm sure it's worse than it is back home," I said, thinking that wherever you go there's always some statistic-laden bore to tell you his sun shines stronger, his snow lands thicker, his mist sits heavier, or his rain pours harder than it does anywhere else, especially compared to England.

Yet months later, as autumn settled in, I realised the wizened Canuck was right. It doesn't just rain in Vancouver, it pours…

…and pours…

…and pours…

…and pours…

On average the city sees 168 days of rain per year, receiving almost sixty inches of water. In comparison, London gets just twenty-three inches per year washing over its historic streets. The volumes are so great in Vancouver that radio jockeys quip about record-breaking runs of torrential rain, banter that starts when the first Pacific storm drops anchor and starts pumping.

"Oh myyyy gawwwwddd, it is *pourrrrrrrring* out there," the RJs would wail. "Could we be on track to beat the current record of twenty-eight days of consecutive rain set in 1953? Se-hereeeeeeiously not?!!"

With the first autumn storm stalled over the city, the counting began. By my reckoning, and the warbling RJs, it wasn't until seventeen washed-out days had passed before the skies cleared, offering brief respite from boots and brollies. The deluge had been a force to be respected, a phenomenon to be feared. I was amazed. In awe. But more than anything I was shocked, disturbed by the torrent.

How could this stunning city I'd enjoyed through the long summer months become such a dismal washout?

Never before had I seen, or imagined possible, rainfall that dumps on your life, drenching your will to live. This was major league rain; yet somehow the city continued to function. Unlike flooding in the UK, no amount of water could stop the Pacific

Northwest. Vancouver kept going, as the storms kept coming. Those in my class who'd grown up in the area didn't bat an eyelid. Others double-took and acclimatised. One hoarded umbrellas.

It was impressive, but damp. A remarkably damp achievement of man over liquid, made even more remarkable by how long it lasted.

October: Wet.

November: Soaked.

December: Soggy.

January: Drenched.

February: Dripping.

March: Saturated.

April: Moist.

(Yes, I said it... *moist.*)

And all the way through the wet season our classes kept going. By the time the sun appeared again in late-spring 2004 I was a transformed man, wise in the ways of the moving image. What would have taken Neo in *The Matrix* mere seconds to upload had taken my class almost twelve months to absorb. Of course our way involved far less bullet-dodging, and flappy leather coats.

But the upload was complete.

As the city packed away umbrellas, I began to focus on what lay in store. Having buried the niggling concern as to where life would lead after VFS, it was now hideously unavoidable, free of its bolthole, loving its fifteen minutes of fame. I assessed the obvious option – testing my new credentials back home – but pained memories of tearfully slumping against a London passage still haunted me.

A plan to stay in Canada took hold. Surely the Canadians would let me put their education to use within their fair nation? Surely it therefore made sense to stay and work within their prosperous film industry?

It would be daft not to try.

The obvious step – so obvious even a bureaucrat in Brussels

would have thought it – was to stay in Vancouver, but my ever-restless itchy feet demanded a move, and I didn't blame them. They weren't keen to slosh through another trench-foot winter, and they knew that Canada holds not one, but two powerhouses of North American film production.

And so instead of staying in British Columbia I looked east, to a city once nicknamed Hogtown, T-dot to recent dwellers; a city known for its attractive lakeside setting, Maple Leaf hockey fanatics, and soaring telecommunications tower. I was set on a move to the most populous part of the Great White North, the pragmatic, commercial hub that is Toronto.

The city had been declared free of SARS, but I still feared the move. It was a wild card play, a shot in the dark. Thinking *strength in numbers*, I planned to take the leap with others at my side, so gathered a coalition of the willing, consisting of fellow classmates Sarah, Kim, and Juan. The four of us would target T-dot, crossing the country by car, and on arrival we'd put our training to use, grab a slice of the pie, and in so doing make our mark on Canada's film industry.

We were the brave, the hardy, the adventurous, the all-conquering… but within two weeks, we were the two.

As our impending departure loomed, for reasons both disparate and of no import to this tale, Kim and Juan dropped out of the Toronto mission, leaving the red-haired American, Sarah, and myself to debate whether we'd soldier on. We met to discuss options. Within minutes it was clear there was little room for manoeuvre: a plan had been set in motion, a cross-country route mapped out, and a haulage trailer hired; but above all, our decision turned on a simple fact:

You don't mess with rental bookings.

Hire companies are ruthless on fees, charging up to $50 for a late cancellation, forcing you to complete at least ten minutes of paperwork.

Yes, ten minutes. Of paperwork.

Hideous, form-filling, paperwork.

No. Thank. You.

The choice was simple: either Sarah and I take on a 5,000km road trip, deep into the unknown, to live in a strange and frigid city, lacking contacts, with no guarantee of finding work, or we cough up fifty bucks and fill out a form.

It was a no-brainer.

VANCOUVER FILM SCHOOL:

Lessons learnt:

- All together now, "Don't pick up used needles in back alleys!"
- If you look beyond appearances, you can make out the human behind the crack addict, but that person is long gone
- There's always some statistic-laden bore, wherever you go
- 'Moist' has developed into a somewhat despised word, but when describing Vancouver's wet season, it's a necessary weapon, *like it or not*
- Always ask admissions staff what doors their education will open
- If you have the choice between a $50 cancellation fee and a cross-continental, life-changing road trip, the decision should be obvious

CHAPTER SEVENTEEN

"Guuuuuuuud morrrrrrrning, folks..." the weather guy warbled. "It's another brisk day out there, so be sure to wrap up *real* warm."

Toronto, February 2005.

"Don't forget to cover every siiiiiiiiiiingle part of your face as, ha-ha, we're predicting frostbite within four, yes, four minutes of skin being exposed to the great outdoors... ooooohh, that's gotta huuurt... In other news today, two homeless men died last night due to hypothermia..."

It was cold. Damn cold.

Shivering under five duvets, I licked at a glass of water that had long ago turned to solid ice. Overnight, temperatures had plummeted to −36° Celsius; inside it was barely a degree warmer, wafer-thin walls struggling to retain a tenth of the heat pumped out by a decrepit heater.

Surveying the scene, I thought back to that $50 cancellation fee; I winced, instantly regretting it, both eyelids freezing tight. Burrowing my head into concrete pillows, I couldn't help but think: *Should've paid the fee, should've paid the fee, should have paid the fee, should've paid the fee...*

Four months earlier, a contrasting scene: on a balmy September evening, as shorts and skirts tumbled from neighbourhood bars, Sarah and I rolled into Toronto having crossed the continent in my twelve-year-old Subaru station wagon.

It had taken two weeks to complete the journey, in which time we'd departed Vancouver for Seattle, sped through Washington and Idaho's dense forests, been awed by Montana's 'Big Sky' country, scaled Wyoming's Yellowstone National Park, slogged past the farmlands of South Dakota, the lakes of Minnesota, and the dairy herds of Wisconsin, popped into Chicago, zipped round Lake Michigan, skimmed Indiana, shot by Detroit, and eased into Toronto as the first hints of auburn tinged the city's prolific trees.

God I hoped it was worth it. We both did.

Yet as a team, success seemed possible.

Relying on one another had been integral to our road-trip; as I drove, Sarah acted as navigator, helping me dodge suicidal deer in the forests of Wyoming, keep awake on the straights of the prairies, and avoid plus-sized cars between the blocks of Chicago. Teamwork had helped us relocate to Toronto hiccup-free, and teamwork would keep us on track.

Sarah knew me well enough to recognise my regular bouts of career-based hysteria, so would act as a calming force, talking me off the ledge. Conversely, I knew she'd need gentle nudging and quiet encouragement to keep plugging away at a taxing job hunt in a foreign city. And initially it worked well, until our peaceful balance was shattered by a bump in the road so big it would have unhinged Tintin & Snowy, Lewis & Clarke or even, *God forbid*... David & Victoria.

The bump came as a question:

"Your friend Sarah just interviewed for this position. Are you sure that isn't awkward?"

It was a justifiable question.

What *the hell* were we thinking?

You see the bump was entirely...

...well, hold on, let's start a little earlier, in more peaceful times, as Toronto welcomed two new residents to its leafy streets.

Rising from the shores of Lake Ontario, Canada's largest city sprawls over 250 square kilometres of mostly forgettable, low-rise land. A handful of highlights include the rugged, remarkably wild Don Valley ravine, the 533-metre high CN Tower, and the downtown district's warren of tunnels that connect offices, apartments, parking lots, and malls, providing warm passage through the deep winter freeze. In just over 200 years Toronto has matured from a muddy colonial outpost (originally named York) to a cosmopolitan metropolis of almost three million people, boosted by Sarah and myself as its latest additions.

On settling into a new city, the first two boxes to tick are finding a place to live, and a place to work. Unsurprisingly, the former was easy; I prayed the latter would be too. Yet confidence was high, as having completed a year's worth of film training – in Canada, no less – I expected to find a receptive jobs market.

Parallels to previous surges of confidence concerned me, but surely this time it had to be different? Now I was offering employers something useful, something they demanded. I was trained; I was ready. Like a man fulfilling everything his beloved has asked of him, so I too had shaved my back and thrown out the porn.

But would she reveal fresh demands?

Not willing, or wanting, to consider such a hideous scenario, I tackled the Toronto jobs market with vigour, applying to every vacancy, chasing every lead, knocking on every door.

And sharing the same goal, so did Sarah.

Disappointingly – some might say predictably – employers weren't half as responsive as we'd hoped, so when opportunities were found we'd jump at them, whatever the hours, pay, or location, regardless of whether or not the vacancy matched our VFS training. It was an unruly approach that would inadvertently, inescapably, see us hurtle towards that awkward 'bump in the road'.

The obvious looming issue was that Sarah and I were looking for the same jobs, searching the same sites, contacting the same people, following the same leads, chasing the same interviews... at the same time.

Which leads to that justifiable question.

The flash point cropped up after just five weeks in Toronto, prompted by Sarah and I being asked to interview for the exact same job on the exact same day. It was an awkward opportunity, but one still worth pursuing, as it had come from a Hollywood colossus, 20th Century Fox.

The Toronto office of the world-famous movie studio is located in a glass-coated tower block near the bustling intersection of Bloor & Young, where two of Toronto's busiest streets converge. Staff there oversee the promotion, distribution, accounts, and marketing for Fox's activities in Canada, as well as running a separate, secret department that continuously spies on the Canadian government for Rupert Murdoch's News Corporation. (Okay, that's not true, my lawyer tells me to stipulate, *but I bet a part of you wants to believe it.*)

On a crisp day just before Halloween, pumpkins adorning doorsteps, the hint of winter in the air, several staff in that satellite office were preparing to interview candidates for the lowly role of 'Publicity and Promotions Assistant', whose job it would be to maximise bums on seats at Fox movie releases across Canada. It wasn't the perfect job, and wouldn't flex a tenth of the skills we'd just learnt, but it would mean a major studio name enhancing one of our CVs.

Such a totem is priceless.

Across town, Sarah and I also prepared, wrapping in multiple layers to protect against the day's chill, a temperature that matched the brittle state between us. There was no hiding the competitive atmosphere, as our usual inane chatter was paused for Fox's combative day. The hostile mood prompted a new mantra:

This is weird, this is weird, this is weird, this is weird…

But having both agreed to interview, the awkwardness had to be ignored, so we hid it behind platitudes, weak grins, and observational humour; yet there are only so many times you can wish each other good luck, pull holiday resort smiles, and point out pets that look vaguely similar to their owners.

Silence took hold, as we strode on past replica homes and pristine lawns, past aging oaks and crumbling stairs, over fallen leaves, unwanted flyers, and blowing litter. A child laughed in the distance. A car sputtered past. A postman dropped mail. The street scene caught my eye like never before. Anything was more appealing than discussing what lay ahead.

"They'll probably offer it in-house," I said, trying to ease the tension.

"Of course. There's little point in even going," Sarah responded.

We laughed, not slowing a step.

"A-ha-ha-ha-ha------- ha------- ha -------------------- ha."

Ouch.

On we walked, past breakfast cafés and Irish pubs, places in which we'd tried to follow hockey games and Canadian football. I wondered, *If one of us gets this job, will we be the same?* but the need to secure work pushed the thought aside.

Then it began to rain.

To be honest, it didn't begin to rain, but it should have.

In a movie it would have been thunderous.

If you want to imagine this walk backed by Samuel Barber's 'Adagio for Strings', best known as Willem Dafoe's curtain call in *Platoon*, feel free to do so. Although I may be over-egging the drama of two friends battling it out for the same job, there is a point, I assure you, and music will help me make it. If you don't know 'Adagio for Strings', feel free to add your own soundtrack, but anything by Katy Perry probably won't do me justice.

We carried on. In the distance, our destination appeared.

A pang of guilt stabbed me. I knew I'd prepped for the interview, but Sarah hadn't. Admittedly I hadn't done a huge amount of preparation, but at least I was entering with *some* ammunition.

As with any interview you need to know what they want – it's a sales pitch, after all – and then you need to offer it. Following that simple ethos I'd looked into Fox's current releases, studied the role of a Publicity and Promotions Assistant, then listed ways I'd boost audience numbers. One such marketing ploy targeted Jimmy Fallon's *Taxi*, a Fox re-make of a French movie. While the American version was a sad indictment of studio production,

I knew disliking it would be of no use to a diligent Publicity and Promotions Assistant, whose prime task is to maximise ticket sales, regardless of a film's quality.

My *Taxi* marketing plan was simple, centring on the fact – yes, fact – that most taxis have an odour able to scare North Korea into giving up nuclear weapons. Furthermore, cabs are used by thousands of people every day, making them ideal places to sell products. Putting those two truisms together, my idea was to produce *Taxi*-branded air fresheners, giving them to cab companies for free, who'd in theory hang them front and centre in cars across the country. A fresh odour, a more pleasant journey, a cheap product, and in large letters the *Taxi* release date, all of which would be hard for passengers to ignore.

It was an easy hit, ticking all the right boxes.

I felt ready; Sarah, I knew, was not. It wasn't my fault, but it still left a lump in my throat, like that awkward feeling when realise you have no change to give to a busker you've been listening to for ten minutes, leaving you no choice but to shuffle off, red-faced, mouthing hollow apologies.

Time to ruminate on such ethics was over.

Lights changed, cars stopped, legs swung into action. We crossed Bloor & Young, just a few buildings from our date with the decision-makers.

Sarah was to be put through the grinder first, but hating the idea of waiting in the lobby I wished her luck (for the fortieth time), said farewell, opting to stay outdoors. I couldn't stomach the prospect of sitting in the lobby, festering on how we'd rapidly gone from supportive pillars to temporary foes, knowing the health of our friendship demanded neither of us get the job, while our careers required the opposite. It was lunacy to tackle Toronto in such a contentious style, yet there we were, fighting for the same piece of turf.

And with that cheery thought in mind, twenty minutes later I stopped pounding the concrete, and entered the Fox block. It was time to go into battle against my one and only friend for over a thousand miles in every direction.

"Your friend Sarah just interviewed for this position. Are you sure that isn't awkward?"

Was it awkward?

It was about as awkward a situation as one could possibly face, but Sarah hadn't run out of the interview shouting about our friendship being more important than their poxy job. Neither would I.

After asking the question, the interviewer stopped.

He wanted an answer.

"No, it's fine. It's an exciting position. We both want to try for it."

True, yes, in a shade of grey.

He peered at me, pausing momentarily as if to see whether I'd reverse my position, then nodded, lost interest, sipped coffee, perused CV, and the meeting continued, as I set about telling him ideas for increasing Fox money across the disparate Canadian provinces.

Posters adorning the identikit meeting room electrified the air. Smash hits such as *Master and Commander: The Far Side of the World*, *The Transporter*, and *Minority Report* fought for attention, shouting, "This is a 20th Century Fox place of business!" but no sooner had I been awed than I was chilled, their subtext whispering, "We're a business fuelled by successful choices made by successful people, now interviewing a particularly unsuccessful person."

Uh-oh. I waffled on, eyes down.

The bespectacled interviewer listened intermittently, allowing me to fill the room with plans to target teenagers and create cross-promotional tie-ins, but his attention waned, likely having heard similar pitches throughout the day.

As I was ending my apparently soporific spiel, his interest finally piqued when I broached the subject of my *Taxi*-branded air fresheners. His ears twitched, eyes widened, nose flared: a cartoon dog alerted to a hidden bone.

Lastly his left eyebrow rose imperceptibly, just enough to communicate a Columbo-esque thought.

"Have you been to our offices recently?"

"Never," I answered. "Why?"

The eyebrow rose again.

"Let me get this straight; you're suggesting that we brand air fresheners and distribute them to cab drivers, for free, within the city?"

"Actually across Canada."

"Right, across Canada, right…"

"…That's the basic idea. It should create awareness, attract the right age group, be cheap to produce, useful to cabbies, improve the smell in…"

"…Yeah, yeah, I know. I was listening. It's just… never been here?"

He looked at me straight on, probing my face. A tall, thin, well-kept man in his mid-thirties, he'd have been well suited to film noir had he been born eighty years earlier. His piercing eyes and furrowed brow left little ambiguity. He may as well have grabbed me by the collar and shouted, "Liar!!"

In return I slowly shook my head, smiling meekly. There's little else you can do when facing such unexpected cynicism. I desperately didn't want to appear confused – it's not a good interview look – but it was hard to avoid. I was baffled. I probably looked like I was trying to figure out long division, or how to convert Fahrenheit into Celsius. After several awkward seconds he stood up, told me he'd be back, and then slipped from the meeting room. Already in 'weirder than reality TV' territory, I stayed, wondering what I'd done wrong.

The wiry interviewer reappeared carrying a mysterious box. He gently laid the box on the table in front of him, sliding it to the centre, like a barrister submitting a 'case-closed' piece of evidence.

"Never been here before?" he repeated.

"Nope," I answered, although at this point I was beginning to doubt myself. *Maybe I had been there before?*

I didn't recognise the place, but maybe I'd sleepwalked into the building, or stumbled in drunk one night. Oh God, maybe I'd taken a dump in the box. Had I taken a dump in the box? I could have taken a dump in the box. Technically it was possible. It seemed unlikely, but all things are possible, and he was apparently convinced I'd been there before, so maybe I *had* squatted over his box. Suddenly it was clear. The obvious answer to his repeated question was that there had to be a turd in the box. My turd.

There was no other explanation.

He pushed a finger under the box, gradually lifting it off the table, raising one corner higher and higher, until the lid opened, spilling its contents across the table.

Oh crap, here we go…

But what tumbled out was no dirty protest, which I instantly realised to be the most idiotic item I could ever have imagined to come tumbling out of a movie studio stationery box. Instead, what tumbled out were hundreds and hundreds of *Taxi*-branded air fresheners; my *Taxi*-branded air fresheners. They lay in front of me, completed, manufactured, piled ten deep.

I couldn't believe it; somehow I'd come up with the exact same promotional idea as their marketing team. No wonder he was sceptical as to whether I'd been snooping around his office. Anyone would be.

Even a drunken poo was more likely.

We both stared at the air fresheners, speechless. They looked exactly as I'd imagined them, the logo of the film and its release date on one side, a still from the movie on the other, and the *pièce de résistance*, an all-conquering, bio-bashing stench that overwhelmed everything within a ten-foot radius.

I picked one up, flipped it over, checked it closely, looked him straight in the eye, and cracked a line I instantly despised:

"You stole my idea."

"How did it go?" asked Sarah.

"Er, kinda well, kinda well…"

Leaving an interview with a smile across my face that could fit a genetically-modified banana revealed how it went.

"I'm pleased for you," she said, genuinely meaning it, and I believed her, knowing she loved seeing people around her do well. I wished I could have been that cool. I wished I could have told her I expected the job to go her way, but the air freshener incident couldn't be ignored. When I told her about it, she too was convinced the job would be mine.

Ignoring previous lessons learned, going against all known advice and common sense, I gave up job-hunting and waited for the Fox call-up. It was a self-backing move I've never again played, and for good reason: I've never since walked into an interview and sold them the exact same idea their marketing department cooked up six weeks earlier.

If dictionaries were to be updated on a daily basis with pictures of people to reflect words, in the autumn of 2004, by the words 'smug' and 'git', there'd have been tiny shots of my banana-smile face. I was THE smug git. I was in the zone. I was in territory usually reserved for playboys, dictators, and inexplicable celebrities.

In *Seinfeld*, dating, or sporting terminology it's known as 'The Kavorka', a period of uncanny confidence that you can't create or buy, that occurs naturally, that can't be stopped or increased, that will provide money, bedfellows, and goals aplenty, until you realise you have The Kavorka, for at that very moment it will vanish, leaving you desperate to regain it… but to no avail. The Kavorka is a little known force, but it can be identified the world over.

For instance, how is it that Italy's Silvio Berlusconi, ex-PM and infamous 'bunga bunga' trailblazer, held power year after year? Did he have The Kavorka? What about Tony Blair winning a third term, despite his Iraq war lies? And how does Kim Kardashian stay in the spotlight? The woman is the very embodiment of The Kavorka. Plus, she's too self-involved to ever question how she got it, thereby going down as a lifelong Kavorka legend.

Clearly my air freshener episode was a distant fourth to Berlusconi, Blair, and Kardashian, but it still left me with enough confidence to twiddle thumbs, killing time as I waited to hear from Fox.

In the meantime, Sarah and I had made a big decision. We'd been living for seven weeks in a two-bed Victorian duplex, but it was time to branch out. The head-to-head job hunt was, I assumed, not going to happen again, and even though our friendship had held up post-interview, cabin fever weighed heavy, driving a need for immediate change.

Put simply, we needed friends.

The third most important box to tick in a new city is a social life. Without it, you're immigrants living in the shadows. Sarah had heard me re-hash my stories a hundred times – the poor girl needed a break – so classifieds were opened, scanned and re-scanned, until we had a shortlist of rooms to check. We were to move apart, make new friends, share those friends, and thereby integrate into Toronto faster.

The daunting process of another move began again.

'Share with six young professionals in a large house off the upbeat bars and clubs of Bloor Street. Large private room attached to back of house. Shared facilities,' read mine.

'Single woman in need of roommate in beautiful apartment with large rooms. Women only,' read Sarah's.

I couldn't shake the feeling I'd be doing *slightly* more for the team by sharing with six complete strangers, returning to student life, to the *thump-thump-thump* of noisy neighbours, but it had to be done.

The 'large house' sat in the middle of a street of detached, red brick properties, mostly three storeys high, boasting wide porches and attractive flowerbeds. Some homes carried the hallmarks of family life (small bicycles, broken toys); some screamed *Animal*

House (crushed cans, string lights), with my prospective pad firmly one of the latter.

Inside the house I found a traditional shared house set-up, revolving around a central living space, shelves lined with DVDs, wine bottles topped with molten candles, tatty throws over tattier sofas, and the usual selection of prized remotes lauding over a mug-stained coffee table. On the same floor was my 'attached' bedroom, a room that was spacious, private, and quiet.

Tick, tick, tick, all as advertised... *sold.*

There was just one hidden flaw. And it was a big one. In my haste to sign up I'd failed to ask whether the room was warm. For anyone moving to Toronto before the start of winter this is a *crucial* question. Not asking about warmth was why, three months later, my eyelids were frozen tight, my bedside water was rock solid, and I was forced to sleep under five Norwegian duvets.

'Attached', I quickly learned, meant attached.

The mid-winter cold was to permeate my inner core because my room had been casually tacked to the back of the house, built over a flat roof using little more than plywood planks, nails, and a smattering of lino. At $-36°$ Celsius I'd have been warmer in an igloo, yet instead of going into the garden and sensibly building myself an ice home, I bought a hot water bottle, a dodgy heater, and enough duvets to warm an Arctic sled team.

And still I was cold.

Yet on moving in, the house was ideal.

Autumnal breezes refreshed my room. Birdsong filled the air. Leaves settled all about. I slept deep. Little did I know of the glacial conditions to come, so being blissfully ignorant, I settled in, socialised, and celebrated a successful move. All I needed now was that Fox call-up.

And within a week, news arrived.

Although you might expect Fox to have judged me a fraud, convinced I'd stolen their air freshener idea, so hated me, my personality, and above all, my smug-git-grin, I have to disappoint; the

Taxi coincidence had done the trick. I was to work at 20th Century Fox, one of world's largest movie studios, and a significant part of News Corporation, a global conglomerate with a finger in every media pie imaginable, a foothold in every country that matters.

This… was… The Big Leagues.

Several days later I walked back into Fox's shimmering tower near Bloor & Young, kicking off my first day within the News Corp. family. At the end of an open-plan office I was assigned a desk, a pile of newspapers, and a daily task: to trawl through Canada's mainstream media searching for mentions of Fox in articles and comments, filing them for future reference.

It wasn't glamorous, but it was something.

I was now part of the Hollywood studio entertainment machine, a small cog, but a functioning component nonetheless. Every cog plays its part, and I reasoned that in order to one day be a gong-scooping producer I'd need to understand them all, from the bottom up, be that catering, financing, or putting bums on seats. As part of a publicity and promotions team I'd learn how to sell films, a skill as essential to silver screen success as optioning diamond-in-the-rough scripts, or tracking down a zeitgeist lead for your low budget feature film.

And while I settled into flogging Fox's cinematic happy meals, so Sarah was securing shifts on film and TV shoots, work far better suited to our VFS training, but work taken on a freelance basis. It paid well, but required a constant hunt for the next job, with some gigs lasting no longer than a day.

It's an uphill battle few can fight for long.

Especially if you decide to jump on ice…

As Christmas loomed, so did a momentous event that would yank Sarah out of the freelance game far earlier than expected; just as we were beginning to settle into Toronto, so our lives were to fall foul of bad luck, poor timing, cheap alcohol, and a lethal swathe of black ice.

Worst of all, it was entirely my fault.

The unfortunate incident began with a plan to spend Christmas in Niagara Falls, an eighty-minute drive away from downtown Toronto. It was an innocent suggestion, kicking off a bizarre chain of events that only Nostradamus, the Oracle, or Yoda could have foreseen.

Without them at our side, what hope?

And so unwittingly we packed bags, took to the highway, leaving the city for a festive excursion near to one of the world's finest natural wonders. If Yoda had been at our side, he'd have turned us around, warning:

"In life, several things there are, everyone needs to know. By the side of a pool, do not run. A woman's age, do not ask. 'Bomb!' in an airport, do not say. After plentiful wine, on ice do not jump. Get you, karma will."

But we had no such advice, so on Christmas Eve the two of us checked into a shabby hotel on the Canadian side of Niagara Falls, set in a landscape defaced with other such concrete monstrosities. I'd thought, and hoped, the area would be developed in line with its famed wonder, but sadly it was crafted in line with mankind's insatiable desire for cheap rooms and all-you-can-eat buffets, leaving the waterfall the only attractive feature for miles around. On the upside, visitors can burn cash in a handful of twenty-four-hour casinos, and if that's not the best way to ruin a stunning landscape, then what is?

Christmas Day began amidst this unnatural, post-modern setting of touristic gluttony, children nowhere to be seen, neon lighting the landscape. Without our families nearby, we were unsure what to do, so I posed the popular question, 'What would Jesus do?' The answer came back thus: he'd pray to Dad, open a birthday present, whip on a robe, and nip down for a cheeky flutter.

If a cheeky flutter is what Jesus would do, then it was damn sure what we were going to do, and so began a rather unusual

December 25th. Once out of our rooms, descending from the twenty-second floor in a sluggish lift, I decided to promptly embrace the spirit of a Niagara Falls Christmas Day:

"Bet you we're going to stop on the fourteenth floor," I told Sarah.

She looked at me with a gaze of mild disdain, followed by a slight shrug. It should have been taken as an indication of disinterest, but instead was taken as encouragement to continue, partly because men can't read body language, but mostly because we prefer to act first, face consequences later.

"It'll definitely stop on the fourteenth floor. You just watch," I added, driving the point home; after all, it was Christmas Day and heaven forbid anyone actually enjoy themselves.

And then, as though the Ghost of Christmas Bores had torn himself from explaining chess to teenagers, instead blessing my tedious gamble, the lift slowed at the fifteenth floor, coming to a dramatic halt on the fourteenth. Nerves tingled. Sarah bristled. And a rather large man from Vermont thudded in.

I stared at Sarah. She stared at me. I stared at the man from Vermont. He avoided eye contact, presumably noting my wide eyes and mischievous grin, red flags warning him: *engage at your peril.*

The silence held sway as we dropped to the ground. Once the man with the University of Vermont cap had scurried off, we exited, alight with intent.

"Casino, now," I whispered. "We find the first one we can, then the first gaming floor we can, then the first roulette table we can, and I'm putting ten bucks on number fourteen. It sounds dumb, but I have a feeling about…"

"It isn't dumb, hurry up, Charlie!!" said Sarah, pulling me through the lobby, dodging tourists in *Maid of the Mist* waterfall viewing ponchos. Outside, sub-zero air hit hard, slowing us briefly, but our pace quickened as we eyed the nearest casino, the two of us marching with devout purpose.

Within sight of the mighty waterfall our target loomed, the

imposing, vulgar, yet immensely alluring Casino Niagara. Our stride lengthened as we skidded towards the main entrance, dodging traffic and doormen, ignoring the bright lights, focusing only on where we'd find the nearest gaming table, knowing full well the exercise to be a time-wasting mission, yet nonetheless consumed by adventure.

We rounded a corner to see the goal ahead, a packed gambling floor filled with the abundant faithful. Once inside, the closest roulette table was targeted, the short distance crossed, a wad of dollars pulled, and as the croupier called "last bets please" about to drop the ball, ten bucks slammed down, a chip was returned, positioned over fourteen, leaving a breathless pair itching for the next spin.

A fellow punter offered a seat; it was waved away.

This was no time for sitting.

With bets placed, the croupier spun the wheel, and threw the ball. The assorted gamers watching with tired passion, most risking far more than a paltry ten bucks, but none more gripped than those two panting newcomers.

Clunk, clunk,

jump, jump,

bump, bump,

clatter, clatter,

click, click, click,

slowing, slowing, slowing...

Settling…

Stop.

And there it was.

For a moment I thought I was God.

For a moment Sarah thought I was God.

For a moment the others questioned God.

Now I did need a seat.

I'd been silenced.

It was unreal.

It was impossible.

It was Number Fourteen.

"Winner, winner!" the croupier said.

He had to suspect foul play.

Or that Jesus was in the house.

Number Fourteen had just earned me $360.

But it wasn't the money I'd remember.

Not by a long shot.

I was… *wow*… I was floored.

Ten whole seconds of dumbfounded shock ended, followed by the usual jumping, whooping, and high-fiving enacted by winners worldwide, then calm was restored, winnings scooped, and the two fortuitous freaks walked to the exit, watched by every eye-in-the-sky, and green-faced gambler in the room.

Cold air was needed with a side order of reality. A sharp intake in the outside freeze slapped me back to the real world. The unusual events of the past forty-five minutes couldn't be understood or replicated. It was what it was, and there was only one thing left to do: spend the winnings the way God and Jesus intended, on a heavy downpour of cheap wine and dirty tequila.

After changing into 'big spender' clothing we settled into the closest restaurant that passed for fine dining, and began to splash the cash. Yet unbeknown to us the day was still to play its final hand, as lurking in the shadows was karma, planning its revenge, livid at my Number Fourteen prediction. Eyeing our fun it licked its lips, as we drank enough cheap plonk to tee it up for an easy victory.

Never off the clock, karma went to work.

You see the planet doesn't let average humans predict what lies in store for them. That's the preserve of the gods – whoever or whatever they may be – so if any of us mere mortals, even accidentally, behave like them, punishment is swift. For us, that punishment was meted out on exiting the restaurant, the result of a bottle of wine too many, Sarah jumping for joy, and the aforementioned large swathe of black ice… stumble… crash… crack…

Owwwww!!!!
Sob.
Hobble, hobble, hobble.
Game over.

I've never gotten over the guilt of Sarah being the one punished for my curious win, but I'm convinced her broken ankle was karma's payback. Once back in Toronto I tried to shoulder the burden, meeting her every day post-work, helping her navigate the city's icy streets, but even with spikes on her crutches it was impossible to function normally in a sub-zero setting.

We both knew that from the moment her bone fractured our time in Canada had been irreversibly changed, benching plans to meet new people, stagnating Sarah's career, forcing us to exist in Toronto, rather than to flourish.

It was a game changer, so although this odd gambling tale may seem a bizarre tangent to my story of seeking career success, there is reason, as our paths were now bound together, linked through adversity, soon to be tied even closer, as we fought to keep the film dream alive. Even though our Toronto adventure had taken a beating – needing crutches, a cast, box set TV, and six-to-eight week's recovery time – we were determined to succeed, ignoring any and all signs to change tack.

Blind Career Obsession was back with a vengeance.

And then, just to make things worse, an additional layer of stress was dumped on the pile, as my life at Fox skidded to a crash. It seemed as though karma had taken an embarrassed look at Sarah's broken ankle, realised that seven brandies might have clouded its Christmas judgement, so had decided to redress the situation by taking me down too.

I'll be the first to admit it, fair's fair, I was the one who deserved a broken ankle, but it still seemed a tad harsh.

Yet karma had decided.

"We'd love to keep you on, but it's just not possible," said my boss.

"Fox can't arrange a permanent visa?" I asked.

"We just can't justify it. We need to hire someone with Canadian citizenship. There's no way around it."

She sat back, looked down, shuffled papers, scanned a sheet, then looked back at me with that workplace double-take meant to indicate surprise at your inability to disappear. I took the hint, thanked her, and slipped out, returning to my desk with a black cloud hanging overhead.

Needless to say, there would have been ways to extend my visa, but it wouldn't have been worth the time and cost for someone in my role. If I was being hired to head a department, pinched from another studio, or had the ability to produce award-winning scripts from my backside, a way would be found; but there was no justifying it for my lowly job.

I'd been given a month, then it was time to move on.

Decisions were once again out of my hands, action was once again needed; on a daily basis the world seemed less and less like my oyster. It was late-February in northern North America, and the oyster theory was on a gurney, in need of life support. I desperately wanted it to survive, truly believing in it, but the world had other ideas. At every turn were barbed-wire borders, worn-out rubber stamps, and triplicate layers of bureaucracy. With my time at Fox running short, it seemed only a matter of weeks before Sarah and I would be forced to part ways, neither of us able to work in each other's countries.

Was this the end of the line?

That was how it appeared, but as so often happens, when one door closes another opens, yet this time the door that creaked open was a beguiling portal few would recommend passing through.

It was a door of our own making, one that came from being beaten and demoralised. It was a door forged by a determination, a stubbornness, to pursue our shared goal to the end. And so, in an effort to beat the limitations of the oyster theory, and as a result of thinking way, way outside the box, Sarah and I arrived at a solution that had the power to change everything; that would allow us to take control; that would allow us to make the impossible possible.

The animals were taking charge of the zoo.

As with many big decisions it began with an innocent conversation about the weather, morphing into a discussion about surviving Canada's intense winter, eventually feeding into the well-worn topic of where we'd go when it was time to leave the Great White North...

...ending forty-two minutes later with a plan, an unusual and somewhat terrifying plan, a plan to take the path less travelled, a path that would be... game-changing... *dern, dern, derrrrrr.*

And what was that plan?

Prompted by desperation, spurred on by our film dream, we decided we'd join forces and live in America, a goal we'd achieve by entering into a marriage between friends. It was a solution we arrived at because nothing else seemed possible. It was our last chance saloon, the final roll of the dice. We'd relocate to the entertainment industry's beating heart, to the magnetising, polluted city of Los Angeles.

And once there, we'd marry.

Our stay in 'T-dot' had been poorly timed from start to finish, coinciding with the most bitterly of cold months, but that was all forgotten; there were now bigger fish to fry. A new plan was in play, flipping the oyster theory on its head.

Just seven months after entering Toronto, with the naïve goal of becoming part of its film community, we'd been beaten, battered, and (literally) broken, but we chose to look ahead. As the city's snow disappeared into its cavernous sewers, it came time to say our farewells.

My final day at 20th Century Fox was marked with a slice of cake, hugs from the accounts department, a strong pat on the back from my closest colleague, and a final exit through Rupert Murdoch's shiny doors, "Good luck in your future endeavours!" ringing in my ears.

If anything was true it was that we'd need luck. Murky waters lay ahead, reminding me of police chief Brody's unforgettable line in *Jaws*:

"You're gonna need a bigger boat."

We were going to need a *damn* big boat. The waters ahead would be infested with bureaucratic sharks, deadly triplicate forms, and razor-edged rubber stamps.

We were gonna need a goddam cruise ship.

JOB NINE: PUBLICITY AND PROMOTIONS ASSISTANT

Lessons learnt:

- Toronto can be ridiculously, horrendously, appallingly cold. I can see why so many Canadians live on the west coast. Bring a jersey, that's all

- Going into battle against your only friend for a thousand miles: inadvisable

- Always prep for an interview. Arrive with answers to their questions, questions for them to answer, and ideas to prove what you bring to the table

- If you've thought up the same marketing idea as your potential employer, try not to look guilty or able to break into the building

- A globally-famous company on your CV is worth five unknown companies

- Karma is patient, ruthless, but also prone to festive error

- When sailing into troubled waters, you're gonna need a *damn* big boat

CHAPTER EIGHTEEN

Two become one.

Those words flashed bright – neon signs on a US highway – as career and friendship hurtled towards common ground, colliding as subtly as the Internet and porn. I couldn't help but wonder, *is this a bridge too far?*

In a blink, a retort bounced back; it was instinctive, primed for this very moment, a quote by ancient Chinese philosopher, Confucius, who said, "Choose a job you love, and you will never have to work a day in your life." I held the line close, my shield of validation, because if accurate, our plan made sense.

His two-and-half-thousand-year-old theory still resonates: if you love your career, your working life will be more rewarding than if you don't. (You'll still likely slog through long, arduous days, but it's better than the alternative.)

And *that* was why Sarah and I had chosen to pursue our dream, to combine forces, and move to LA. Together we'd make it work. What else could we do? Return to our distant homes, reset, and start again? Fuck. That. We were willing to take a giant leap to avoid such a regressive scenario.

At least that was the plan.

Once back in the UK, sharp days followed sharper nights. April is what it is: rain, sun, snow, hail, heat, and cold; it's gloriously unpredictable, yet I was focused on the far more predictable burden of paperwork, *damned paperwork*, as I compiled must-have documents for a visa interview at the US Embassy.

Yet it wasn't to be.

Following our departure from Toronto, Sarah and I sped to New York, after which I flew to London with the aim of returning to America within weeks. Yet once home it didn't take long to realise I'd guesstimated a grossly simplistic timeline, as the quicksand of bureaucracy drained my will to live, demanding background checks, fingerprint scans, address verification, and more, forcing me into a holding pattern, waiting on documents that would likely take months to arrive.

I won't bore you with the details of what hurdles needed jumping – that much can be researched online – suffice to say that before you come close to an embassy interview, you need every document in place, notarised, in triplicate. Until you have the required paperwork to hand, you're stuck in limbo, unable to plan ahead, left wondering how to fill your days.

But I wasn't to wonder for long.

For once again, an oyster came a-knocking.

"What the hell is going on over there?!"

"#&@***!!"

"What?!!"

"$***@#!!"

"Calm down, woman! …Christ… I can't take this…"

I'd only popped to Steve's house for a cup of tea, but instead of small talk and biscuits I found myself watching him shout through his mobile at a mystery person with whom he seemed to be having trouble communicating.

He held the phone from his ear, and whispered, "Manager in the Caribbean's having issues, and I'm spending half my week talking her out of resigning…"

It didn't sound like an offer for a cup of tea.

I found the kettle, flipped it on, and continued listening to his transatlantic tirade. Steve was a man with many fingers in many pies, and one such pie was a booze cruise tour that took punters on a four-hour rum-and-snorkelling excursion in the US Virgin Islands. In theory it was a fine way to make money, but in practice it meant supervising staff thousands of miles away, dealing with problems that should have been sorted on-island.

"Just work it out at your end, Sharon, for God's sake," Steve blustered. "If it's a small purchase then just get it!! ...No... No... I'm sorry, I didn't mean to shout at you... No... Yes, absol... You're doing a fine... But I need... No... If we just... Okay, sorry... Fine, we'll speak later, goodb..."

The phone thumped on a cushion.

"Christ alive!"

"The usual?" I offered, sympathetically.

"It's endless; the same staffing problems every time. Honestly, if I could replace them with robots I would!"

"What's up now?"

"Where do I start? The cruise has gone feral. Payroll issues, new hires, maintenance, licensing, business development, asset sales, security, petty theft, insurance... The manager wants to leave. I'm begging her to stay, but we need a replacement. In the meantime, I need to talk her through every job, wasting my time. It should have been simple, but's it's turned into a bloody nightmare."

I sipped my tea, attentively.

"Anyone out there who can take over from her?"

Little cogs quietly stirred.

"Nobody. It's hopeless. We'll have to sell the business soon."

Little cogs ground faster.

"There's literally nobody to take it on?"

Little cogs span hard.

"Nobody. I'm out of options. I'm speaking to her again later, but she's resigning this evening, I'm sure of it. She's had enough. We'll have to let the junior staff go first, then wind up the operation. It's a real shame."

Little cogs flew at full speed, accelerated by easily excitable itchy feet. I quickly 'did the math': I was waiting on paperwork, my career on hold; Sarah was in New York, a four-hour flight from the Caribbean, her career also on hold. We both needed a cash injection. Why not go to the Virgin Islands for a month or two, save the day for Steve's company, be local heroes, bank some money, then proceed as before, with paperwork by then in place, ready to roll?

It seemed daft; it seemed impulsive.

It seemed too good to be true.

Adventure came into view.

It would surely be shot down.

"When are you speaking to Sharon?" I asked Steve.

"Sometime this evening…" he replied, adding, "but, you know, don't let me trouble you with all this…"

And then, à la Baldrick from TV's *Blackadder*, I grinned the grin of the mad and dim-witted, stroked my stubbly chin, raised a bushy eyebrow, and thought his famous line, *My Lord… I… have… a… cunning… plan.*

Of course I didn't say it out loud, not wanting to scare Steve at this most opportune of moments, so leant back, trying to mask any sense of hope in what I was about to convey:

"Welllllll… er… what if a friend and I went to the Caribbean and took over? I've got nothing on my plate at the moment, so could…"

"Yes."

I tried to upsell, unaware he was already sold.

"Well, I just think we could…"

"Yes."

Steve's eyes burned bright.

"When do you need someone to…?"

"How soon can you fly?"

An overview of my to-do-list took all of four seconds.

BEST LAID PLANS… OFTEN GO AWRY

Lessons learnt:

- "Choose a job you love, and you will never have to work a day in your life," said Confucius, so kicking off BCO for millennia to come

- Always talk to people about what they're up to, their problems, and how they plan to solve them – you never know where opportunities may lie

- If you stumble upon the chance to work somewhere exotic for however short a period, and have nothing but thumb-twiddling in the diary, wait for those little cogs to spin, and then *carpe diem*

CHAPTER NINETEEN

The trauma, oh, *the trauma*.

It started eighty-two seconds after leaving the airport, and continued for over three gruelling hours. Eighty-two seconds was the time taken to walk through the terminal's automated exit doors, suck in a lungful of tropical air, take in our lush surroundings, look for Sharon, spot Sharon, determine Sharon was beyond breaking point… and to hear her first words.

Eighty-two seconds.

And then the trauma began.

In just four days I'd gone from hearing Steve's transatlantic tirade, to meeting Sarah in Puerto Rico, to the two of us boarding an eight-seater 'prop' plane, bound for the tiny volcanic specks that make up the United States Virgin Islands (USVI). After a forty-minute flight, engines powering down, blades sweeping through the humid air, we hopped from the compact aircraft, and ambled across the blacktop at Cyril E King airport in St Thomas, USVI, both of us flaunting 'pinch-me' grins, mesmerized by our new holiday-island home.

Those moronic beams disappeared fast when a compact middle-aged woman from the American Midwest began to exercise her final act as manager of The Olivia II Cruise Company, dumping several months of pent-up frustration on to our jet-lagged shoulders. Cursory greetings over, we jumped into her jeep, and so began a detailed explanation of everything we'd need to know in order to run – and potentially save – a troubled booze cruise operation; it was a tsunami of information that didn't let up, gathering pace as we sped past all-in-one resorts, pirate-themed pubs, and discount jewellery shops, en route to the company's waterfront HQ.

After fifteen hours of transatlantic and cross-Caribbean travels

I was shattered, on the brink of seizure, yet to show weakness would have been a pitiful start. Remembering a trick I'd learnt during my soporific pan-European drive several years earlier, I covertly pinched the inside of my thigh, harder and harder as the lecture rolled on, forcing myself to stay awake, and in so doing limped to the end of Sharon's encyclopaedic initiation.

The following morning: *panic*.

Waking with thighs as raw as a wrestler's nipples, it swiftly transpired that thigh-pinching only keeps the body conscious, not the mind. I hadn't stored a single byte of Sharon's upload, leaving me clueless as to how to run a cash-strapped Caribbean booze cruiser. Shouting across to Sarah's bedroom only confirmed the worst; she was – pun intended – in the same boat.

I considered asking Sharon for a re-briefing, but tender thighs prompted the idea to be hastily shelved. On second thoughts, we'd do this the old-fashioned way, by jumping in the deep end, by teaching ourselves the need-to-know. The plan incited flashbacks to the film job I'd stumbled through in New York, learning everything from scratch, but I'd survived that ordeal, just, and I could survive this one too, because once you get past self-doubt, there's very little that an averagely intelligent human being can't accomplish.

People proudly display idiocy the world over – as confirmed via a million YouTube clips – yet if in need of success under pressure, such as finding an emergency toilet when liquefied by the runs, or shedding love handles before a wedding, we're all capable of doing what's needed.

As the saying goes, 'necessity is the mother of invention', and on that wretched Caribbean morning our necessity was to figure out how to navigate the complex intricacies of booze cruise tourism. It was time to knuckle down and hit the books, but before studies began, there was just enough time to appreciate the near-equatorial island to which we'd arrived.

I drew back the curtains and breathed in the scene; it was enough to forget the worst of woes. On all sides was a picture-postcard cliché ticking every escapist box: a honeymoon-getaway-cum-student-deadbeat-paradise.

Crystal clear waters, little fluffy clouds, searing heat, feral dogs, cantankerous air conditioning, and Bob Marley on permanent repeat – you can't help but know when you're in the Caribbean. Far removed from the downpours of southern England and the ice sheets of eastern Canada, I was elated to be back in a land where business is conducted in flip-flops and sunnies.

With a half-hour to kill before the workday began, it seemed criminal not to kick off proceedings the local way, so I schlepped from the manager's apartment, shuffled across the narrow deck, and tumbled over the side, straight into the warm, embracing waters of the Caribbean Sea.

Sorry, did I forget to mention something?

Yes, the manager's apartment was *on board* the boat. I was literally sleeping on a booze cruiser. My new home boasted a deck on all sides, a bar on all levels, and Instagram-views from all windows, but there was one drawback that I was to be reminded of mere moments after climbing back on board.

"Get off the damn boat, or stay on for the day!!" shouted the skipper.

This apartment moved.

Adhering to the skipper's deadpan reminder, we got 'off the damn boat', for a cerebral marathon lay ahead, immersing ourselves in the how-to points of booze cruise management. First up would be getting to grips with the basics, checking out the fixtures and fittings, finding out exactly what we had at our disposal; and there was only one way to begin: by taking a tour of the ramshackle warehouse located alongside the boat's guard-dog protected mooring point.

Stepping ashore from the 115-foot steel cruiser into a steamy day, Sarah and I sipped at the humid air, unused to its sedative effects. We took a moment, acclimatising, pores clogging. Behind us, the crew threw lines, the captain calling commands; we turned, and as *The Olivia II* eased out, the two of us revelled in our first daylight glimpse of the colossal beast we were now managing.

She was big. She was classy. She was the Meryl Streep of vessels: attractive, experienced, a proven success, yet expensive to run. *The Olivia II* was similar to an Oyster Bay fishing boat, sitting low in the water, upper decks to her stern, with a long, open deck to her midst and bow; a simple, ideal space to entertain large groups of rum-swilling tourists. The *QEII* she was not, but a floating haven of Caribbean debauchery, she was.

As the boat disappeared round the headland, off to scoop up thirsty day-trippers, we turned to tour the bulky warehouse, pushing open its ten-foot high corrugated-iron door, gingerly peering inside.

Lying within was a veritable Aladdin's cave, forty-foot long, thirty-foot wide, lit by a weak bulb, shards of daylight stabbing through cracks in storm-beaten walls. On shelves and hooks rested every conceivable item to have kept the ship in business – engine parts, rope, life jackets, flares, tool kits, sprockets, used oil, railings – all of which looked impressive at first, but on closer inspection were worn through, rusted out, or had been pillaged for parts.

We picked up a few items, tossing them back down again. Junk. Recycling at best. Of more interest was a small manager's office overlooking the harbour. Aside from a handful of idle cockroaches and insatiable mosquitos, it was a standard two-desk workplace, made luxurious by an efficient air conditioner, and a full-length window that overlooked the active dockside.

As I poked about the dusty, litter-strewn room wondering how to begin the clean-up, something caught my eye, something that demanded further inspection. It appeared to be a hidden door sunk into the end wall, a door that had been bolted and nailed shut, covered in posters, concealed by printer paper, obscured by boat parts.

What could lie beyond? Piles of cash? A body?

"A vacuum cleaner or a mop, either of which will come in

handy for you to help tidy this place," said Sarah, in that wonderfully pragmatic way women master from the first time a man irritates them (an event usually taking place remarkably soon after birth).

I shrugged, knowing she was probably right, then set about clearing the door, kicking away boxes of paper, tearing off posters, pushing aside boat parts. Having found a hammer, I eased out every nail, about forty-five in all, so many in fact that I began to question my task.

Is this door holding up the building? Am I about to open Pandora's box? Have I sleep-hidden another turd?

The last nail fought hard, but could only resist for so long until it came free, pinging to the floor, leaving just the bolt to open. I heaved at it, but the stubborn slug wouldn't budge, salt air having formed a rusty sheath. I took to the workshop to search for a can of WD40, assuming I'd find one lurking in a cobwebbed corner alongside a copy of *Playboy* dating back to...

"Ta-da!!!" Sarah sang. It was justified, for in my absence she'd yanked open the obstinate bolt. Of course I should have thanked her in a gentlemanly fashion, but there was an inexplicable breakdown between my brain and mouth.

"I loosened it," tumbled out.

Mr Darcy was on leave.

Together we pulled at the door, hard, then harder. It refused at first, then gave in, eroded hinges remembering long-forgotten purpose, swinging back fast, leaving us off-balance, slumped to the floor.

In awe, we stared at what lay beyond.

"Heaven be a place on Earth!"

"Praise be on high!"

But it was no church, at least not the religious sort.

Beyond the mystery door lay a spit-n-sawdust bar, replete with reggae music, Red Stripe beer, and fifty shades of rum. Open to the elements, it was squeezed between two dockside buildings, clearly built to mop up tips earned by the neighbourhood's deck-hand workforce.

My liver winced.

There was only one appropriate course of action; I jumped into an office chair, slouched back, and uttered five magical words I'd repeat with alarming regularity over the coming months:

"Two rum punches please, barman."

Mystery solved, drinks in hand, it was time to get back to business. The books required attention. There's little need to go into the minutiae of that onerous day, so I'll make it easy, I'll go '80s:

Picture a montage of Sarah and me flipping through financial information, paperwork stacking up – Dolly Parton's '9 to 5' blasting in the background – us taking a break, jumping in the sea, being shouted at for swimming in the wrong place, laughing with a fisherman at our mistake, him pointing at an urchin sting on my foot, horror on my face, me running around like Benny Hill, then back at work, the boat returning, darkness falling, studying under smoky light, the pile of books shrinking, and finally us high-fiving, 'Eye of the Tiger' scoring the moment.

An '80s montage: tough times for dummies.

On the upside, the books were in order, except for one issue: the crew were being paid a fraction too much, without clear reason. It was an error I wanted to remedy fast, so the following day I informed the bank to lower future payments, so setting in motion events that would lead to my first – and most terrifying – lesson in small business management.

"WHAT THE FUCK HAVE YOU DONE?!!!"

"I, er… What's up, Sharon?"

I knew what was up.

Or down, as the case happened to be.

"Where's my FUCKING SALARY?!!!"

"Well…"

"What's THE FIRST RULE of management, Charlie?"

"I, er…"

"YOU DON'T FUCK WITH SALARIES!!"

"Sure, but…"

"You've cut my FUCKING PAY PACKET!!"

She was right. We had. But it was higher than her contracted amount.

"The thing is, Sharon…"

"The THING is?"

"The THING is," I mimicked. "We did THE SUMS!"

"Oh, you did THE SUMS?!"

Then Sarah spoke, calming a tone that was plummeting into the farcical.

"We did the numbers," she said, "and noted the crew were being paid more than the company was supposed to pay them, so docked a small portion this month to cover the error. That's all. No harm intended."

Sarah's cool, confident approach pulled us back from the brink.

"Why didn't you tell us?" asked Sharon. "You should have just told us. And I'd have told you that we were on higher amounts because new contracts were agreed but never drawn up. You can check with Steve."

"We'll check and reset things if that's the case," Sarah replied, adding, "sorry to have caused a panic."

"That's fine, just check with me in future."

And with that Sharon swept from the office, leaving behind an obvious message for management students worldwide:

You don't fuck with salaries.

Having checked with Steve, cleared the issue, and re-informed the bank, we took lunch at the water's edge, erasing the day's stress with a glorious vista of gently bobbing yachts and cotton-ball clouds. Even after such a confrontational experience, I felt content, revelling in my tropical challenge. As I dug into the local dish of jerk chicken, plantain, beans, and rice, I couldn't help but compare my workday to my friends' lives, wondering where they were at that very moment, five hours ahead, on an average afternoon in the city of cities, the frenetic global epicentre of commerce and culture that is London.

Mostly they were nearing another commute home, sofa-bound, having already banked four-to-five years of traditional career time, and mostly they were fairly-to-extremely discontent. At the other end of the spectrum, I was working on a Caribbean island, living on board a booze cruiser, and yet, as idyllic as that setting may have been, something still irked me.

It was a question, a rather premature question:

Am I too old for this?

Action movie stars have toyed with this quandary for decades (usually while brandishing an AK47, jumping from a burning helicopter), but it tends to come as a statement – "I'm too old for this shit!!" – and is generally said because the star very much is 'too old for this shit', boasting more wrinkles than a cadaver's foreskin, on more drugs than a Tour de France cyclist.

But was I 'too old for this shit'?

At twenty-six it could hardly be said that anyone's too old for anything, but there were still people questioning my Caribbean stint, throwing out sucker-punch hints before I'd even stepped foot in the tropics:

"Edward just got a job with Mega-Wealth Bank running their 'Bag-a-Tycoon' department… he's on at least six figures…"

"Julie's a brain surgeon at St Bart's, saving lives, producing angels from her backside…"

"Dave's just opened a terrific gastro-pub, with plans for three more in Richmond, Bath, and Gentrified-Upon-Tyne…"

"So, you're going to run a booze cruise boat in the Caribbean? How… different… That's nice. Well done you… well… done… you…"

With "well done you" ringing in my ears, I began to question why there's so much pressure to join the nine-to-five crowd. *Why the intense need to conform?* And then, as I sat there picking jerk chicken from between my teeth, it hit me.

Being part of the system isn't about conformity.

It's about staying on par.

Put another way, you look like a bit of a sad act when the people you left school with are in charge of entire departments, while you're taking orders from a guy who can barely shave; but that's the downside to veering off the approved path. So be it. You make your choices. You live with them.

Fortunately my mother encouraged travel. She never laid down demands, which is to her credit, as it couldn't have been easy hearing endless offspring success stories, only to inform the group her son's latest achievement has been to break open a mystery door in his Caribbean booze cruise office, providing one-step access to a dockside rum bar.

Thump!

Thump!!

Thump!!!

The noise shook me back to the day. It was Sarah, knocking on her desk, having noted I was daydreaming into troubled waters.

"You want a re-fill?" she asked.

"I sure do."

What the hell was I doing?

There are times to be reflective and there are times to just be; this was a time to just be. Of course I wasn't 'too old for this shit'; I just needed to have the courage of my convictions. That's not to say you should never question your choices, but if you find yourself on a three-month working holiday, there's little need to examine the details; just throw yourself into the day-to-day.

And what a day-to-day it was.

During the high season, the population of St Thomas swells daily, a symptom of having the second busiest cruise ship terminal in the

Caribbean, accommodating up to three gargantuan vessels back-to-back. Two more can dock at a nearby port specifically designed for the biggest leviathans of the industry, and in peak periods others just weigh anchor, all of them dumping thousands of holidaymakers on to the roads and beaches of the 80km-squared landmass.

Heading straight into the heart of the terminal, pulling up beside those behemoths of pleasure, *The Olivia II* would have a daily appointment with around 120 passengers, mostly American, some of whom could be counted as two, if not three people. Relying on cruise ship staff to direct their sleepy guests to our sturdy gangplank, we'd soon be ready to depart, as punters slapped on sunscreen, or bagged a shady corner to help them survive the rising mercury. After a headcount, lines would be thrown, and the skipper would ease out, following his tried and tested route into deeper waters.

It was a well-oiled machine topside, but below deck things were a different matter, as ageing pistons and moribund mechanisms ground into action, many of them massaged to life that very morning by our mechanic, Kyle, a miracle worker able to keep *The Olivia II* running when many would have consigned her to the scrapheap. Assisted by WD40, and a lot of TLC, out to work she'd sail, securing crucial earnings for another day.

Usually a simple business formula is key to success, and *The Olivia II* was no different: collect hedonistic tourists; transport to picture-postcard beach; supply snorkelling gear; leave to paddle and sunbathe; scoop up; offer bottomless jugs of rum punch; return to cruise ships merry and tanned; collect tips.

And at the end of one such afternoon a realisation suddenly, in double-vision, smacked me between the eyes: *We* are *running a successful operation, doing exactly what we set out to do.* The Olivia II is *a success, a beacon for all who would try and turn a profit in the tropics.*

We're legends.

We're champions.

"We're screwed."

As my hangover reached its climax, Kyle showed no mercy, listing off the boat's latest mechanical failure: "Your Thingy McNeedle has worn through," I could swear he said, adding, "I'll need to order the part now. It'll take about a week to arrive, costing four or five thousand bucks."

His words kicked me into a higher gear of pain.

"Urggggggggggggggggghhhhhhhhhhh…"

"Say what?"

"We're screwed."

"Yep, tell me something I don't know."

Grandiose visions of booze cruise leadership vaporised. Regardless of our best efforts to improve her bottom line, the ship was hamstrung by an insurmountable problem: her age. Every time we thought profits looked positive, a tiny 'Thingy McNeedle' would break, gouging the current account.

It was a sorry state of affairs, yet Sarah and I weren't management consultants parachuted in to save a business, we were film graduates sent to keep it ticking over. And so that's what we did, plugging profits into maintenance, keeping *The Olivia II* afloat to the end of our stint in St Thomas.

As our time on-island neared expiry, Steve told us he'd lined up a skilled manager to take control. It bode well for the business, but a return to reality for us. Three months of babysitting the boat were over. Our postponed move to LA was back in focus, back topping the agenda.

It could wait no more.

Before we knew it, our departure tickets had been booked, and the clock was ticking. Soon enough we'd be the ones dumping three hours of corporate frustration on to the next guy, after which we'd be free to hit the road.

But where would that road lead?

Although my long-awaited papers were still pending – background checks taking far longer than expected – we decided to continue on to LA. We'd do it in reverse, sorting paperwork once in mainland America. We had no idea if it would work, but figured taking action *had* to be better than wasting time.

As we packed bags to leave *The Olivia II*, Sarah and I were seemingly on the same page, prepared for what lay ahead, yet 'seemingly' hid a whole world of anxiety. The enormity of what we were about to do was becoming clearer by the minute: we were about to depart our tropical playground for a momentous event, hurtling headfirst towards one of the most serious, life-defining, life-changing experiences two people can share.

This shit was real.

Ladies and gentlemen, please fasten your seatbelts.

We're expecting turbulent air.

JOB TEN: CARIBBEAN BOOZE CRUISE MANAGER

Lessons learnt:

- There's very little that averagely intelligent human beings can't accomplish
- Pinching the inside of your thigh keeps the body awake, not the mind
- You don't fuck with salaries
- You may have discord with your team, but once grievances are aired and solved, peace *can* exist. Following the salary issue, Sharon and I put it behind us. She was integral to keeping *The Olivia II* afloat, teaching me that management is a learning curve; errors will be made – be sure to fix them fast
- You're not too old for anything at twenty-six (or thirty-six, or even forty-six, but any later and you might want to avoid Turkish oil wrestling)
- People will always question unusual decisions; to take the path less travelled you need to be confident, ignoring the naysayers, focusing on the upsides
- Detours are detours – after a while the original plan will be back on track, with all its pros and cons still firmly in play

CHAPTER TWENTY

Fade up.
'A LIFE IN LOS ANGELES NEVER TOOK PLACE'
Fade out.

That has to be the most irritating way to start a story.

Revealing the outcome of a tale at its beginning is infuriating. It's criminal. It should be banned. In North Korea it probably is. And yet filmmakers occasionally do it, showing part or all of a story's climax straight after the opening credits; oh, sure, they'll throw in a twist in the final minutes, but by that point the 'surprise' is so blindingly obvious the kid in the back row crawling down his girlfriend's oesophagus has already figured it out and got back to business.

So why do I hate this format?

You need tension. You need drama. You need conflict. But most of all, you need a story to keep you on edge, right to the bitter end.

With that in mind, I apologise for the reveal at the top of this chapter; it pained me to adopt the very style I loathe, but I knew I had to, as the implosion of two people's lives shouldn't be treated like a Mills & Boon tale. On top of which, there's little to tell: after departing the Caribbean, all that followed was a short flight to New York, and an interminable drive over the rutted interstates of Middle America, listening to audiobooks all the way to California's 'City of Angels'.

And then, on arrival, second thoughts.

After much pleading from family and friends to carefully consider the ramifications of taking what would be an irreversible step, we delved back into the US immigration system, deeper this time, seeking a complete, all-angles picture of what lay ahead. After poring over web forums, government advice, and horror-story news reports, it gradually became clear that a marriage of convenience isn't just frowned upon, it can land you in deep water.

As in deep, jail-time water.

We were probably in trouble for even considering it, as that's how twitchy governments can be about people trying to beat the system, and as website after website confirmed our plan's inconvenient truth, the penny dropped, bounced back up, and smacked us between the eyes...

We'd reached that point.

The end of the road.

There's little point going into greater detail about our time in LA; it can be summed up as two people drinking box wine, browsing websites written by the been-there-done-that crowd. In a city famed for its drama, comedy, horror, romance, action and adventure, I can't offer anything more than a French art-house production filled with moody conversations and disappointed faces. We should have been wearing berets; we weren't. We weren't even in a smoky bistro.

What I can offer is a picture of unadulterated frustration, not the teenage sort, but the 'we-came-a-long-way-for-nothing' sort. We were two soft-skinned twenty-somethings unwilling to spend years playing cat-and-mouse with an unforgiving, vengeful government. Many may try, but we weren't built for that kind of battle, or the pressure it would put on our friendship.

We knew there were legal ways for me to work in the US, but I was back to the 'Canadian conundrum': that no company would bother applying for a work visa for someone at my junior level, especially not in such a competitive industry.

The outcome was too obvious.

It truly was the end.

Sarah could have stayed in LA, but she wanted to return to New York, so we booked a ticket to London for me, a ticket to

New York for Sarah, and with that, the dream was over. My career wasn't to flourish in Los Angeles. Sarah and I weren't to be bound by a shared journey. Far better we part company, and seek an alternate route; far better we take a step back, and do things the right way.

It wouldn't be easy, but it was how it had to be.

And apologies to all, for there is no twist. Real life rarely has them. We were two people who needed to stop swimming against the current.

For the current had won.

NYC TO LA: REALITY BITES

Lesson learnt:

•   If it feels as though you're swimming against the current, and you're being told by people that you trust that you're swimming against the current, and deep down you know it's foolish to fight the current, then at some point you'll realise you need to about-turn and swim *with* the current

CHAPTER TWENTY-ONE

"PUT YOUR FUCKING BACK INTO IT!!"

London.

"ARE YOU MAN OR BOY??"

September 2005.

"YOU CAN LIFT MORE THAN THAT!!!"

He was right. I could; so I stopped, turned, and grabbed another vicious load, lugging the rubble mere millimetres off the ground.

"YAAAAAAAAAAAAAAARRRGGGGHHHH!!"

Reality hurt.

Really fucking hurt.

But I liked it.

The pain of manual labour echoed the state of my London return. It was as palpable as a punch to the face, a blow to the gut.

The effort was excessive. Unnecessary. Masochistic. But I wanted it. I needed it. The pain beat back self-pity. It occupied the mind. It was punishment, reparation, and escape in a simple, repetitive task. It was a daily reminder of our LA volte-face, yet also release from that very same fiasco.

And at the end of the day it was a job, a way to stay busy, an honest day's work. It was all I deserved, all I could justify, so I dumped the leaden sacks, swung round, and marched back for more.

Hubris, n. *In ancient Greece: The sin of thinking you are above the gods, or forgetting to give them credit when they have helped you. Of course they don't tell you when they help you, you are just supposed to know. Committing hubris ALWAYS leads to nemesis, the gods' punishment.* (urbandictionary.com)

And so it came to pass that once again I'd fallen foul of the age-old vice of hubris – having believed, fleetingly, that I could beat the system – and due to unforgiving, righteous wisdom, the gods did vent their fury, dishing out the most ancient of ancient punishments, that of manual labour.

Yet I was enduring manual labour with a most modern twist: shifting junk, rubbish, and rubble for a newly-formed dot-com business, sorting it to be recycled, or eternally condemned to a distant landfill. In other, less obfuscating words, I had become… a bin man.

"We're all in the gutter, but some of us are looking at the stars," Oscar Wilde once quipped; well, I was firmly in the gutter, not a star in sight. It wasn't Plan A, or even Plan Z, but being a bin man was where I'd landed, where I had to be.

Nature – nay, hubris – demanded it.

There'd be no fanfare, no welcome home party. There'd be no picking up of pieces, no throwing myself back in the rat race. There was just a need to find a hole, and bury myself deep within it.

With Sarah and I having parted ways, beaten by borders and a menacing system, we were set adrift, two become none. And with our move in tatters, sails torn to shreds, I'd given up, unsure where to turn. Fortunately for the rudderless and dissolute, there's almost always a port in a storm, but nomad beware: while some offer thick harbour walls, five-star comfort, and free HBO, others barely offer calm water, let alone star-studded entertainment. At best you'll get intermittent CNN, *en Español*, with a side order of scurvy.

Yet in September 2005 any port would do. A storm was raging; I needed safe haven. If he'd let me drop anchor, I cared little if the harbour master demand I shift junk, lug rubble, sort rubbish, or wear a polka-dot bikini to accompany him for a night-in watching box sets of *Glee*.

And so as 'Don't Cha' by The Pussycat Dolls topped UK music charts; as film fans unwound to Keira Knightley in *Pride and Prejudice*; and as coalition troops rolled tanks across Iraq and Afghanistan, so I donned a bright yellow uniform, steel-capped boots, and worn-through leather gloves, picked up the day's duty list, jumped in a refuse truck, and went to work.

Hubris couldn't have been happier.

And yet landing at the bottom rung of society's ladder didn't irritate me half as much as I'd expected.

Trailing my time in the US by becoming a 'Truck Team Member' for Clear Your Junk should have been the final blow, the end of times, the moment when all hope is lost, but it was far from it. Instead, it was a break from my pursuit of pinstriped success, and an unexpected shield, because on hearing of my newfound career status Londoners were left staring at their feet, unsure what to say.

"You've become a… professional waste merchant?"

"No, a bin man."

"A professional waste…"

"No, a bin man."

"Er, well, that's… so… er…"

There's only so much pity that can be dealt out in any given year; only so many times people can hear woeful tales. I'd be told to, "hang in there," or that, "things happen for a reason," and then the person would disappear off, moving faster than a social climber spotting minor royalty.

It was a revelation.

I'd found career kryptonite, a sure-fire way of being left alone, of being able to deal with my return, minus the intrigue and drama.

And best of all, I didn't have to swallow my pride.

I had none left.

On returning home I didn't dare look for work in the film industry. The LA experience had seen my career aspirations stagnate within a matter of weeks, leaving a gaping hole in my confidence. The pinstriped dream lived on, but it was a fallen star, shamed by a box office flop. It needed to rest and recuperate, hopefully reviving its status after a break from the limelight.

And so I shifted junk, trying to forget the past, trying to avoid the future. It was tough, backbreaking, often putrid work… but it was work.

At first I prayed nobody I knew would see me, but after a few days I relaxed into it, and as the weeks rolled by I began to wonder why society looks down on those tasked with removing our waste. It may not demand a university qualification, but it's an important part of keeping our cities clean, and as far as varied work goes, I couldn't have asked for more.

One moment we'd be at a building site shifting sacks of rubble, the next we'd be at a derelict house emptying a rotten cellar, then at a condemned pub clearing out coagulated kitchen fat, crawling over rat droppings, reaching for a blockage… okay, on second thoughts, it wasn't quite the dream job.

I still can't walk past a skip, wheelie bin, or rubbish truck without fetid memories flooding back. One whiff of month-old milk and I'm thrust back to those noxious days clearing out a dead person's possessions. One waft of a dump truck's pervasive odour and I'm back at the wheel, windows open, gasping for air. One sight of a writhing maggot and I'm catapulted back to an afternoon emptying infested cupboards at a court-ordered flat clearance.

London was showing her pestilential core.

At heart, she's a filthy bitch.

On the upside, I was now plumbed into the glorious world of the 'white van man', and after a month within his gang my mood began to lift. Little did I know that to be welcomed into his fold is a badge of honour. They're a much-derided group of wolf-whistling gents, but as part of their clan you realise why they lean out of vans whooping at passers-by.

It's the call of the wild, a celebration of freedom.

I used to think it was something to do with peer pressure, a lack of brainpower, or an overabundance of testosterone, but having had the privilege to walk in their fine, Adidas-logo'd shoes, I now know the truth.

They (*mostly*) love their work.

There they are, cruising the city, maxed-out radios piercing the concrete jungle, meeting divorcees, singletons, retirees, and students – visiting between "nine and two, but no promises, guv" – all of whom they help for a special rate, cash in hand. It's freedom, variety, business, and pleasure. No wonder they're wolf-whistling at passers-by. They're marking their territory, revelling in the job.

It comes back to that crucial point: happiness leads to success.

The discovery that white van men like, even love, their work was a relief, as it meant being surrounded by relatively happy people. It made the junk job not just a port in a storm, but a comfortable refuge. It made settling back into London a breeze (albeit a rather pungent one).

One day we even ended up at the house of Rachel Stevens, a singer from teen pop band S Club 7, who at the time I thought to be the prettiest woman on Earth. It was surreal to be shifting her junk, but I did it with a smile, turning ever-so peachy whenever she looked my way.

And so as the weeks rolled by, my confidence grew. I was on the mend, the LA flop fading to a closed chapter. Self-esteem stretched, rising from a deep hibernation. After a few more months I knew I'd be ready to tackle the rat race, ready to put film back in my sights, ready to fight the good fight. Self-esteem would be fully awake; I'd be primed for victory, but...

...as the saying goes, 'Man plans and God laughs', and as I planned, far on high a thunderous chortle erupted, which could only mean one thing...

...crack...

...crunch...

"FUUUUUCKKKKKKKK!!!!!!"

Everyone in the business knows you should lift with your legs, not with your back. I knew I should lift with my legs, not with my back, but after almost four months in the job on a cold December day, shifting rubble from a sodden pile of construction waste, I played it fast and loose. I broke the rules.

I lifted with my back.

It was foolish; no genuine white van man would have done it, but I was a novice, not even able to wolf whistle, so in a split second of stupidity my life as a Truck Team Member was over.

It was a back injury that pulled me out of the beautiful waste business, but it was a timely accident, needed to extricate me from a career change that was rapidly becoming all too comfortable.

Following the bad lift, a doctor's visit, advice to quit, my resignation, and a much-hobbled festive season, it came time to plot new coordinates. The junk job had been a refuge in a storm, but the storm was over. After four months of shifting shit, followed by several weeks laid up, I'd had time to gather my thoughts, pick up the pieces, and re-grow my balls.

The wisdom is that, 'a ship in port is safe, but that's not what ships are built for'. My grimy harbour had kept me safe, but it was no longer needed. It was time to weigh anchor. Raise the mainsail.

And take her out to sea.

JOB ELEVEN: TRUCK TEAM MEMBER

Lessons learnt:

- Committing hubris *always* leads to nemesis
- It appears that in return for safe harbour I'd be willing to don a bikini and watch back-to-back episodes of *Glee*
- Career kryptonite is a useful weapon
- White van men are some of the happiest people around, but wolf-whistling should probably stop. Just pee on a lamp post
- When the weather clears, it's time to once again set sail

CHAPTER TWENTY-TWO

We wish you a merry Christmas,
We wish you a merry Christmas,
We wish you a merry Christmas,
And a fuuuu-cking sore back.
Happy New Year, asshole.

Guzzling prescription pills, I winced at the coming months, praying for a foothold, for stability, praying to grasp the ladder and never let go.

They say January is the best time to job hunt. Those unhappy at work wake on the first of the month with steely resolve to improve their lot, so resign, freeing up space, creating movement in the market. That movement is evidenced by a surge in vacancies, jobs that pop up across the web, and that activity attracts vultures, circling, waiting for their chance to feed.

Swooping high and low, scanning the savannah, my search was refined, efficient, targeted, and it didn't take long to spot a fresh kill.

The sighting took place in mid-January, on perusing mandy. com, the ultimate stalwart of the media industry's lo/no pay sector. It may sound like a porn site, but rather than offering cheap titillation, it seeks cheap labour. As usual I skimmed it fast, expecting little of use, but halfway down I suddenly stopped, taken aback by a previously unseen posting.

What is this imposter?

I backed up, slowed down, and re-read.

The ad detailed an opening for crew on a London-based feature film, with those hired needed to raise finance during pre-production. As with most listings I looked closer, studying the fine print. I noted it was paid, tick; noted they were taking people at entry level, tick; noted the start date was within a week, tick; noted I had the requisite skills. TICK.

I sat bolt upright, yelling out, my back still not fully recovered. I tried again, easing up, and then re-scanned the text, checking for traps.

Am I missing something?

It seemed too good to be true, an ideal match. I was fascinated by film finance, loved the creative arts, and wanted to combine the two. An application was duly dispatched. Knowing the stiff level of competition in the film industry I wasn't holding my breath, but I still prayed something would come of it.

Literally.

I knelt down and prayed to the Lord of Career. Admittedly I may have tumbled over, floored by back-related pain, but the bottom line is that I was on my knees, face to the heavens, begging for divine intervention.

Dear Lord of Career, Alan Sugar, and every gatekeeper across the world, hear my prayer. Please, I don't ask for much, but I'm running on fumes. Gimme a break. All I want is a good job in the world's most alluring industry. Is that too much to ask? For Christ's sake, show me some goddam love…

Spiritual, I know.

And so imagine my surprise when I received a reply, not a month later, not a week later, but that very day. Assuming it to be an automated email I ignored it, at first, but curiosity piqued my interest, forcing me to click it open, and once done I proceeded to stare dumbfounded at the words before me.

It was personal. It was positive.

I'd actually received a 'we're interested' email from a London production company. Immediately the trip to Canada, the wait, the return, the film school, the Toronto freeze, the *Taxi* air fresheners, the Caribbean stint, the LA U-turn, the junk-humping… all morphed into one ecstatic phrase:

'Worth it.'

The email was an offer to interview for the position of Assistant

Producer on a feature-length movie, working initially within a film finance team. *Wow.* There was literally nothing in that description that didn't make me want to drool. I responded eagerly, but not too eagerly, pausing an hour before punching out a reply.

Pausing is a tactic often used in the dating world, but in that environment you triple the amount of wait-time, and never use the word 'keen'. But I was keen, oh so very keen, as thousands are who search for media jobs every day, drawn to varied days and abundant creativity. I knew the job sounded promising, but I also knew to proceed with equal amounts of enthusiasm and scepticism.

Unsurprisingly, by this stage in my career I'd amassed a colossal warehouse of scepticism, yet the force of hope was alive and well, hanging around like a Labrador at a toddler's birthday party, hoping a treat will come its way, even if it means eating gob-smeared cake off the feet of three-year-olds.

And seeing as hope is the strongest force of all, I licked my lips, wagged my tail, and one week later leapt on board the Tube to north London, hoping to re-invigorate my comatose career.

Feed me, kids.

Drop gob-smeared cake.

Just give me a goddam job.

Sweaty palms. Polished shoes. Nervous smiles.

It could only be interview day.

As with most interviews, it began the usual way – cordial, polite, efficient – yet on heading home I realised that something was off.

Even with Blind Career Obsession I could sense it.

Subconscious alarm bells had been tinkling away from the moment the meeting began, but I paid them no heed, focused only on securing the job. And so I ignored the interviewer's lack of interest in my CV; I ignored the state of his threadbare office; I ignored his awkward smile.

I shut it all out.

This was 'next step' day.

On finding his converted loft space, I'd met Tony – producer, interviewer, and company owner – who'd told me he was hiring a small team to work on his next film. He needed a group he could rely on to raise finance, as his time would be split finishing another project; once the money was in place, we'd then assist him producing his next film, taking plum jobs from script-to-screen.

He assured me it would be a busy schedule in a creative setting, somewhere I could latch on to Britain's film ladder, ensuring an upwards climb. Delusional dreams of working in an LA studio were replaced with realistic goals of impressing in a tenacious London outfit. All I needed to do was shine in the interview, and seeing as I had my foot through the door, confidence was high.

It was a new year.

The gods were smiling.

Once underway, I operated on autopilot, being the person I now knew a film producer would want to hire.

"How much did you learn on your film course in Canada?" he asked.

"Every facet of filmmaking."

"Great, great… have you worked on any features?"

"Yes, but not for a while."

"Great, great… are you comfortable talking to people on the phone?"

"Very much so. I've grown up with the technology."

My last answer wasn't quite so blunt, but it was something along those lines – "Yes, I'm very good at talking to people…" – which received another "Great, great," response. It seemed an odd question, but I didn't challenge it, my autopilot intent on delivering a smooth ride.

Create no waves. Win the day.

And with that mindset guiding me, nothing was a problem. Tony must have had similar programming, as the interview was tantamount to synchronised skating, the two of us spinning to a perfect finish. Considering our performance, it didn't surprise me one bit when Tony came straight out and asked me to return for training the following Monday, training that would likely lead to a full-time job.

I didn't bat an eyelid.

Or ruffle my sequins.

It seemed a natural progression after such a killer interview. A new chapter lay ahead. I had an *actual* start date, at an *actual* production company, where I'd work on an *actual* film. All along this is how I'd wanted career to behave: an application, an interview, an offer, and the pinstriped goal drawing ever closer.

It should have been a moment of unparalleled joy, but I left with a pragmatic feeling of having achieved what I'd set out to do. There was no skip in my step, just a sense of having ticked the box.

It wasn't until riding the Tube home that I reflected on why I hadn't skipped down the street, and in so doing began to analyse the finer details of the interview. I knew something was off... but what?

After seven minutes of penetrating thought, scrutinising every word and line Tony had ventured, the truth hit me: it had been *way* too easy.

Looking back, I could have said anything and been offered a job. I could have walked in shouting profanities, carrying Tony's wife in my arms, naked, upside down, as she performed acts illegal in several nations, and he'd still have offered me a job. That was one concern, but in examining the interview further, another issue emerged. It was something he'd mentioned several times, but in muffled tones, in a way that suggested he had to say it, but didn't want to.

It was summed up by one specific word: scheme.

It swirled around the carriage, as if whispered by all aboard. I knew it was a dirty word, associated with Ponzis and dodgy developers, but it was hard for Tony to gloss over it, the 'scheme' being central to his film-financing plan. To a novice it sounded like it *could* be a good idea, but at the same time sounded like it *could* be tantamount to robbing an old lady in an underpass.

The word referred to the Enterprise Investment Scheme, a government-approved way for businesses to raise money. These days I'm clued up as to how it works, knowing it covers a variety of investments, such as putting your money into new wind farms, retirement homes, or even low budget film productions. Usually the investments are worth doing, but as with any sector, cowboys lurk.

Having just met the man it was impossible to know if Tony was businessman or cowboy. All I knew was that the word 'scheme' carried concern, but I figured that I wasn't yet in a position to judge if it was too good to be true, a decent way to raise money, or a barefaced scam. The only way would be to work it out from within the company, grabbing the bull by the horns.

Decision made, I could ignore those *damned* alarm bells, for now, but they hadn't been silenced; time would tell, but I felt able to enjoy the moment, so exited the Tube, tail wagging fast.

"Hello madam, can I have a moment of your…"

Slam.

Beeeeeeeeeeep.

I checked my list. Sixth rejection of the day. A hundred and eighty calls to go. Thoughts of jumping on train tracks weren't easily dismissed.

I glanced over the script: *Hello sir, can I have a moment of your time, I'm looking to see if I can help you save tax, and help the British film industry at the same time… Yes, it is intriguing… Well, the first thing to know is that this is a government-backed project…*

I groaned, partly because I'd written the script, partly because I loathed delivering it, but mostly because – when they didn't slam down the receiver – I'd become remarkably successful at parting people from their hard-earned money. I felt like a Bernie Madoff Oompa Loompa. I was his Ponzi underling, rolling Violet Beauregarde to the de-juicing room, as fat cats Wonka and Madoff high-fived each other, tossing dwarfs into the chocolate river.

And just like Wonka's minions, I was part of the problem, assisting in a golden ticket scam, willing to do anything to make it work.

Well, almost anything.

"Hold on a moment, dear," said the next number. "I'll take a seat and listen to you properly." The elderly and lonely would always offer an ear.

"Oooooh, that sounds like a lovely project, pet," she said, after I ran her through the scheme. "And I love British films. My grandson, Peter, is working for a film company in central London. Do you know him?"

"I might well do," I said, "but it's a big city." I imagined Peter happily meeting me in a dark alley with a baseball bat.

"How much do you need, dear?" she asked. "I can send you five pounds in the post. Will that help?"

Pangs of utter self-loathing.

"There's really no need. Thank you so much for your time. I don't think this will be right for you."

"Okay dear," she said, "well, I hope you make a fine film."

I hoped so too, but not with her fiver. There I drew the line. This scheme was for people with spare cash, not grandmothers scraping by on winter fuel allowance. At least that's what I thought, but to be honest I didn't really know what we were doing; I knew those damned alarm bells were still ringing, but I'd managed to build a defensive wall around them, thirty-foot-high, six-foot-thick.

During the short training period Tony had given five of us newbies a briefing as to the company, the film, and the scheme, which had come across as a better proposition than I'd initially feared. Our new boss, dressed in black suit and matching tie – looking part-media tycoon, part-undertaker – ran the team through the project, using a white board to explain its finer points.

Day one had started with a commute across London, via Clapham Junction, Victoria, and Euston, so I was glad to be in the warmth of Tony's office, intrigued to find out more about his film financing plan. (I wasn't yet calling it a 'scheme' in an attempt to keep an open mind; in an attempt to stay positive.)

"Right," said Tony, in a chirpy, tour guide manner, "the scheme works like this... oh, wait, let me start with the film we're raising money for..."

The way he added in the film as an afterthought was a worry, but I gave him the benefit of the doubt, assuming he was a producer focused on funding first, production second, because without money, there is no film.

"The project is called *Ulrika's Secret*," he continued. "It's a romantic murder-mystery set in London and Brighton."

Hmmmmm, guess that'll work, thought I. Sounds plausible. Not exactly the action-adventure blockbuster I was hoping for, but potentially a story that could sell tickets. Who was starring, was the next obvious question.

"No star attached yet, but we hope to book Elisha Cuthbert."

And I hope to shit diamonds.

"It's going to be a really exciting project, but we're behind schedule, and we need to raise at least fifty grand in order to get going."

He eyed us up, flashing a wide grin.

"That's where you come in."

"We'll be working on the film once it's funded, won't we?" asked one of my fresh-faced colleagues.

"Of course, of course. Once we have enough money we'll go into production, and you guys will assist in making it."

That got our attention.

"How long do you think it'll take to raise the money?"

"That's up to you guys. I've raised three hundred grand, so it's just a hundred extra we need, then we can get cracking. I'd hit the phones myself, but I need to finish my last project. There's re-shoots needed, and..."

"Hit the phones?" asked a confident co-worker, mimicking the exact query I feared to ask.

I could tell Tony was irked.

"That's the… only way. It works like this…"

He went on to explain the Enterprise Investment Scheme, which took a while, so I'll stick to the highlights:

The 'scheme' is essentially a way for people to limit their tax bill. Interested parties invest a lump sum in an approved project, such as a lugubrious British feature film, and the government lets them take thirty per cent of the amount invested off their income tax bill. It should be a win-win. The 'schemes' lead to productivity, as well as people – read myself and esteemed colleagues – finding jobs, helping drive the economy, generating taxable income. And the investment, in theory, provides a solid return, potentially leaving the investor twice up on the deal.

On paper it seemed like a no-brainer.

When calling the forty-eighth octogenarian of the day it seemed far from it. The only way to survive the experience was to play Phone God, pretending to be all-powerful, judging who'd be passed over, and who'd be squeezed to the max:

"Helllllllllo, Brigadier General Jones here, this is a listed number, my man, just who do you think you are calling me…"

Squeeze.

"Yeah, 'ello who's that? Come on, chummly, I ain't got all day, I gotta get to Geneva for a meeting…"

Squeeze.

"Oh my gosh, that's like totally amazeballs… oh, so sorry, hello there caller, Tara speaking!"

Squeeze.

"Oh, how nice to have a sweet young person call me at this time of day… now, what might be the nature of this call?"

Pass.

Unless it's followed by, "Well, dear, before you start, I must say your generation's a disaster, and if you think I need help with my taxes, well, young man, I could teach you a few things about saving money…"

Squeeze.

It's important to keep cold-calling flexible; know when to turn a pass into a squeeze; know when to walk away. Some calls will work, some will be as successful as an obese Internet dater using a swimwear model's photo – it'll never get the desired result, but top marks for trying.

Overall, though, database phone lists are disturbingly efficient at picking out high net worth individuals who'll listen to a pitch and dig deep. The chance to legally keep money from the government is as tantalising to most people as high-end hookers are to Gulf billionaires, so for many the hard sell was over the moment they'd heard the words "save you tax". One mention of the word "minimise" and you're off to the races; throw in "potential profit" and you've sealed the deal.

The scary thing about cold calling is that you don't know how good you are until you try it. Turns out I could sell dikes to the Dutch, but only over the phone. There's a confidence I have in telesales that I lose in person. It's obvious why. On the phone I can sound like Roger Moore. In person, I can't.

Of course in life you work with what you're given, so I put Roger to use, unearthing investors across the country, calling homes from Abbots Langley to Zouch. Every day I enthused, complimented, and cajoled, pushing myself to pole position for monies raised, bit between the teeth, eyes on the prize.

I soon discovered that with an ambitious team, mountains can be moved, including the feat of raising £100,000 within five weeks, but that's the magic of ambition; it can be blind, greedy, and callous, driving a team to dial 15,000 numbers, milk the market, and meet their targets.

Tony knew all too well what fuelled our fire, using a small group of hungry media grunts to do his bidding. We were an eclectic team, hailing from across Europe, all in our mid-twenties, all desperate to notch media success. Ambition wasn't just alive, it was rabid, and with our target hit, electricity tinged the air.

Phone-jockeying was done.

Production could begin.

A multicoloured bar chart on the office wall had been tracking our progress to £100,000. The top line, ink still wet, had been diligently filled in, with little fireworks scribbled all around to emphasise our landmark achievement. We proudly sat under it, discussing the next step.

"Thanks for all your hard work," said Tony, ogling the chart.

"You've done well, really well," he added, smirking a touch. "There's a slight glitch, though. We need to push production back a bit."

Alarm bells.

Those damned alarm bells.

"Huh?"

"Yep, we're, er, still a bit short. I need you guys to raise a touch more."

"What? When are we going into production?"

"It's not clear," he said, "but keep fundraising. We're almost there. We start soon. We just need a bit extra. The strong economy means production costs are spiralling. Help me help you. Raise just another thirty grand, then we'll be there. It won't take long at your current rate. In the meantime, I'm making final touches to my last project. It's all go!"

And with that he grabbed his briefcase, making a sharp exit.

Never assume anything.

A rage rose inside me. Back to the phones to source more cash was what Tony wanted; to impale him over a bed of hot coals was what I wanted. It seemed like an obvious step, but what to do?

The team met to mull options.

"Impale him over a bed of hot coals," said Janet. I nodded my approval, noting she had a look in her eye suggesting she might actually own a spear and a fine selection of combustibles.

"Mass resignation," suggested Pete.

"To go where?" I asked.

Silence spoke volumes.

It's a well-known situation: stalemate. The employer has the employee over a barrel, but needs something out of the employee. The employee wants something out of the employer, isn't getting it, but has invested too much time to quit.

Big stalemate.

Like the least dramatic version of a Mexican standoff, replacing guns with office phones, cowboys with media grunts, we were at High Noon, handsets at the ready, knowing that if anyone flinched we'd all take a receiver to the chest.

The phrase I love to hate came back to bite me: "Whatever doesn't kill you makes you stronger." Bullshit. The media industry was killing me slowly, killing me from the outside in; and every time it smacked me down I'd ask myself, *how many more times can I summon the energy to tackle the same old problem?*

Tony's request for us to continue fundraising had come at the end of a long line of setbacks, leaving me bitter and confused. I was far from storming into his home, knife in hand, but dark thoughts vexed my scorned mind.

Where was I on the scale of white-collar psychos? Would a rampage come at the next setback? Could I stop it in time? I shrugged, unsure, indifferent, then turned back to the conversation, moving it towards a new plan, a great and worthy plan, a plan inspired by militant wage slaves the world over.

"We'll work to rule," I announced.

"We're on freelance contracts; there is no *rule* to work to," said Pete, shaking his head, sighing heavily.

"Then we'll do what everyone else does in these situations."

"And what's that?"

"We'll kind of do very little."

The Kind of Do Very Little Plan:

You'll need a group of disaffected employees, wait, scratch that, any employees will do, so long as they've got some form of control over their boss, be it talent, contacts, or knowledge about his dubious film-financing scheme.

Next up: You Do Very Little.

All those years studying for A levels, Bachelors, and Masters will boil down to the fine art of taking forty-five minutes to brew a cup of tea, using fifty minutes to send an email, and – my personal favourite – punching in, going to the cinema for a triple bill, and then punching out.

Not subtle, but it never gets old.

You are now ready, my young Padawan, to master the ways of The Kind of Do Very Little Plan.

And so that's what we did. The weeks ticked over, but with our work languishing in first gear Tony was still satisfied, because you don't stop in first gear, there's still some forward motion. Gradually we increased the tally, but it was taking time, lots of time, time I didn't want to waste.

Every week my team of disgruntled phone-jockeys would meet with Tony to discuss the tally, and every week he'd tell us the start date was close, but more money was needed. I didn't believe a word of it, growing ever more keen to break the standoff, but ambition is a debilitating force.

We paused, waiting to see who'd blink first.

Raising less money meant less commission in my pocket, but it couldn't be helped. I should have walked. I should have shouted. I should have gone on a bloody rampage; yet I could see no option except to stay.

The Kind of Do Very Little Plan slowed to such a rate that the majority of my time was spent drinking tea. My bladder was in its fittest state in years. I was desperate to leave, but every time I decided to quit, another tease about *Ulrika's Secret* would keep me there, be it Tony displaying the film's poster, or news of the script being finalised.

I was torn, indecision forcing inaction.

The rewards of staying were immense, the logic of leaving equally so. *I've come this far*, I reckoned, *and I'll be damned if another media grunt takes my job once production gets underway. I'm staying put, like a farmer surrounded by shopping malls, refusing to sell his land.*

So on it went, trudging into a second month, no change on the horizon, still hearing we were close to a start, the standoff still firmly in play, the same daily rituals repeating themselves, one cup of tea rolling into the next, one Tube ride rolling into another… until one day a member of my stubborn dream team stopped bitching about the situation to ask a rather pertinent question:

"Have you guys seen Tony?"

It was a fine question.

I hadn't done much of late, but had I seen Tony?

Couldn't say I had. And none of the others had either.

We mulled over where he might be.

On holiday? Too busy. In meetings? We'd have heard. Dead in his office? We'd have smelt it. In LA sourcing talent? Ha.

Finally my cynicism provoked a question:

"You don't think he's…"

"He's what?"

"You know…"

"What?"

"You know…"

"Gone?"

"Yeah, gone."

We started counting off the days to when any of us had last seen the elusive man, an exercise that took us back a full week. How had this happened? How could we have let ourselves become so disengaged?

Where the hell had the bastard gone?

The usual lines of enquiry led nowhere – mobile, landline, email – as did investigating the car park and his favourite bars. It didn't take long to realise he'd disappeared. Or given up. Either way he was nowhere to be seen, and had left no clue as to if, or when, he'd ever return.

Trigger pulled.

While we'd been brewing tea, the standoff had ended.

Tony had fired first.

And that led to the next realisation: we'd been punching in for a week to an office with no boss. As demonstrated in this book, there are many fine ways to resign or be fired, but to find yourself in a situation where neither has taken place, yet you're still out of work, well, that was something new. My interest in the new experience evaporated fast, replaced with one primal word:

Cunt.

I've been trying to avoid its use, but it's the only way to describe how I felt. To those of you who've ever uttered it in frustration, rage, or descriptive story-telling, you know why it's appropriate. To those of you who find it distasteful, go to your nearest bookshop, pick out 'How to Be Offended by Life, The Universe, and Everything', slap it across your face, and shove it where the sun don't shine.

Ahhhhhhh, that felt good.

Tony had used me to raise money for a film production that was probably non-existent. That much was fact. Maybe I'd been raising funds for him to install a new kitchen, buy a new car, or fly to Vegas to throw it all on Number Fourteen? I had no idea. What I did know was that fighting back wouldn't be easy.

For starters, he was the invisible man, and for seconds, what passed for a contract had been handwritten on a side of notepaper, without an address or company number. It just listed my duties and commission rate, along with a vague promise of a job once 'a period of fundraising' had been undertaken. An employment lawyer would have laughed me out the room.

At the time of signing I'd wanted to question it, but knew that doing so would have meant another media grunt taking my place, one who wasn't so bothered by the small print. Catch-22. And so you bite your tongue, hoping for the best, and if that doesn't work, you're shit out of luck.

We were plain shit out of luck, having been used, spat out, and left to rot. We had no options, no recourse, no forward strategy. We were just another group of disaffected youths – a dangerous situation if armed with clubs heading for parliament, not so if armed with teaspoons heading for the Northern Line.

There was nothing to do except shuffle home, but could we ensure that Tony wouldn't forget us? I looked over the office: zero valuable items, little to smash. There was hardly anything even a gang of hoodies could damage. The ground floor consisted of two-quid phones and plywood desks. Tony's office was bolted shut, a fortress none of us could bypass, but that didn't mean we wouldn't let passing opportunists try their luck, and so my dejected team trooped out, leaving the front door wide open, an invitation to all and sundry.

As the gannets moved in, down the road we bade each other farewell, disappearing to disparate boltholes, retreating to lick wounds and mull options. We probably needed counselling, but instead faced months trawling those tediously familiar job sites, praying for a better break.

I drifted away, direction unknown, north London passing me by. Step by step I turned ever more inwards, consumed by furious fantasy. Tony had electrified my mind, summoning rage rarely seen in an Englishman. Before long I was engrossed in homicidal plans, imagining how I'd take my revenge...

With furious intent I tear out his beating heart, leaving it twitching, searching for blood, failing to find its fuel. I throw it to the floor, leaping up high, landing back on the fleshy mass, flattening it to a piece of butcher shop off-cut.

I swivel, see his wife, and spray her with a full magazine. She's cut down before there's time to pray. I reload, jumping feet first through an oak door, only to face an army of cops. In thirteen seconds they're either dead or dying, so I swing round to the family dog, lowering the gun's barrel, and...

Whoa, whoa, whoa… not even in fantasy slayings can you take out the dog. It's just not kosher. Yet consumed by rampaging thoughts I was out of control, over the line. Internally, lunatics ran amok; externally, rage hid behind a mask, revealed via the ultimate sign of English fury: a slight quivering of the upper lip.

At any moment I was on the brink of a category-five nostril flare, a manifestation sure to be noticed by even the least observant Londoner, who'd do the right thing and alert armed police to a madman on the loose. I crashed on, muttering to myself about killing Tony, all the while smiling at strangers (for the veneer of English civility must be relentlessly maintained).

I walked and walked, trying to lift my mood, eyeballing the city's workforce. All around me they were sucking on identikit coffee cups, speeding to and fro, intent on being somewhere; yet I wasn't angry with them. Far from it. I was jealous – *why wasn't I able to be like them?*

I wondered what it would take to join their frenetic world, to become one of society's 'success' stories, yet at the same time I knew it was an academic thought, for I had nothing left in the tank. I was even out of fumes.

I considered punching something.

And then I slumped against a wall.

What was the point? I'd probably miss.

Fuck it. Fuck it. Fuck it.

It's an odd feeling when you know you're beaten. An empty feeling. There was nothing left to fight for, nothing left to chase. I had just one thought on terminal repeat: *fuck film*. I didn't want to travel any further down that deranged rabbit hole. I'd gone far enough. The hole was too dark, too deep.

So there I was, aged twenty-eight-and-a-half, dreams lying shattered at the side of a piss-stained street, at the end of my tether, ready to let go. I had no interest in contacts, interviews, or opportunities, no interest in moving up the ladder. I'd hit the wall. All I could do was glare at the intimidating cityscape, out of ideas.

And then something struck me.

Something that hurt.

Really hurt.

Thwack!!!

You'd think it would be indistinguishable, being so light, but you'd be wrong; it hits you with the force of a thousand bricks. It hits you when you're weak. It hits you when you're low. It hits you when it knows you won't get up.

It was the final straw.

And it had just broken the camel's back.

JOB TWELVE: PRODUCTION PHONE JOCKEY

Lessons learnt:

- If consumed by BCO, you'll ignore those damned alarm bells, carrying on regardless. *This is not advisable*
- If you could have walked into an interview with the employer's naked wife in your arms, yet still be offered a job, there's probably something amiss
- A Mexican standoff will end at some point. Should you fire first? You won't know until the bleeding begins
- Whatever doesn't kill you makes you stronger? *Bollocks*
- The media industry, like any industry, has its crooks
- If you see an Englishman in the midst of a lip quiver, or on the verge of a nostril flare, call the police, for there's a madman in town
- There really is a straw that can break a camel's back

CHAPTER TWENTY-THREE

Live. Adapt. Survive.

The working world is a constantly evolving landscape, as changeable as teen fashion – and just as baffling – yet workers can learn from the young and fickle, for theirs is an arena riddled with popularity contests. Those that master it do so by adhering to a timeless mantra:

Adapt or die.

It's an ethos that's as equally apt to the working world, because when faced with strife, when beaten, broken, and dejected, when the final straw has broken the camel's back, you adapt, you change, you reinvent… you survive.

And in mid-2008 I was adapting, finally paying attention to the fat lady singing loud and proud. She could be heard in the cheap seats. She could be heard in the streets. There was no mistaking her momentous warble:

"Your career in film is over. A new start is needed.

A New Hope."

Career Wars, Episode XIV: A New Hope

Hair blowing in the wind, two stars setting in the sky, an effeminate robot, his trashcan companion, a newly-inspired mission. Yes, we're in *Star Wars* territory. It's about time. If it floats your boat, or your Millennium Falcon, imagine these words in bright yellow, disappearing into the depths of space:

Earth. Early 21st century.

The self-proclaimed 'masters of the universe' – the Galactic Empire of Sith Financiers, if you will – have pushed the global economy to the brink of ruin. For the people of this small planet, dark times loom. Governments will flounder. Banks will fail. Loan sharks will feast.

But this should have been no surprise.

Doomsayers like Nouriel Roubini (aka Dr Doom, *the clue's in the name*) had for years been warning about harsh times ahead, but it wasn't until mid-2008 that people took heed, the symptoms too obvious to miss: employers downsizing, colleagues disappearing, and national newspapers beginning to bark about an impending cataclysm that would drag us back to the Dark Ages.

That pained, oxymoronic phrase 'negative growth' was on the tips of everyone's tongues, a fearful force expected to arrive in the second half of 2008. It would be the start of something truly evil.

Boom. Bust.

Boom. Bust.

The predictable rollercoaster of capitalist greed and inadequacy has been lurching from high to low for centuries, all the way back to the first recorded bust in 1637 when Dutch Tulip Mania made its mark on history, investors snapping up newly-fashionable tulips, only to see their wealth disappear faster than a falling petal. But we never learn the lesson, regardless of how many times it's taught, for the lure of the fast buck never fades; and so, centuries on from the Dutch bust, the global economy was similarly over-exposed and under-prepared.

Yet despite the gathering storm, the time had arrived for me to take a step into the unknown. With lightsaber at the ready, tunic pulled tight, I was primed, pumped for a quest that would demand Jedi-like strength and resolve, for it was time to take on the ultimate re-think of the ultimate question, that fearsome challenge known as… 'career change'.

Squelch.

Yep, that's the sound of me lightly browning my pants.

It was terrifying to have to reset, but seeing as my first answer to the ultimate question appeared to be magnificently wrong, a new answer was undoubtedly needed. Of course if 'Answer One' was wrong, the next question was obviously, 'how do I ensure 'Answer Two' is *not* wrong?'

I took time out to think, staying with family far from London, mulling options. Distance from a problem can give one much-needed perspective, so I holed up, pulling apart the facts, researching avenues, trying to figure out what it would take to master career, once and for all.

The first thing I noted was that knowing yourself, and knowing what to do with your days, are inseparable. That's the first step: know yourself. Once understood, you're better prepared to tackle (or re-tackle) the ultimate question.

If stuck, consider the following:

- What are you good at?
- What do you like about work (any type of work)?
- What career values are important to you? (Creativity? Good hours? Office-based/out of office? Profit-focused? People-facing?)
- What type of work-life balance are you looking for?
- What level of income are you comfortable living on?
- What career matches your skills and those dynamics?
- Are you willing to put in the effort to pursue it?
- If yes, how do you begin?

It's the last question that can grate the most, because there are few things more frustrating than knowing where you want to be in life, but not having the faintest idea of how to get there. On top of which there'll be mounting pressure, from yourself and those around you, to take the leap, but you might be fearful of the unknown, or handcuffed to your current path, unable to see a way out.

It's never going to be easy, regardless of friends telling you to, "do it now, as life's too short," or, "you'll regret it if you don't." Of course they'll encourage change, keen to see you happy, but you'll be the one anxious about covering your rent, student loans, credit card bills, and twice-weekly therapy sessions.

Life gets pricey.

There are hundreds of reasons to stay in situ, rather than face upheaval, yet career change is far from unusual. Thousands take the leap every year, with many seeing the risk pay off handsomely. Case in point, what do Martha Stewart, James Blunt, Ronald Reagan, Andrea Bocelli, and KFC's Colonel Sanders all have in common? They're all successful career changes.

Stewart was a model, then stockbroker, then caterer, and later billionaire homemaking queen. Blunt was a soldier, then singer-songwriter; Reagan was an actor, then US president; Bocelli was a lawyer, then operatic maestro. And Colonel Sanders was a railroad worker, service station operator, and eventually the KFC legend known to billions worldwide.

It's inspiring stuff; no wonder millions of us want to join their ranks. According to a 2012 monster.com global poll, fifty-five per cent of respondents were attempting to change career (in response to economic troubles), with another thirty per cent open to the idea, if they could find a better line of work. And in 2015, a London School of Business and Finance survey found that (of the 1,000 professionals who took part) forty-nine per cent wanted to change career, the top reasons being increased salary prospects, a better work-life balance, and improved job satisfaction.

Workers want change.

We're all seeking that elusive 'happy state'.

And I was no different.

Knowing I'd misread the film world, or been sucked into a false dream, I knew I had to commit to a sector that best matched my skills, and as I laid low, considering what that meant, a pang of realisation painfully dawned…

There was only one clear option.

Having reassessed my strengths and weaknesses, qualifications, goals, values, ideal work-life balance, and preferred job types, I was left with a front-runner that suited me better than sandals on Jesus. But this was no cathartic moment or earth-shattering realisation, this was a career my teachers – backed by a two-bit super-computer - had suggested over a decade earlier; no, not being a prison guard, far from it; this was a line of work distant in both respect and perception, inherently distrusted by the British public, lumped in with estate agents, politicians, and bankers for the low regard in which they're all held.

So be it. The front-runner was the front-runner; there was no error, no second choices. I'd have to deal with the downsides. Like it or not, they went with the turf. And so I re-aligned my energies to a new horizon, to being part of the very industry I'd trialled fresh out of school, the very profession I'd hastily fled – the dog-eat-dog world of UK print media.

I'd come full circle. *I couldn't believe it.*

How had this happened? After years spent pursuing film work, I was back at square one. It was an absurd, time-warped realisation, but everything pointed to it being one hundred per cent accurate.

Even though two stints of work experience had repelled me from journalism, I knew it was a match for one simple reason: I can somewhat string a sentence together. After all, I didn't take an English degree out of fear of being a successful mathematician, and I certainly haven't been running from headhunters targeting me for engineering jobs. We all have our strengths; it's best to rec-ognise them early on, and put them to good use.

Finally I'd accepted the truth about myself and what career I should be doing, and once acknowledged it seemed blindingly obvious, remarkably do-able. Yet there was one *massively* intimi-dating issue about trying this line of work: in mid-2008 Britain's publishing sector wasn't exactly in its most stellar phase.

It was under siege.

Print titles across the country were up the proverbial creek, as the Internet encroached on prized turf, and the recession became a reality. Unable to withstand the pressure, advertising profits tumbled; but there was worse still to come, with the soon-to-be-ubiquitous smartphone forecast to bring news direct to everyone's pockets, kicked off by the iPhone's game-changing arrival in 2007.

The onslaught had begun, yet it was to this beleaguered industry that I was turning to for salvation. Looking to join the print sector in 2008 was much like becoming a candlestick-maker after the invention of electricity. That's not to say that tens of thousands weren't employed in its captivating sphere, but jobs were in jeopardy, publishers squeezed by technology and circumstance. It was still an alluring career, but it was an industry in flux, struggling to find its way.

Yet with stories of Martha Stewart and Colonel Sanders egging me on, I rolled up my sleeves, preparing for the challenge ahead. Economic woe aside, print media is a competitive sector; around 7,000 students graduate UK journalism courses every year, fighting for a dwindling number of full time editorial jobs, estimated by the government's Labour Force Survey to total approximately 40,000 (in 2015).

Those are daunting stats. To succeed in the industry I'd have to master the skills of the craft (beyond the basics of typing and destroying Tory politicians), so I lined up a crash course in journalism, needing to learn the trade's insider tricks; but this was it, I reasoned – *this was it* – one last scholarly hit that would set me on a lifelong path of contented success.

All it would require would be a brief return to the classroom, a notebook at my side, a few points scribbled down, a hand up here, a correct answer there, a quick test, and the revolving door of higher education would spit me out, a qualification in one hand, and a job offer in the other.

Satchel packed, pencils sharpened, a new hope dawned.

Needing to cram the highlights of a three-year journalism degree into a fraction of that time, I plumped for an intensive nine-week course at a media training facility in east London, keen to experience fast-track career change.

As day one kicked off, the lead tutor welcoming his new students, I found myself in a class of eleven, all of us corralled at first light to an indistinct building filled with educational paraphernalia, foam chairs, and that unmistakeable scent of marker pen on white-board. Circled by his attentive group, sipping from a paper cup, our tutor underscored what was to come, not mincing a word:

"This is going to be the toughest nine weeks of your life."

I hoped "toughest" was exaggerated, but he added, "You're not going to see your friends. You're not going to see your family. You will live here and only here, except to sleep for six, maybe seven hours per night. Any questions?"

Eleven hands shot up.

I glanced over the group. *Christ, I must be getting on.* I was at least five years older than the lot of them. So this is what happens when you change careers; this is why so few adults return to the class-room. It's not a lack of desire for change; it's a lack of desire to be the old fart in the room. I popped my collar, trying to blend in. An anonymous snigger prompted me to subtly tug it back down.

Forget about it; embrace your old fart status. Far better to focus on what the tutor, Niall, was saying, for Niall was done with his wel-come speech.

There was nothing else to be said.

"Turn up… don't be late… let's begin."

I liked his direct, no BS approach. It was refreshing, and exactly how I imagined news editors to behave in the real world. We pulled out pads and pens, looked up, and hung expectantly on his every word.

"What makes news *news*?" asked Niall.

It was a brilliantly simple question from the bearded, six-foot teacher. I had an answer, but fearful of muttering the blindingly obvious, "Sex sells," or "If it bleeds it leads," I kept my hand down.

"It needs to be new," offered one of the men in the class. Eyes darted back to Niall – would this be accepted?

"Yes, it needs to be new, but what *makes* people buy newspapers?"

"The weather," said one of the ladies, adding, "it's always on the front page of the *Daily Express*."

An answer with supporting evidence. Respect.

"Yes," said Niall, "if it's unusual weather."

And we were off.

The list of what makes people buy newspapers (or read free-bies) includes big numbers of anything amazing, local fear, global war, the weird and unusual, landmark events, celebrity gossip, election results, and, of course, cute pictures of baby animals. It was the start of a study into journalism that would delve into every facet of the centuries-old profession, teaching us the essentials – writing articles, managing deadlines, designing pages, subediting, proofreading, and getting the juice out of a defensive interview.

As promised, the course demanded fifteen-hour days, including weekends, right through to the end of week nine. It was unrelent-ing, but efficient. It was bruising, but pragmatic. On crossing the finish line, diploma in hand, I was shattered, in desperate need of a break, but also qualified, ready to hit the jobs market, and if that's not the point of vocational training, then what is?

All that was left was to figure out where to flex my newly-ac-quired skills. Applying to work on a magazine in the UK was the obvious answer, but those itchy feet – those unruly, irrepressibly itchy feet – were on fire, seeking once again to test the oyster the-ory, seeking to explore a somewhat curious target.

A somewhat distant target.

With a fresh diploma to hand, I was determined to maximise its potential, and seeing as a leopard doesn't change its spots, I reverted to poring over maps; yet looking to work overseas wasn't only driven by a desire to travel, there was also a practical reason: the UK jobs market was on the floor, beaten to a pulp. Before long the bell would ring, signalling a trip to A&E, perhaps even the morgue.

And so I set my sights on a distant land; a land plagued by heat and dust; a land that – at the time of writing – holds questionable respect for journalistic integrity, yet still shot to the top of my list, as it was so confident in its economic prowess that it boasted of being impervious to the planet's mounting woe.

Desperate for career success, that was more than enough, but when people asked why I wanted to live there, my answer wasn't the country's audacious self-belief, or abundant media vacancies; it was a response far less mature:

"It's hot, damn hot!!"

I'd already lived in one of the world's coldest cities, Toronto; it was time now to live in one of the world's hottest.

And so I eyed a move to a surreal city, where sand meets sky-scraper, where tradition meets modernity, where survival meets gluttony, the commercial hub of the Arabian Gulf that is...

Dubai.

CAREER CHANGE: A NEW HOPE

Lessons learnt:

- Adapt or die – it's unquestionable logic
- When the fat lady's warbling, listen up
- Know yourself: it's the foundation to answering the ultimate question
- Millions are seeking career change – you are not alone
- If older than those around you, embrace your old fart status
- Being impervious to recession should be reason enough to move to a new city, but "astounding heat" sounds far better in the pub

CHAPTER TWENTY-FOUR

12.30am (Gulf Time Zone).

Touch down.

The chunky door of the Boeing 777 eased open. The Gulf rushed in. Within seconds sweat oozed from every pore. It was 36° Celsius, ninety per cent humidity.

It was hot. *Damn hot.*

The curvy stewardess beckoned me to depart. She smiled uncomfortably, creases in her uniform giving away tell-tale signs of a losing battle, damp lines advancing. I crossed to the stair truck. Palm trees shimmered in the distance. South Asian workers swarmed the aircraft, forklifts emptying its hold.

There wasn't an Arab in sight. Maybe we'd landed into Delhi? Maybe, but the efficacy of the operation suggested otherwise, as did the distant words:

'Abu Dhabi International Airport'.

I'd arrived into the United Arab Emirates (UAE) for a week-long stab at locking in my first journalism job, but you may have noticed a peculiar flaw in my travel plans, a flagrant flaw, one more obvious than hormones at prom. Spotted it? Yep, I wasn't hunting for work in Abu Dhabi; I was hunting for work in Dubai, Abu Dhabi's glamour-puss sister over 100km to her north.

September 2008, a time for *change*, a time for *hope*. As Barack Obama's presidential campaign monopolised both words, trying to convince the American public that politics could deliver, so I too sought a new job, keen to begin what the geek in me was already calling 'Career 2.0'.

But landing into the wrong Arabian city was no error; it was all part of my fast-track career change plan, and made absolute sense on positive days, but was readily tagged 'long-shot' during more pessimistic spells.

As I climbed off the stair truck on to the airport apron, those 'long-shot' words slapped me across the face – *what the hell am I doing here?*

And yet… my brow furrowed… positivity fighting back… *come on, Charlie, you can do this. You have the right qualifications. You're in the right land. You can turn things around, and… WOW, that's hot…*

The day's heat radiated off the asphalt. For a moment I thought I'd stick to it, but the airport's engineers had clearly thought ahead; everything functioned smoothly, unfazed by the late night furnace. I continued along the assigned route, palpitating under floodlights, winding past luggage convoys, support vehicles, and refuelling jets, inhaling sweet wafts of their favourite tipple.

Pace after pace I puffed on, and then, halfway to the terminal doors, as my face began to resemble a Botoxed stroke victim, the appeal of living in a blisteringly hot environment evaporated into the combustible air. I shed my jacket, wondering how humans exist in such intense conditions, momentarily, for the answer slammed me on entering the terminal, a shield of cold air embracing all.

I slipped my jacket back on, lining up for passport control, at which point I clocked the local Gulf Arabs – the Emiratis – protecting the border, taking their sweet time to punch paper and shunt the line. Inquisitive, I stared, having only spied them in central London cafés, sipping coffee, smoking shisha, lounging beside Arabic-plated supercars. How different to see them at their desk jobs, in their desert setting, clock-watching like anyone else.

Sitting in booths along the entire breadth of passport control were about thirty semi-identical staffers dressed in their traditional white *kandora* (a neck-to-ankle robe), all of them boasting identically-trimmed beards, identical Blackberries, identical hands-free kits, and near-identical nonchalant looks, one after the next, after the next. The air around the officials was heavy with an unusual, malodorous blend of damp wood and blue cheese, an aroma I now know to be 'oud', the local male fragrance. The homogenised nature of the line-up fascinated me, but I knew there was a practical reason to it: white clothing keeps you cool in a hot climate, and a resilient cologne is critical in sweat-prone regions.

"Next!"

I gulped, embarrassed by my non-PC musings, but it didn't last long, the passport stamper hitting me with my most dreaded question of all:

"What's the purpose of your visit?"

I knew exactly why I was there, to find a job, but would that be accepted? Might border guards appear, shackles in one hand, a jumpsuit in the other, after which a prolonged and effective cavity search would ensue, followed by jail, man-love, and a one-way ticket home? As with Zimbabwe, the answer was obvious:

"Tourism."

The officer flipped through my passport with the ease of a pro, smiling a beam of toothy perfection. He appeared to be in the mood to chat.

"Very well, my young friend, and where are you coming from?"

"The UK, Heathrow airport."

"Good, very good… No wife, no children?"

I was taken aback, but answered nonetheless.

"No, just me."

He looked disappointed – *or was that disgusted?*

Years later I know that to ask such a question in the Gulf is commonplace, especially if anyone over the age of thirty has failed to prove his semen can produce life, but on first encounter it chafed.

Damn it, I thought, *who the hell is he to ask…*

"Next!"

Passport returned, I glided into Abu Dhabi's marble-floored arrivals hall ready to tackle the UAE's media scene; yet as I waited for my suitcase to arrive, I couldn't help but obsess over a simple, pertinent question:

Was Gavin right?

"You're going to go to Abu Dhabi for a week to find a job in Dubai?" Gavin had asked, in what came across as more 'put-down' than enquiry.

Up until this point it had seemed a watertight plan: go to Abu Dhabi, meet Jack, drive to Dubai, meet media people, pass around CV – with journalism qualification front and centre – find a job.

What wasn't to like?

"Yep, that's the plan."

"Hmmmmm…"

Even though I was set on a move to the Middle East, Gavin's derision added fresh impetus to my plan succeeding. The trouble was, as any job-hunter knows, the outcome isn't up to you. Timing and luck, timing and luck, it's all you can hope for. I knew a one-week timeframe to find work was pushing it, but also knew I'd achieved it in Zimbabwe, was now targeting the UAE – a transient place of abundant opportunity – *and* had that all-important job-seeker's weapon at my disposal: a contact with connections.

All of which led to Jack, an old friend who'd been living in Abu Dhabi for more than six months, who I'd arranged to meet by the airport's taxi rank, in what had seemed a foolproof plan, until I was standing there, dripping, shedding layers faster than an extroverted swinger. Mercifully he arrived on time, screeching to a halt in his beat-up Nissan, saving me from an early episode of heat exhaustion (and certain mockery for collapsing so soon after touchdown).

I loaded up, leapt in, and after answering the usual queries about turbulence and airline food, ran Jack through my recent encounter with Gavin, ending with the anxious question:

"He's not right, is he?"

"Fear not," replied the tanned expat, accelerating away from the airport perimeter, "this is the land of plenty!"

And with that he pumped the A/C to Arctic, slipped on to a ten-lane highway, and gunned the super-charged engine of his plus-sized 4x4. Doubts briefly allayed, I took a break from career paranoia to gaze out over Abu Dhabi, a place that had so far been nothing more than a destination on a ticket stub.

It was the capital of the nation I'd earmarked for my next move, yet on first impressions – speeding past monotonous, jaundiced villas – I was struggling to see its appeal. I thought back to what I knew about the UAE, pulling apart the facts, trying to figure out what I was missing about the place:

Formed from the remnants of the Trucial States (Gulf sheikhdoms under British protectorate status from 1820 to 1971) the UAE could have been a far bigger nation, but Bahrain and Qatar chose to go it alone, leaving seven sheikhs at the eastern horn of the Arabian Peninsula to debate, disagree, squabble, and agree, eventually combining lands to form the United Arab Emirates.

To fully appreciate the country, you need to grasp it within the context of its location, for the UAE has some particularly notorious neighbours. Alongside its northern coast is the Persian Gulf, on the far side of which is Iran, the UAE's long-term Shia rival. To the west of Iran is war-torn Afghanistan, and to its south, politically-torn Pakistan. West of the UAE lies the ultra-conservative oil puddle of Saudi Arabia, and to its south sit ruptured Yemen, and discreet Oman. Up the Gulf from the UAE are the tiny sheikhdoms of Qatar, Bahrain, and Kuwait (famed for being, respectively, unsuited to hosting the World Cup, unsuited to hosting Formula One, and unsuited to hosting Saddam Hussein). Heading on northwest you'll find a fractured Iraq, and to its west a crippled Syria. Further west is divergent Lebanon, and then on south, contentious Israel (aka the former lands of Palestine), and lastly the Arab Spring flop that is modern-day Egypt.

Put simply, the BBC, CNN, France 24, Fox News, Al Jazeera, CCTV, Russia Today, ITN et al. make more hay than prairie farmers out of the region. Put another way, you couldn't live in a more screwed up corner of the globe.

Of course none of that's why more than a hundred thousand Brits live within the UAE's borders, yet as Abu Dhabi zipped by,

I was still struggling to see the lure. Cooked by day, steaming by night, the summer offers an empty moonscape, virtually void of life. As Jack drove on, a blur of roundabouts and date palms flashed past, 4x4s and silver taxis, flat-roofed villas and concrete mosques, neon-lit stores and sprinkler-fed lawns; and between them all, wherever it could, the desert pushed back, filling untended gaps, returning the land to its natural state.

Considering the fortune it sits on, Abu Dhabi is a remarkably bland, understated city. In the noughties and beyond it's tried raising its game, opening a Ferrari-branded theme park, joining the F1 circuit, and building one of the world's most lavish hotels, Emirates Palace, but Dubai still steals the limelight, having surged ahead in expat numbers and manic developments.

Yet whether in Abu Dhabi or Dubai the same downsides lurk, most notably that alcoholic drinks – if you follow the letter of the law – are only legal for people holding an Alcohol Licence, leaving tourists potentially flouting the rules for buying a hotel beer. The country also forbids sexual relations outside of wedlock, flipping the birdie, kissing in public, and even your rant on Facebook about 'how goddam hot it is' could land you in jail (for potentially offending the faith). Yet one of the most common ways to upset the authorities is a mere financial glitch; yes, bouncing a cheque could see you face-to-face with a city judge.

It doesn't exactly pave the way to the Rock and Roll Hall of Fame, so what *really* is the UAE's huge appeal?

All together now – *money, money, money*.

The main lure is the biggest carrot of all: tax-free salaries. Sure, there's sunshine and beaches, but at the end of the day few expats would live there without such a powerful financial incentive.

Guess that's that, I concluded. *Forget what's out the window. Focus on dodging the recession. Focus on finding a job.*

Jack had said the UAE was "the land of plenty," but… *was that a throwaway comment? Was he exaggerating? Would I easily find work? Was Jack… oh no, not again…* I sighed, realising my next question to be all-too familiar:

'Was Jack right?'

"Your name landed on my desk," said the voice.

"Eh?"

"Someone passed me a business card with your name on it."

"Er…"

"We need to meet."

I'd returned to London a day before, was sleep-deprived, confused by what the stranger wanted.

"Okay, er, meet about what?"

"You're looking for a job in Dubai, right?"

The penny dropped. Seeing as I'd only been handing out business cards in the UAE I should have clocked on sooner.

I slapped myself, waking a touch.

"Yes, yes, that's right, back from Dubai, researching work… companies… looking for work, journalism work… there last week… yes, I'm looking for work…"

Smooth. Nothing alarm-bell-ringy about that.

"Oooookaaay…"

Shit, I was losing him. *Take the initiative.*

"What's the job?" I asked.

"My name's Ian. I'm the editor of *Media Minds Middle East* magazine. We've just started printing in Dubai. We're expanding our team."

My heart skipped a beat. It was perfect.

Don't fuck up.

Ian continued, "So, I got your card off one of your friends, who then emailed me your CV. You were at *Media Minds* in London, I see. We're looking for a news reporter, could be a good fit."

What he should have seen on my CV was that I'd spent two weeks at *Media Minds* – a media industry business title – doing work experience at the end of my journalism course, but I was pretty sure that he'd only taken in the words *Media Minds*, not the 'work experience' detail. A question of ethics erupted: should I point it out, potentially jeopardising my chances of getting the job, or breeze past it, dealing with my limited media knowledge at a later date?

The answer was easy.

"Yep, could be an ideal fit," I replied. *Always put 'Number One' first.* "When do you need someone?"

"As soon as possible. We should meet. I'm in Dubai, flying to London tonight, so let's have a coffee near Paddington Station, tomorrow at 11.30am. I'll be at a local cafe. Bell me on this number when you get there."

Call finished, I punched the air, ecstatic my week in Abu Dhabi might actually pay off. Moreover, I was itching to prove Gavin wrong. I hoped to soon be trotting out that despised little line, "I told you so."

The following day I made the far shorter journey to Paddington than Ian's seven-hour flight, but we both made it on time, him sucking on a cigarette. After a momentary handshake, some small talk, and an overview of the job in Dubai, the fashionably-dishevelled man asked me, "So what do you know about the media industry in the Middle East?"

"To be honest, not a great deal. I didn't cover it much at *Media Minds.*"

I wasn't being exact, but wasn't lying either. It was a fine line.

"I can pick it up quickly, though," I added.

"Sure, sure, sounds fine. And when can you start?"

I thought over my responsibilities. Not much had changed over the years: no wife, no girlfriend, no baby, no dog, no goldfish, no car, no apartment, no bills, no interest in staying, and nothing in the diary. To some, it would be a sad list indicative of an empty life. To me, it was liberty.

"Whenever you like," I replied.

"We need someone on Sunday."

"As in this Sunday?"

"As in this Sunday."

It was Tuesday morning.

An instinctive answer spilled out, "No problem."

From his satisfied look I knew I'd locked in the job. We parted company, him telling me to get to Dubai, find the company apartment, and be ready to start work on Sunday morning. Then he disappeared into the streets of London, to be seen again under the bright skies of a Dubai day.

I stood there, grinning at the tourist hordes by Paddington Station, consumed by one simple thought, *'I told you so, Gavin, I fucking told you so.'*

Searing heat, aggressive sweat, South Asian workers, robed Emiratis, hands-free Blackberries. No doubt about it, I was back in the Gulf.

There's nothing like that feeling of stepping off a jet into the unknown, of being the blank canvas, of immersing yourself into unknown idiosyncrasies – and there's nowhere more idiosyncratic than Dubai.

At the time, Dubai had perfected its role of playing mischievous teen to Abu Dhabi's didactic sibling. Abu Dhabi was, and by all accounts still is, supremely wealthy, yet jealous of its attention-grabbing sister; conversely Dubai was, *and by all accounts still is*, an alluring flirt, maxing out its credit card. And in October 2008 it was business as usual, Dubai pushing to be bigger and flashier in every way, which meant spend today, worry tomorrow, and…

Build. Build. Build.

Dubai has been called many things – both flattering and insulting – but the one thing you can't label it with is unambitious. From the moment you arrive you're met with a palatial, sparkling airport that makes its European and American rivals look like neglected toilets at a council-run music festival.

If only that were true for the rest of the city.

There's little that can prepare you for life in Dubai, unless you've managed to spend time living in the head of a town-planning toddler. The landscape is so eclectic it's as if a bucket of bricks had been thrown over a crèche floor, leaving a think-tank of four-year-olds to plan the city's development. A Big Ben skyscraper here? Yes. A palm-shaped island there? Why not? A Barbie doll hotel with an Islamic arch at its centre? Of course. The world's biggest mall? Clearly, but how about an even bigger one? Oooh, goodie. And no crèche-designed city is complete without a 163-storey building as its centrepiece. Hang on, while we're at it, let's also have a falcon-shaped district with replicas of all the world's favourite landmarks.

Nice idea, Timmy, gold star for you.

It's a city of extremes, of records, of rich and poor, of debauchery and conservatism, of greed and generosity, of hospitality and segregation. Dubai is everything to some, nothing to many.

Departing the airport, I began to contemplate where I'd fit into this supposed 'desert miracle', but within seconds I was finding it hard to concentrate, the driver's gymnasium odour knocking me sideways.

Gagging, I lowered the window, gasping for air.

As my vision returned, heat invading the cab, the driver grumbling in Urdu, I was captivated by Dubai's haphazard skyline, by the lights, towers, cranes, and construction sites, by the workers high above finishing off the world's tallest tower. I'd barely seen a fraction of the city during my networking drop-in with Jack, so found myself staring in disbelief that this surreal vista was now 'home'; yet there was scant time to digest it, my perspiring driver desperate to offload his fare, flooring it, tailgating two inches behind the fastest car ahead.

We shot on down the city's fourteen-lane ribbon of jugular blacktop, the heat suffocating us both. Overwhelmed and exhausted I raised my window, unable to fight the inevitable, slumping into the hideous embrace of the driver's eau d'armpit. It stung. Trying to breathe, I pulled my T-shirt up over my nose, then immediately realised the car's acrid pungency was in fact a team effort.

We sped on, stifled by mutual loathing.

"Who are you?" asked the stranger.

Thirty kilometres from the airport the taxi had pulled off the highway, swinging into Dubai Marina, a luxury enclave now known for hosting some of the tallest residential structures worldwide, but at the time best know for Jumeirah Beach Residence, a 1.7km-long chain of bulky, beige towers.

The area is one of a handful of communities where foreigners can buy property, following a decision in 2002 by Sheikh Mohammed, Dubai's sovereign ruler, to designate it a freehold district. Eyeing maximum profit, developers thought big, building sky-high on whatever slice of sand they could get their mitts on, creating a waterfront sub-city in less than a decade.

And bang in the middle of this gold rush development was my company apartment, where Ian had told me I'd be sharing with three male colleagues, yet the stranger at the door was *definitely* female. Moreover, my increased heart rate attested to the fact that not only was she female, it appeared I fancied her too.

"I'm Charlie," I answered. "I'm moving in… and you?"

"I'm Kirsty. I'm staying a few nights."

"Great, er, good to meet you. Do you know which room's mine?"

"Oh, yeah, the guys told me. It's… that's it… down the passage on the end. The main bedrooms are taken, so you've got the visitor's room."

That sounded fine. I pictured a double bed with en suite bathroom. I pictured myself soaking away the day's long-haul journey.

"Actually, I think it's the maid's room," she added. "Just follow the passage. It's after the washing machine, drying area, and storage boxes."

The soaking plan drained away.

I walked the narrow passage, losing light the further I went, passed a washing machine, clothes rotting in its door, passed storage boxes piled high, and then turned, taking in my new digs. First thoughts were, *thank God I'm not a maid*, followed closely by, *how can they treat maids this way?*

The room was a cell. A fiery cell.

Barely big enough for a man to lie flat, all four walls could be touched from the same spot, on top of which it lacked air conditioning, the architects possibly forgetting that domestic staff are also human, meaning the airless chamber maintained a temperature similar to the inferno outside. To top it off, the window was sealed tight, a cocoon of misery. A simple, single bed slotted into the space. An overhead bulb doused the room in a clinical tone. Yet I wasn't complaining; it was what it was. I needed a job. I was there to do a job. It was time to buckle down.

And so I lay on my single mattress, sweating majestically, struggling to breathe the fetid air of my latest abode.

Career 2.0 was underway.

Brimming with more confidence than Vladimir Putin wrestling a bear, in late-2008 Dubai's publishing sector was buoyant, expanding, even as its UK equivalent hunkered down, facing an uncertain future.

Like the region's other publishers, my new employer, FRM Media, was riding the city's property boom, its profit margins bloated by real estate ads. Dubai's developers were awash in a tsunami of wealth, fuelled by international money, as investors licked lips, realtors spoke of unprecedented returns, and third parties leached off the oasis, sucking it dry before it reached its inevitable implosion.

To a man looking for a new start it was ideal. Instead of sombre pints in London pubs, Dubai teemed with positivity, with opportunity, with proactive people, adventurous risk-takers, and those starting afresh. It suited me, surrounded by the like-minded and like-motivated, living in a city with its head in the sand, where people believed the 'Great Recession' could only affect others.

It was fantasy-warped hope, but while it lasted Dubai powered on, sweeping me up in its frenetic energy, and so a day after arriving it was straight into a tour of FRM Media's open-plan, spacious offices, based in the aptly-named Dubai Media City, following Ian as he motored through the various departments.

Peering into boardrooms and cubicles, it appeared to be a thriving business, brimming with teams of mostly young British staffers working in advertising, sales, PR, marketing, and across a range of weekly magazines; the only issue was, "Er, where's the *Media Minds Middle East* team?" I sensed I should have asked about colleagues during my brief interview, but it was too late for regrets. The reality was all too clear: there was no one else, just Ian.

We *were* the editorial team.

Deep end spotted, I prepared to be thrown in.

Short on hands, straight away I was dispatched to interview industry experts, sent to attend press conferences, and ordered to track down news leads. We were promised extra journalists, but until they arrived it was a sink-or-swim scenario, so I furiously trod water, desperate to stay afloat; I arrived early, left late, and skipped lunch, going the extra mile to survive the start of Career 2.0. The approach was draining, but worth it; I just about kept my head above water, even though my initial articles needed re-writes. Ian told me that was normal for a newbie, but "learn from your mistakes, and make damn sure they don't happen twice!"

As treading water became second nature, my confidence grew. I felt able to deliver, but after just four weeks on the job things took a decidedly strange turn. Following a mundane request to research a feature article, I was to stumble across a shocking accusation about my new employer, suggesting the company was playing it fast and loose in what I'd come to call the 'Wild, Wild East'.

The episode began auspiciously enough:

"I want you to write up something close to home," Ian said,

as we sat in a meeting room, shivering under a broken air-conditioner. "It's a piece focusing on magazine growth, franchising, and the publishing sector in the Middle East. I want you to dig deep into the potential of the market here, what titles are coming to this region, who's making money, who's losing money, and where the money's coming from. Twelve hundred words within two days."

It was my time to shine.

And I knew exactly where to start.

Seeing as *Media Minds Middle East* was a sister title of *Media Minds* in the UK, who better to ask for information on Gulf magazine franchises – most of which were licensed by British publishers – than the UK's *Media Minds* editor, based right there in the heart of London?

With little time to waste, I found his number and dialled his direct line. He answered straight off, step one proving easier than expected, but once I explained the reason for my call, the conversation rapidly nose-dived.

"The thing is, Charlie, I'd love to help," he said, professionally, and with much courtesy, "but I really shouldn't be talking to you, particularly about magazine franchises in Dubai... I'm sure you understand why."

"Er... well, I'm afraid not," I answered. "I just thought that seeing as we're a sister company you might be able to help my research into..."

"Ah, there's the problem. It appears your employer hasn't been entirely honest with you about your magazine."

Worn out bells tinkled away.

"Oookaaaayyyy..."

"Yeah, sorry, I feel bad being the one to tell you this. You see, *my* management are in litigation with *your* management. It appears to us that your management copied our *Media Minds* brand and concept, launching it in Dubai without our approval or input, all of which means that I really can't speak to you about magazine franchises, or anything else for that matter."

Silence.

Fuuuuuuuuuuuuuuuuuuuuuuuuuuck.

"Charlie?"

"Ummm, yeah…"

Not another one, was all I could think. *Not another bunch of bastards, please don't say it's so. Not again.*

Of course the irony of the situation hadn't passed me by, yet I wasn't laughing; instead I was shocked by how idiotic, not ironic, it must have seemed for me to be calling him for information on – of all possible topics – the pros and cons of magazine franchising in the Gulf. In fact, it must have seemed beyond idiotic; it must have seemed offensive, downright antagonistic. But above all I was embarrassed, unable to find a sentence to fit the moment.

"That is… news… to me," I said, knowing that I needed to be honest. "I genuinely had no idea."

"Well, no problem, but obviously you see why I can't talk to you. If you move to another company and still want to research this topic, then don't hesitate to call back, but as it is, I'm afraid I can't help."

Considering the situation he couldn't have been nicer, but the call left me wanting to shrivel up, shame silencing my day.

What the hell have I signed up to? Should I back out, job hunt, leave the country, or suck it up and stay put?

At first glance, jumping ship might have been a reasonable response, but I hadn't discovered anything criminal, just allegations, and my employer hadn't lied to me, yet also hadn't been fully open. It's not an employee's right to know everything about a company's operations, so I couldn't complain about being kept in the dark, and for all I knew it was just a paperwork error, a clerical oversight.

Even so, the discovery rocked me.

I carefully considered the call, the potential lawsuit, and how it might affect Career 2.0, then weighed my options, re-assessing FRM Media in as cold and clear a light as possible, against the backdrop of a deepening global recession.

The result was fast: *STAY PUT.*

And so I ignored the allegations, never asking management about them, praying they would never re-surface. And they never did. *Ask no questions, hear no lies, don't rock the boat,* was the theory. I adhered to it religiously, burying my head deep in the sand, mimicking those around me, slipping into life as a fully committed, card-carrying Dubai expat.

Contrary to my initial assessment of the UAE, working within her borders came with many upsides, such as only paying Dh110 (£18) to fuel a gas guzzler, not fretting about your apartment being unlocked 24/7, and living within the most vibrant social scene I'd ever encountered. Soon enough I'd embraced the city for what it was: an adult theme park offering abundant sunshine, eclectic entertainment, and world-class sporting events, backed by fat, tax-free salaries.

Many Westerners were there purely to party, but whether footloose and fancy-free, or married with children, people of all ages turned out for the city's hedonistic climax: the Dubai Friday brunch.

Weekends in most of the Middle East are Friday/Saturday, as Friday is a holy day for Muslims. Dubai is no different. Each Friday half the city diligently follows the call-to-prayer, funnelling into mosques for their Day of Assembly prayers. At the same time, the Western faithful gather at Friday brunches for their weekly call-to-dine, with hundreds of hotels laying on Bacchanalian feasts. For a flat fee (averaging about £65) you get three to four hours of bottomless gluttony, usually starting at midday, after which happy hour prices keep you keen, leaving you raring for a club at 5pm, asleep by 11pm, waking groggy at 7am.

In a conservative corner of the globe it's incredible that such revelry exists, but it does, and it thrives. The good times roll on. There's no one to spoil the party. No dissent. No doubt. No tabloid ridicule. No government advice. No brakes, and no red lights.

I found it a whirlwind of excess, a dangerous liaison. It's how life should be lived, at least for a while, and as the world sunk deeper into financial gloom, thousands arrived to join Dubai's Teflon decadence.

It was riotous.

It was relentless.

It was bound to end in tears.

HEAVILY IN DEBT, DUBAI CALLS IN THE BANKERS
(New York Times, 25/11/08)

The good times shuddered to a halt the day Dubai's government admitted to holding $80bn in debt, almost one and a half times the emirate's gross domestic product. The panic button was slammed, crisis bankers swooping in from across the globe to try and contain the fallout.

It was the most shaming news the authorities could have released, but the Internet super-charged the situation, cooking up rumours that Dubai's jewels (including Emirates Airline and Dubai Ports) could be sold to cover the bill. Yet the most hideous aspect for Dubai's ruling elite must have been suggestions that arch rival Abu Dhabi might buy their prized assets, allowing the far wealthier emirate to own massive chunks of its spendaholic neighbour.

Newspapers the world over latched on, ecstatic that supposedly untouchable Dubai had been hiding eleven-digit debt figures, having squandered gazillions on phallic towers and man-made islands. The words 'property bubble' spread like chicken pox in a primary school, journalists quickly identifying the root cause of the government's woe.

The turning point had come months earlier, July 2008, with the housing market topping out, after which investors melted away, smelling weakness, unwilling to push the game any higher. And so began Dubai's misery, because without any more mugs willing to buy unbuilt apartments, or join over-extended property chains, there was only one outcome… Game Over.

Within the year, prime real estate prices would plummet around sixty per cent. Thousands were left owning multi-million-dirham cubes of empty air, many buildings never reaching fruition, leaving banks at the mercy of defaulters, and the government facing its own colossal bill, having invested billions in the construction of a cityscape in which prices had dropped faster than you can say, "Pop!"

Although Dubai's woes weren't so bad as to shock markets in London, New York, or Tokyo, the perfect storm of private and public failure hit the local economy hard. The golden goose was dead, and any company suckling on her previously supple teats was dragged into the fallout, including FRM Media.

Regardless of how hard our dogged sales teams pushed, advertising collapsed, developers pulling up the drawbridge, the words 'project on hold' reverberating around the emirate. The crisis had arrived and taken up residence. Like a squatter gaining access to a Knightsbridge mansion, it changed the locks, sold the chandeliers, took a dump in the hall, and refused to leave.

The dark days had begun.

"The sun will shine tomorrow, as sure as eggs is eggs!" said our editorial chief, trying to assuage fears, but failing in the clearest definition of the word.

"What the fuck does he mean?" begged a colleague.

"Who knows," I answered, "who knows?"

It was spring 2009. Jobs were disappearing across Dubai, yet the downturn affected the city in an unusual way, in a way that's best summed up as 'out of sight, out of mind', the laid-off disappearing overseas – residency visas cancelled – leaving only the employed to populate the city. But within that population distinctions formed, my team joining a marginalised group, on the one hand employed, yet on the other hand in a grey area, failing to be paid on time.

As the months rolled on, our salary situation grew progressively worse, payslips arriving five, six, then seven weeks late, in a country that provides no easy recourse for the mistreated employee. By October, as my time in Dubai reached the twelve-month mark – shortly after the Dubai Metro opened, and more than a year after the $600 billion Lehman Brothers collapse – our salaries were ten weeks late. Colleagues were struggling to pay rent, loans, and school fees.

Some couldn't even afford to Friday brunch.

As I'd previously learned, "You don't fuck with salaries," but around the world times were tough, and with a scarcity of options there was no easy way out, so despite management sneering they could pay us five per cent of one month's salary, if collected in cash from a public park, and despite being told to evacuate via the fire escape to avoid Ministry of Labour inspectors, and despite hearing reports of luxury cars abandoned at the airport, expats ditching debt and fleeing west… we let the problem slide… and slide… and slide…

…until one day:

"Have you heard the news?"

"What news?"

"*The Sunday Times* has been pulled from every shelf in Dubai!"

The watershed moment.

The Sunday Times of London, a newspaper printed under licence in the UAE, had lampooned Sheikh Mohammed in a cartoon depicting him drowning in a sea of debt. It was distributed on November 29th 2009, and before you could shout 'censorship' legions of flunkies had been dispatched to shops, supermarkets, and service stations to retrieve every copy, in an effort to stop anyone being tarnished with such distastefully accurate satire.

Of course, once the 'flunkies-are-censoring-newspapers' story had done the rounds, the cartoon received a far wider audience online than the print version could ever have enjoyed.

The episode was a wake-up call.

If the government wasn't making progress improving its fortunes, what hope for the rest of us? It was going to get worse before it got better, and that would mean even later salaries. To drive the point home, it wasn't until the last day of November that we received our August salaries; FRM was now twelve weeks behind. It was crystal clear the crisis wouldn't be over by Christmas.

We'd reached our limit. There's only so much you can take before the union man in you jumps on his soapbox and shouts, "Strike!"

Except that you can't strike in Dubai, it's against the law, leaving us with only one option: that little used, but deadly tool of mass resignation. My small team, now numbering four journalists, was going 'musketeer'. If one of us left, we'd all leave. Mid-December was decided as the last point we'd wait for the company to hand over every paycheque owed.

If they failed to do so, we'd walk.

As December rolled around it became clear how events would unfold, marked by FRM shutting down our staff accommodation. It was a direct kick straight to the soft and tenders. The situation was moribund.

It had taken months to reach the musketeer moment, nobody wanting to be unemployed during the worst downturn since the 1930s, but at the same time nobody wants to punch-in for free. It would soon be time to jump ship into the freezing waters of unemployment, praying for a life raft close to hand.

One thing I knew for sure about my next step, I didn't want to write business news. I hoped to move into lifestyle journalism, yet as I looked ahead I couldn't help but ponder the film industry, for the pinstriped producer's seductive charms had never faded from the recesses of my wandering mind. But the daydream lasted mere moments; he was pushed back to the shadows. I had no interest in his empty promises. Been there. Done that.

Got the T-shirt.

Closing the lid on such ludicrous thoughts, I focused on

finishing articles for what would be the last ever edition of *Media Minds Middle East*, published in mid-December 2009. At the same time, Dubai received a $10 billion bailout from Abu Dhabi, allowing it to service a small portion of its debt, but it still had a staggering amount more owed to creditors. The loan changed nothing. The economy was on the rocks; FRM was up the creek.

As the magazine hit shelves and coffee tables across Dubai, was confirmed by management that monies owed wouldn't be paid out, not to us, not to any of the company's struggling staffers, so that very afternoon my entire team exited through FRM Media's slick, steel-framed doors one last time, with a message to the boss trailing us out the building:

"See you in court."

Then we melted into the dependable sunshine of a Dubai winter's day, the grisly prospect of court battles and lawyer's fees stretching far over the horizon.

Career 2.0 had crashed to a halt.

And the recession marched on, four more scalps to its name.

JOB THIRTEEN: BUSINESS NEWS REPORTER

Lessons learnt:

- If an interviewer seems to have misread your CV, and it's working to your advantage, go with the flow
- There's nothing like touching down to a new life in a new country
- Learn from your mistakes, and make sure they don't happen twice
- One way to be unfazed by nefarious allegations: bury your head in the sand and pray they go away
- There are few countries as supportive of the oyster theory as the UAE
- You don't fuck with salaries, even during a recession

- There'll be times you'll need to 'lawyer-up'. It was a necessary evil that took eighteen months to reach a winning verdict. As an added bonus, under UAE law FRM Media had to pay back double what was owed. Then our lawyer doubled his fees, keeping the surplus money. *Lawyers be lawyers,* I concluded

CHAPTER TWENTY-FIVE

I felt sick. I felt something.

What is it?

I felt as though I'd stepped off a two-week cruise. Queasy. Unsteady. *What is this?* Tingles. Quivers. *It isn't love… but what?*

I paced the room, a palm-roofed shack on India's west coast. Warm wisps of sea air snuck through ill-fitting shutters.

The feeling had started an hour earlier, as I took stock of my now familiar situation – unemployed, single, ever so angry.

Following the musketeer move, with nothing to plug my nine-to-five, I'd departed for India, seeking cheap living and natural beauty. On arrival I'd met Kate, a friend also keen to travel the country's west coast by train, from Mumbai to India's southern-most tip, Kanyakumari, a distance of around 1,600km.

I'd given myself three weeks off before tackling the next job hunt, a process I'd barely considered, let alone planned, yet on arrival into Goa, approximately 600km south of Mumbai, with little but novels and card games to occupy the mind, my thoughts had migrated inwards.

And so that's how I found myself at ten in the morning, pacing a Goan shack, mulling over my next move, diagnosing an odd sensation; but then again, there *was something* familiar about it, something I recognised, something akin to how I'd felt when planning travels in far-off nations.

And then – *wham* – it hit me.

It had finally happened. I was actually feeling positive, even confident, about my impending job hunt; in fact, I was actively enthused.

How the hell had this happened?

It was unsettling, like seeing your Chinese doppelganger, or enjoying a friend's improv night. How dare I be upbeat; that's the domain of the successful and confident, of the calm and controlled, of those on the right path.

Holy of holy craps.

Was I one of them?

I retched. A touch.

With so much time spent *looking* for the right path I'd never expected to actually *be* on the right path. Maybe this was a mistake. Maybe I'd drunk too much the night before. Maybe, but no. Kate's a teetotaller, and in her company I rarely drink more than the Queen at a garden party.

This was for real.

I truly *had* entered the realm of the confident job-hunter. I truly *was* looking forward to the next step on journalism's career ladder.

Who knew that being on the right path could feel so… good?

Christ, I sounded like a runner-up in a beauty pageant.

Thousands, I expect. They do exist. They're not a total myth. They are them, that lot, those people who've found their path, whether that's working for financial gain, creative plaudits, a family business, or any of the hundreds of other ways in which people find career contentment.

Being on the right path for some is pure accident, but for most it's a meticulous plan born from introspection and self-awareness, resulting in a lifestyle that provides as much 'happiness' as you can reasonably expect; for you can never expect complete happiness, that would be absurd. There have to be lows to be highs; there has to be quiet to be noise.

And in the workplace, you should hope for pleasure, but expect *some* pain, which is fine, as long as it's manageable, reasonable… minimal.

It's a compromise; some people are willing to take on more stress, usually in return for a higher salary or status, while others look to take on less stress, usually in return for a lower salary and a more enjoyable workday. In every industry there's a vast grey area;

in journalism, news writing is likely to be more stressful, less creative (but probably better paid) than features writing, but the latter should be more fun, with far better perks.

The split was stark, features calling to me.

I wanted to be shot of business news, dropping it to write about food, travel, hotels, and restaurants. It wouldn't all be joy and plain sailing, but I was sure the pleasures of the job would vastly outweigh the pain; it therefore *must* be the right move, which left me wondering whether I'd done enough to lay the ground for a sideways shift into lifestyle journalism.

Victory. Loves. Preparation.

At FRM Media I'd had the opportunity to experiment with features writing, because beside me sat the writers of a men's magazine, penning witticisms on all the usual lads' mag topics. With little time to waste – wary that salaries were arriving later by the month – I quietly met with their editor, offering to write up anything he could throw my way.

After some gentle prodding, over the next few months I had the pleasure of interviewing a twenty-two-year-old model for their 'You're a fit bird and let's hear your story' page, along with test-driving a new Lexus, reviewing a local crab shack, and filing an Australian adventure travel piece.

In journalism, expanding your portfolio isn't easy (deadlines and contracts usually block the way), but it's far easier if your employer has sister titles willing to take your work. If that's the case, you file what you can – reviews, interviews, features – because once published, you'll be locked and loaded, primed to shift into your chosen genre, whatever that may be.

And so having banked even just a svelte portfolio, I felt ready for the push into features, armed with ammo, leaving me able to trundle along India's railways fretting only about Delhi belly and train collisions; seeing as neither occurred, after three weeks of inadvisable street food and twelve-hour train rides, Kate and I parted company at the southernmost point of India, her heading west, me back east.

At almost 100km away, the nearest airport was a beachside runway in Kerala's state capital, Thiruvananthapuram, a place I'll never be able to pronounce, yet somehow found, stumbling over directions all the way to my economy class seat, bound for Dubai. I was itching to return, itching to put my portfolio to the test, itching for a good shower, and, well, just itching, having spent three weeks riding the rails, pooing through a hole in the floor.

There was just one cliff left to scale: I'd need to find a job in the thick of the financial crisis, at a time when even the most devoted of job-changers were shelving CVs, committing to the nine-five. It was a hurdle, but I had faith in a theoretical truism holding strong – that Dubai was still Dubai, a transient place of abundant opportunity… *recession or not.*

Double Dip. Austerity. Bailout.

In 2010 those three terms were infecting common lexicon at a rate to match the billions being inhaled by the world's failed banks. Yet in the UAE, only two words mattered: Burj Khalifa.

The 828 metre-high building's official launch on January 4th 2010 was intended to herald stellar times for Dubai, but instead marked a new low for the city-state. Right up until January 3rd 2010, as evidenced by road signs, metro markers, and city tourist maps, the unmistakeable superstructure due to open a day later was, without doubt, to be named Burj Dubai.

But on January 4th the name ceased to exist.

Which begs the question – what does it take to buy naming rights to the tallest tower ever built? Well, about $10 billion oughta do it. That's because, having loaned Dubai that very sum in mid-December, it became apparent that Abu Dhabi wanted more than just a thank-you note.

They wanted a shout-out.

And what better way to remind humanity that it was Sheikh Khalifa, Ruler of Abu Dhabi and President of the UAE, who saved his naughty neighbour from financial ruin, than for his name to adorn Earth's most epic skyscraper?

It was a stroke of unsubtle genius.

And so from January 4th 2010 a lightning-fast edit took place, minions covering road signs, replacing metro markers, and most likely setting fire to a million tourist maps, thereby erasing the name Burj Dubai from history, presumably leaving Sheikh Mohammed, Ruler of Dubai, to stare at his Babylonian marvel, wondering where it had all gone wrong.

Yet it wasn't *entirely* his fault.

The world was in the doldrums; and to his credit he blamed no one, aside from the media for supposedly exaggerating Dubai's debt crisis. Of course it's easy to imagine stiff words were had in private, but in a system where he's at the top of every tree, the buck stops with him. Fortunately for Sheikh Mohammed his misfortune was about to be overshadowed by *far* worse spendaholics.

The financial crisis, Phase Two, was inbound.

Batten down the hatches, it's time to talk euro. In the dysfunctional family of nations that make up the European Union, national debt in economies both whale and minnow had spiralled to stratospheric levels, and none more so than in Greece, a nation that was fast becoming a byword for astonishing indebtedness. In late-2009 Athens had revealed the true extent of its government borrowing, standing at a cool 300 billion euros (its highest ever level), kicking off an IOU fiasco that would plague the EU for years to come.

The small Mediterranean nation, which hadn't turned international heads since hosting the Summer Olympics in 2004, and before that since inventing the Olympics in the time of the chariot, was now making headlines on a daily basis, its fictitious accounting thrust into the public domain. And with the truth out, soapbox commentators began to warn of a mysterious phenomenon:

Double dip.

That's not a drinks party faux pas where drunk Uncle Tom

re-dips his carrot stick into the communal hummus, but a term used to describe economic recovery, followed by a return to recession. And in early-2010 many countries, including the UK, were anticipating double dip, reckless politicians having over-borrowed and overspent, feeding a perfect storm of banking and governmental ineptitude. In a blink, austerity became the new buzzword, bailout its odious sidekick.

Europe's debt-ridden nations were numerous, but only the worst offenders made it into the ultimate gang of financial flops, the very mention of their name inciting citizens to flee for higher ground.

They were... *bom, bom, bom*... the PIGS.

In Dubai, anyone who thought they might head home changed plans, extended contracts, and offered to babysit the boss's kid. This was no time to depart. Portugal, Ireland, Greece, and Spain (the PIGS) were about to spin their little tails, spreading muck across the planet.

And there I was, in the middle of that unrelenting travesty, out of work, praying that Dubai was *still* Dubai.

I was confident the city offered opportunities galore in normal times, but it had taken a sharp knock. Even so, it remained the premier hub for international firms doing business in the Middle East, and an unrivalled holiday destination for Gulf nationals overflowing in black gold. Rising from zero to hero in little more than a decade, Dubai had become the most modern, safe, and reliable city for thousands of miles in any direction, a status that wasn't even close to being challenged.

And with that assurance in mind I searched on, seeking vacancies, which meant once again being hounded by a most unwelcome question:

"How's the job hunt going?"

Urgh, the most tedious question in unemployment.

When searching for work it crops up on a daily basis, always asked with good intention, always received with covert loathing.

I assume most people share my instinctive reaction to it, at least the immediate thought process, which sounds like this: *If it were good news, you'd already know, so assume there's no news, and back the **** off…*

And yet, that feeling, that queasy feeling in that Goan shack; it had had a lasting effect, altering my outlook. Contrary to covert loathing, I found myself unleashing pedestrian inanities like, "Yeah, really good, mate, banging out CVs," or, "Wicked, dude, making contacts, got irons in fires…"

For God's sake, I sounded like an extra off *Gavin and Stacey*. But I couldn't stop. I was on the up. I felt confident. I was *sure* Dubai would deliver. Finding a job, I truly believed, was only a matter of time.

Now, seeing as you've got this far into my tale of career strife, you'll most likely be expecting a downward swing into depression and depravity, an epic fail to match YouTube's *Girl gets hit by massive wave* but I'm going to have to disappoint, for not only did a life raft did come along, it appeared within a mere month of my job hunt beginning.

I know, *unacceptable.*

I feel ashamed to have written such positively dull words. I'm sorry, and to repent I'm going to whip myself with a sort of medieval flagellatory device designed by the Spanish Inquisition's most sought-after torture squad. Assume that just happened. Youch. I repent. That hurt.

Like, a lot, Felipe.

The life raft was an offer to interview at Dubai's oldest English-language newspaper, in need of staff having let people resign without finding replacements. That's fine, for a while, but there's a limit to how much you can fasten your belt. At some point it'll be too tight, locking up your gut, leaving you unable to excrete for a week. That's the point *Khaleej Times* had reached, having realised its belt was so tight it needed a laxative to release the pressure… which is where I came in. (*Admittedly I'm beginning to regret this metaphor.*)

The broadsheet newspaper needed a features writer on their

weekend magazine, focusing on food, film, events, and travel. It was perfect, and they clearly needed someone fast, because within a week of applying...

Identikit meeting room. Corporate posters.

Tea and coffee sideboard. Venetian blinds.

Notepad and pens. A stranger to impress.

It was all so horribly familiar.

At least I knew the drill: keep it simple; tell them what they want to hear. Yet even though I knew what to say, I was still on edge, desperate to be 'workplace happy'. How to calm those nerves?

You know it: *be prepared.*

And so I'd studied for the interview, jotting down ways to improve the magazine, listing potential articles to suit its predominantly female audience, trotting them out on cue as the meeting unfurled. Maybe it was my suggestion to include film reviews, or my offer to write up desert retreats, but something must have clicked, because within forty minutes we'd arrived at the most promising, yet troublesome, stage of any interview:

Salary negotiation.

It's a tough skill, mastered only by the brave.

A friend in ad sales once told me he'd stood up and walked away from a bruising numbers game, treating his potential employer in the same way I'd treat a souvenir vendor in Marrakesh; lo and behold the employer gave chase, offering him the exact amount he'd targeted. That shows courage. That shows self-awareness of what you bring to the table.

And I too was intent on maximising my salary, but it wouldn't be easy, partly because journalists are content creators, not money generators, but mostly because being unemployed during the greatest recession in living memory is a weak place from which to negotiate; it's Tibet v China. Moped v Truck. Drunk v Staircase.

"If all goes well, what do you think of the salary level?" asked the editor.

"Well, to be honest, it's a fair bit lower than my last job."

"Yes, but it's a recession, everyone's tightening."

"Are you sure you can't go any higher?"

"No."

"Hmmmmmmmmmm," I said, pretending to mull it over. "You drive a hard bargain. Well, are you sure you…?"

"That's as high as it gets."

"I'm in."

Salary negotiation? *Dream on.* Considering the economy, my junior level, and unemployed status the conversation couldn't have gone any other way. They were holding all the aces; they knew I'd be elated if offered the job.

Four days later, they were proved spot on. Having received an offer at their suggested pay grade, I wasn't just elated, I was ecstatic. Career 2.0 was back in play. I was finally on the right path, caring little where it led. I just wanted to be on that yellow brick road, enjoying it for as long as possible.

No more worry. No more concern.

Just mile-upon-mile of contented skipping.

Several weeks later, as I commuted a congested highway to begin my first day as a features writer, I couldn't help but think over the chaotic route I'd taken to get me there; I'd covered some serious mileage:

Fourteen jobs, seven countries, four continents.

Guiding safaris, serving soup, critiquing scripts, marketing films, inebriating tourists, removing junk, writing news, and even eating my way into Accident & Emergency. An oyster theory at my side. An ultimate question. A pinstriped goal. A second career. And finally, the yellow brick road.

Over the centuries more extreme paths have been taken – carpenter to Judgement Day decider being a notable case – but I'd never imagined my path would be so winding, or that after starting out in rural Zimbabwe, years later I'd be in another wilderness, punching-in on the fringes of the Arabian Desert.

Career works in mysterious ways.

Yet even though I was happy with where I'd landed up, I wasn't so sure about my new commute, driving into Dubai's main industrial district, Al Quoz, an area strewn with desolate warehouses, spit-stained alleys, budget strip malls, and the infamous labour camps of the Arabian Gulf.

Laden with dust and diesel, it's where tourists don't venture. No sightseers come. No selfies are snapped. Away from the malls and five-star hotels, this is the reality behind Dubai's success. The so-called 'camps' are actually low-rise dormitories housing thousands of workers in dubious conditions, and there they were, at the side of my commute, hidden in plain sight.

They've been written about enough; there's little for me to add, except to say that to live in Dubai, or even to visit the city, you have to accept they exist – *as they are* – or you shouldn't go. Alongside cheap fuel, cheap labour props up the region's economies; the camps are therefore common across the Gulf, so even though you may, *and should*, dislike the system, you can't change it.

You accept they exist. Or you leave.

With the financial crisis rampant, I wasn't going anywhere, so I did what expats do: I gazed pityingly at those penal buildings, swore I'd donate more to help the labourers, and drove on. It's all you can do.

Just a few turns later, the camps were out of sight; instead, before me rose the colossal *Khaleej Times* facility, shimmering in the desert heat. Another 'day one' was about to begin, another bout of faces, names, and politics.

It was 'newbie time'.

Compared to FRM, life at a daily paper was scaled up, supersized; the building never slept, crammed with a printing press, delivery crews, marketing teams, and an open plan editorial floor buzzing with journalists.

At the side of that floor sat my five-strong team, pumping out lifestyle articles, surrounded by the constant hum of typing, talking,

and tea brewing. It was an instant fit, and within days I was penning a variety of pieces, from restaurant reviews to profile pieces,
while remembering that I was on the payroll of an institutionalised
newspaper, one that adhered to a strict editorial code.

Writing up Munich's Oktoberfest highlighted the challenges of
working within that code, as you're not allowed to mention alcohol,
pork, or sex in UAE media (with at least two of those being integral
to even a sober Oktoberfest experience). After much begging the
editor allowed me two uses of the word 'beer', thereby lessening
my reliance on 'hop-based beverage', the locally recognised code
for 'beer'.

It was an obstacle, but rather than deter, it intrigued, offering
first-hand insight into the constraints journalists face in controlled
societies. It was a window into another world, a world I'd never
expected to experience.

It was interesting. It was unusual.

It was a fit.

And so that's where I found myself, mid-2010, working at an
English-language newspaper in the Arabian Gulf, excited about the
months ahead. Much like my second safari job some fourteen years
earlier, I was content, but – and it's a *big* but – you may remember
why I walked away from that job, so would being a features writer
also fall victim to my irrepressibly itchy feet?

Or was I now older, wiser, and *truly* content?

In a word… Yes.

I was working a job that suited me, within a team of relaxed,
decent people, experiencing a varied life; that's as good as it gets.

That's all I ever wanted from Career 2.0.

So that's that, I hear you say. Are we done? You've found your 'yellow brick road'; can I delete this book, or let it gracefully gather
dust?

Why the hell are you still writing?

A fair question. I was in the right job, on the right path, so should now be wrapping up this tale of hit-and-miss career confusion, yet as the more astute among you will have noticed, there are several pages still to go.

That's because... this story isn't quite over.

That bastard.

That smarmy, slick bastard.

Always close. Always lurking.

He just wouldn't bugger off.

Sitting there, legs crossed, smug smile on his chiselled face; he was stubborn to the end, slouched back, picking invisible dust off his impeccable trousers.

His impeccable, pinstriped trousers.

He was the dream that never died. He was inspiration, perseverance and despair. He was a shadow.

He was back in my life.

Fast-forward to late 2011 and the pinstriped prick had returned to taunt me, having waited just the right amount of time, long past the end of the honeymoon phase, once the daily grind of being a features writer had firmly kicked in; he knew it was only a matter of time, for 'the grind' always kicks in, whether you're a product taster at Cadbury's, or a career-hopping journalist in Dubai.

He'd waited ever so patiently, and then sprung into action, materialising in daydreams, during quiet moments, and on brake-light-commutes, prompting long-forgotten desires to surface, demanding attention.

He knew how defenceless I was against his ways; even so, I tried fighting back. I tried rationalising. I knew the film industry had broken me once before. I knew I'd gone to great lengths to retrain and find work, changing country for a new career, a fresh start. Yet his power to entice me towards pinstriped glory was potent.

It was only a matter of time.

Sure enough, within weeks of his resurgence I found myself glancing over job sites. It was ludicrous, but there I was doing it all the same. I knew it was a bad move, a fool's errand; nevertheless, it was evident my subconscious just couldn't drop the idea of one day being that *goddam* pinstriped producer.

And with that suicidal goal agitating away, making me believe I wasn't on the right path, I scoured the web, searching for an opportunity I knew could destroy everything I'd worked so very hard to build.

I tried to stop, tried to work smarter, tried to focus on better interviews, reports, and reviews, but nothing worked. During workday lulls my eyes returned to those familiar sites, lured back to that masochist dream.

And then, after seven weeks, the listing I craved lit up:

> Assistant Producer needed at busy Dubai film company.
> - International shoots, commercials, and features.
> - Apply online. Experience necessary. *CLICK HERE*

On seeing it I paused, tense, teetering at the threshold.

Peering over that precipice I suddenly realised why the pinstriped menace still held sway, why my fingers were once again hovering over a film job listing – more than a decade after they'd first done so – and why I was now on the verge of tumbling back into the abyss, having only crawled out of it three years previously; for at that very moment unseen bytes of memory had colluded, forging the perfect answer to my imperfect predicament, recalling a line spoken by Leonardo DiCaprio in 2010's *Inception*: "Once an idea has taken hold of the brain it's almost impossible to eradicate." In other words, this U-turn was… inevitable.

There was no point in fighting it.

In a flash I saw my past repeated in my future, but also opportunity, a fresh line of attack, and two little words enticing me on…

CLICK HERE

I dragged the mouse over that persuasive link.

And clicked it open.

A cold breeze blew close, turning my head. I twisted, peering high and low. There was nothing to be seen, but I knew what it was.

It could only be him.

And right on cue, from deep within, that pinstriped tormentor chuckled wryly, folded his newspaper, looked up, and whispered:

"Now you're fucked."

THE END *(of the start)*

JOB FOURTEEN: FEATURES WRITER

Lessons learnt:

- Pooing through the floor of a moving train requires thighs of steel
- Victory. Loves. Preparation. Know yourself, and plan ahead
- Even in dark times, Dubai offers opportunity
- Sometimes it works in your favour to be a corporate laxative
- Salary negotiation is of little use if the other side holds all the aces
- 'Hop-based beverage' is a very silly phrase
- Never forget: once an idea is seeded, it's almost impossible to shake
- Dreams don't die… but are they worth pursuing?

EPILOGUE

There is no end, just hope.

Without hope we're nothing. Without hope we'd never try to date 'the one'. Without hope that kid in *Love Actually* would never have burst through airport security to chase a girl *way* out of his league. And without hope – yes, I'm going there again – Luke Skywalker would never have destroyed the Death Star, as 'The Force' is just hope and self-belief, amped to eleven.

Maybe if the Galactic Empire had employed better electrical engineers, or done its due diligence into 'weak spots and aviation through-flows', he might have failed, but it's too late for recriminations; best just to start over.

Build, destroy, and build again.

Isn't that the ultimate lesson from *Star Wars*? If at first you don't succeed, try, try again. The Empire rebuilt, and tried again, and again. That's inspirational. We should learn from such single-mindedness, for in that Sisyphean approach can be seen the greatest force of all:

Purpose.

It keeps us building, destroying, and building again; it keeps us learning, improving, striving for a better tomorrow. It keeps us out of trouble, *and creating trouble*, but we need it. We're not beasts of the field; we have greater purpose than eating and defecating.

Purpose is key.

A goal will guide your purpose, and with both in play you'll have something powerful, something enduring, something that'll keep you busy and productive to the end of your days – and that's a win-win.

That's all any career needs.

The pinstriped producer inadvertently gave me a goal, one I tried to shake, but one that's nonetheless guided my days; it wrenched me from a dream job as a magazine features writer, pushing me into life as an 'Assistant Producer... at a busy Dubai film company', but several months later the new boss and I fell out, going our separate... well, that's another chapter for another day.

For now, my main take-away from fourteen jobs over fifteen years is that career is a fluid entity, affected as much by your ambition and education, as it is by your family, contacts, the economy, or an untimely swathe of black ice. You need to be flexible, but as long as you have purpose and a goal, you should – at least you *could* – be happy, *if your goal is achievable*.

To figure that out, you need to know yourself.

Start by answering these simple questions:

- What makes you happy (in a working context)?
  - Numbers/words, being indoors/outdoors, being fast/slow-paced, being in a big team/small team/alone, etc.?
  - What are your interests, and why are you drawn to them?
- What are your values?
  - As in, what do you hold important? Helping people, entertaining people, living a varied life, being creative, being challenged, being on the road, earning big money, being the boss, being famous, etc.?
- What type of work matches your happiness and values?
- What type of work is realistic for you, considering your age, background, experience, etc.?
- If you have a goal, is it achievable?
  - Is it realistic, or is it unsuited to your skills?
- If looking to change career, what's stopping you?
  - Are your hurdles surmountable?
  - Will you need to retrain?
  - Can you stomach the effort?
- Are you now able to answer 'the ultimate question'?
- Do you want to test the oyster theory?

- Are you ready to beat the rat race?
- *(See www.hiredfiredfled.com for more)*

After reading my tale it should be obvious that while it's worth searching for your 'yellow brick road', there's no guarantee that you'll find it, and even if you do, you might be lured away, hoodwinked by masochistic obsession.

I searched for longer than most, answering 'the ultimate question' twice, and who knows, I could go on; I could be like KFC's Colonel Sanders, career-hopping until I too launch a fast food chain; maybe, or maybe I'll run chalets in France, or open a publishing company in Dubai; maybe I'll go on to become the premier vendor of anti-panda bear grenade launchers (saving mankind from their genetically-engineered warmongering). In a world of options it's anyone's guess, but whatever the outcome, every path starts with purpose and a goal.

At least these jobs have taught me a thing or two, summed up succinctly in a line by Las Vegas rock band, The Killers, "…while everyone's lost, the battle is won, with all these things that I have done…"

The journey has made me who I am today, far clearer on the parameters of the oyster theory (how best to combine travel and work), and somewhat clearer as to what I should be doing with my days on Earth, but only somewhat. I fear *the ultimate question* will haunt me until the day I die.

Take from these pages what you will; hopefully a smile, maybe a thought-provoking moment, maybe a saccharine feeling that you didn't have to go to such idiotic lengths to find your own path. And if you're on an equally meandering journey, maybe fearing the future, just remember that millions are with you, and that everyone walks a different line.

That said, most differences are superficial; when you strip away the doctors' coats, workmen's overalls, military uniforms, and pinstriped suits, deep down we're all seeking the same thing. As a wise friend told me long, long ago: *success doesn't lead to happiness, happiness leads to success.*

Follow that mantra; seek happiness, after which you *should* find a successful future. At least that's the theory.

To be honest, it's, er, still being field-tested.

And while I seek work, pinging out my erratic CV, the rat race continues to taunt me, one rejection at a time:

"Sorry you haven't been successful in this round of recruiting, but please try again… we wish you well in your future job search."

There is no end, just tomorrow.
Hope on.

ACKNOWLEDGEMENTS

This is the section of every book that no one reads, but every author writes, as it's important to thank some notable people. Of course, I should start with my mother, but I need to start with Ben Flanagan, for suggesting I write this, even if he doesn't remember doing so. It started with you.

A big thanks to my mother for supporting my endeavours over the years, both in emotional, financial, and whip-cracking terms. Thanks also to my stepfather, who's always quietly nudged me in the right direction.

Thanks to my editors: Caitlin Cheadle and Adam Zacharias; you're both tough, encouraging, and I couldn't have done it without you. Thanks to my fastidious proofreader, Helen Baggott. Thanks to Heather Pomar for your perceptive feedback. Thanks to my other readers, especially Emily Bueno, Rocco Cafferelli, Kate Paxton, Ned and Olly Jacobs, Karen Ann Monsy, and my eagle-eyed mother. And to Paul McLennan, my ex-flatmate, thanks for supporting my efforts and dragging me to the pub when the pub was needed.

To the thousands of people who didn't employ me over the years, thank you. You've made me a thick-skinned bastard.

I'd also like to thank those people who've not only employed me, but also guided and inspired me. Mentoring is something that's needed in spades, and is appreciated by juniors in any industry. There'll always be people looking for leadership, and those more senior should try and offer a few minutes every day. Nobody is so busy they can't spare a fraction of their week.

On that note, I'd like to thank Gordon Catherwood, one of my English teachers at school. He gave his time and money to take our class to the theatre, and strove to ensure we'd develop a love of literature, creative writing, grammar, and syntax. I hope I haven't let you down.

Thanks to Mark Kermode and Simon Mayo, whose Wittertainment film reviews have kept me amused for many years, helping to fuel my passion for the silver screen. The producer dream might have been dropped sooner if you guys weren't so damned engaging; I'm fairly sure that's a compliment, so let's just say it is (and while we're at it, let's also say hello to Jason Isaacs).

A big thank-you to the United Kingdom:

You're a self-deprecating, oft-mocked nation, but I love you. You're a bastion of liberty and openness in an increasingly controlled world. The more I've lived overseas the more I've appreciated what you bring to the table. It's no wonder people are clamouring to join our island nation; it's a beacon of creativity, tolerance, inspiration, natural beauty, and architectural gems. It's a tenacious land, one that's fought on the right side for decades, and in so doing has paid its dues for sins committed in the past. Yes, there's the weather, which Brits moan about incessantly, but trust me when I say that it's far better than −36° in Toronto or +50° in Dubai. On that note, if you do live abroad, Britons back home don't judge you. They understand the need for cheaper living, more space, and more sunshine; and on your return, you're always welcomed back into the fold.

It's home, whether I live there or not.

And to that pinstriped producer, whoever you were… thanks.
Or up yours.
The jury's out.

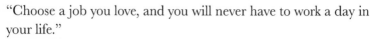

WORKING WORLD WISDOM

"Choose a job you love, and you will never have to work a day in your life."
  – Confucius

"A man is a success if he gets up in the morning and gets to bed at night, and in between he does what he wants to do."
  – Bob Dylan

"Success comes from curiosity, concentration, perseverance, and self-criticism."
  – Albert Einstein

"By working faithfully eight hours a day you may eventually get to be a boss and work twelve hours a day."
  – Robert Frost

"Don't confuse having a career with having a life."
  – Hillary Clinton

"If you don't wake up in the morning excited to pick up where you left your work yesterday, you haven't found your calling yet."
    – Mike Wallace

"You will never feel 100% ready when an opportunity arises. So just do it."
    – Unknown

"The future belongs to those who believe in the beauty of their dreams."
    – Eleanor Roosevelt

"The future depends on what we do in the present."
    – Mahatma Gandhi

"You just have to keep trying to do good work, and hope that it leads to more good work. I want to look back on my career and be proud of the work, and be proud that I tried everything. Yes, I want to look back and know that I was terrible at a variety of things."
    – Jon Stewart